Testimonials

"What I loved about Toad's Place is that they let you do more than just show up and set your band up and play. You could actually curate some kind of show that was interesting to people, different."

—CYNDI LAUPER

"I have fond memories all around of Toad's Place. We always loved playing there. It seemed like every show we did there was great. It's a great club."

—AL ANDERSON OF NRBQ

"I've always said that the best way to tell if a band is any good or not is to hear them in a club like Toad's Place. We love that joint!"

—HUEY LEWIS OF HUEY LEWIS AND THE NEWS

"I loved Toad's Place! It gave aspiring artists and musicians in Connecticut a chance to discover who they were musically and the freedom to strengthen what they would need in order to have any chance of having a career in music. Looking back, I can clearly see that Brian applied the same kind of commitment, veracity, and focus that he did when I used to see him in the dojo (karate school). Long live Toad's!"

—MICHAEL BOLTON

"There was always a heightened sense of excitement when you played at Toad's. Everybody knew it was the best place to play. And Toad's has this active roster of national acts coming through, which is very attractive. A great place to see a show and hang out."

—CHRISTINE OHLMAN

"When you play at Toad's you feel like you've hit the big time. It has that aura."

—CYNTHIA LYON, EIGHT TO THE BAR

"I couldn't say enough about Toad's Place. It's such an important piece of American music history! Soul is one of those things that's impossible to describe, but you know it when you feel it. And Toad's Place has it overflowing out into the streets."

—ZACH DEPUTY

There's a place just around the bend
The same place where it all began
It's the best, man, you just can't beat it
And later on, when the place gets heated
Get ready, 'cause it's a wild weekend.

—NRBQ, "IT'S A WILD WEEKEND"

THE LEGENDARY TOAD'S PLACE

Stories from New Haven's Famed Music Venue

BRIAN PHELPS AND RANDALL BEACH

Globe
Pequot

Guilford, Connecticut

Globe
Pequot

An imprint of Globe Pequot, the trade division of The Rowman & Littlefield Publishing Group, Inc.
4501 Forbes Blvd., Ste. 200
Lanham, MD 20706
www.rowman.com

Distributed by NATIONAL BOOK NETWORK

British Library Cataloguing in Publication Information available

Library of Congress Cataloging-in-Publication Data available

ISBN 978-1-4930-5860-0 (paper : alk. paper)
ISBN 978-1-4930-5861-7 (electronic)

∞™ The paper used in this publication meets the minimum requirements of American National Standard for Information Sciences—Permanence of Paper for Printed Library Materials, ANSI/NISO Z39.48-1992.

To my family: Maria, Jessica, Kaylie, Brian Jr., my deceased parents Everett and Barbara, and my brother Timmy, for their love and encouragement —Brian Phelps

To my wife Jennifer Kaylin, for her love and support; and to my daughters Natalie and Charlotte Beach, for their love and loyalty —Randall Beach

CONTENTS

Brian Phelps's Preface

This whole crazy story started with a broken window.

In April of 1975 I was in my junior year at the University of New Haven and also taking classes at a karate school I owned above Cutler's Records in New Haven, around the corner from a new arrival on the block—a French restaurant called Toad's Place.

One night an off-duty soldier on leave from his station in Germany got a little too drunk and smashed the window on the karate school's front door. He also stole the sandwich board sign we kept at the sidewalk entrance.

We heard the glass breaking, so we ran downstairs, saw the shards, and noticed the sign was gone. We figured whoever had broken the glass door had also stolen our sign and couldn't be far. We started walking around the neighborhood and found the sign outside Toad's.

There were about five of us, and my buddies were all warmed up for a fight. We weren't going to let the window smasher get away. We walked into Toad's Place; I hadn't been in that space since it was Hungry Charlie's, a couple of years back.

I shouted, "Does anybody know who put that sandwich board sign out front?"

"It's that guy over there," one of the patrons said.

We were getting ready to move in on the perpetrator when a big fellow with a welcoming, easygoing smile approached us. I soon learned this was Mike Spoerndle. He was one of the restaurant's owners and he was also the bouncer. Mike didn't have any back-up.

"Let's talk this out," Mike said. He asked us to hold off as he called the cops.

I said, "Okay, we'll wait for the cops to come." I asked my friends to back off.

The cops didn't come right away, but we had the guy corralled in the corner, by the popcorn machine. He had no way out of there. When the cops finally showed up, they arrested him. The next thing you know, he's disappeared; he was back in Germany. It was the weirdest thing: Why would he break the window?

But this is when my relationship with Toad's Place and Mike Spoerndle started. He said, "Come in any time you want." He gave me a pass to get in for free and told me, "Come in and talk; hang out." That was the beginning of our friendship.

I never got the money for the broken window. But my whole life changed because soon afterward I became a part of Toad's Place.

As nutty as it sounds, everything would be different if that guy had never broken that window.

Randall Beach's Preface

My earliest memory of Toad's Place is from the fall of 1977 when I beheld the spectacle of Meat Loaf on stage. He was sweating profusely and roaming back and forth while clutching a long red scarf and belting out "Paradise by the Dashboard Light."

And I thought, *What a great place this is! I'll be back.*

But I couldn't imagine that the performers I would see there in the years to come would include the Rolling Stones, Billy Joel, and Bob Dylan.

I arrived in Connecticut in January 1975, the same month Toad's opened its doors. But for the next two years I worked and lived in Wallingford, a one-horse town about twenty minutes north of New Haven. Eventually I developed the habit of getting on I–91 and driving down to Toad's, which was just then beginning to blossom as an exciting venue for live music.

In January 1977 I moved to New Haven to begin a reporting job with the *New Haven Register*. After seeing more great acts at Toad's, including Talking Heads and the Ramones, I talked my editors into letting me pioneer the rock music beat at the *Register*. This enabled me to get free tickets to cover shows at the New Haven Coliseum (where I saw Queen and the Who), but it was the performances at Toad's that I much preferred, for their intimacy and close vantage points.

In addition to the Stones, Joel, and Dylan, I enjoyed Cyndi Lauper, David Crosby, Donovan, the Roches, Roger McGuinn, Rickie Lee Jones, Iggy Pop, and dozens more. I was also able to snag backstage interviews with Tom Waits, John Prine, Commander Cody, Warren Zevon, and "Weird Al" Yankovic. The atmosphere at Toad's had a way of putting them at ease.

When Brian Phelps told me in the fall of 2019 that he was working on a book that would tell the amazing storied history of Toad's Place, I suggested he bring me on board for a collaborative effort. I was gratified he quickly agreed to forming this partnership.

The Toad's story is how two partners, Brian Phelps and Mike Spoerndle, used their passion and skills to make Toad's nationally known as a major music venue despite holding only about 750 people. While working on this book I have often thought about how sad it is that Spoerndle died so young, at fifty-nine. I also regret he wasn't here to tell me all about how he got Toad's started and propelled it forward.

But Brian is still at the helm and has done a remarkable job keeping Toad's going amid all the changes in the music industry. He shows no sign of quitting, even though as I write this in April 2021 the COVID-19 pandemic has forced him to shut down his club for more than a year, and he faces more months of uncertainty before he can again throw open the doors.

The Toad's saga embodies what many of us experienced during those wild, fun-filled nights of the seventies, eighties, nineties, and beyond. Paraphrasing Billy Joel, one of the legendary artists who graced that stage and who I was privileged to see there: We loved those days.

CHAPTER 1

The Toad Is Born

IN JANUARY OF 1975, THREE YOUNG FRIENDS IN NEW HAVEN, CONNECTICUT, POOLED their meager resources to open a French restaurant they called Toad's Place.

I'll give you a sense of what those times were like politically and socially: America was in a post-Watergate stupor. Five months earlier, Richard Nixon had resigned in disgrace because of that scandal and was replaced by Gerald Ford, a calm caretaker.

The Vietnam War, which had polarized the generations and killed more than fifty-eight thousand US soldiers, was finally winding down. Four months after Toad's opened its doors, US involvement in Vietnam would end with the fall of Saigon. On television we would watch the frantic helicopter evacuation of the few Americans still there as the South Vietnamese government surrendered to North Vietnamese troops.

I turned twenty-one in the spring of 1975, but Nixon had abolished the draft two years earlier. Like millions of other young American men, I had caught a lucky break.

In early 1975 on the grounds of Yale University, which surrounded the new restaurant and soon-to-be-music club (forget about that Veal Cordon Bleu), students were no longer protesting the war en masse as they had in the late sixties and early seventies. Like me, they didn't have to worry about being drafted and being sent overseas to fight and perhaps die in an unpopular war. They were ready to party!

Yale had gone co-ed in September 1969, but Yale men still needed an off-campus site where they could hang out, drink, listen to music, and pick up women. And the women were up for some action too. Now, right there on York Street next to Mory's, the storied but stuffy and staid dining club for old Yale chums, the young Yalies would have their own place, Toad's.

There were thousands of other college students in the New Haven area looking for a social outlet, thanks to the nearby campuses of Southern Connecticut State College,

Clockwise from top left: The Ramones, Southside Johnny, Lenny Kravitz, Samantha Fox, Sum 41, Molly Hatchet, Barenaked Ladies, Buster Poindexter, and John Dalby.

the University of New Haven, and Quinnipiac College. (Southern and Quinnipiac have since become universities.) They provided a great, marketable melting pot. Oh, and the drinking age was eighteen.

The intimate, cozy atmosphere of Toad's (at that time you could squeeze in only about four hundred people) offered an alternative to the large concert venue a few blocks away, the New Haven Coliseum, which had a seating capacity of about eleven thousand people. The Coliseum was an ugly concrete structure that had opened in 1972 with a performance by the Beach Boys. It had replaced the rundown New Haven Arena, at which in December 1967 Jim Morrison, the charismatic lead singer of the Doors, got busted by the New Haven police. Morrison was pepper sprayed by a cop backstage then proceeded to blast the Pigs at the start of the show and got hauled off to the police lock-up for "performing an indecent and immoral exhibition." He later got revenge by writing and recording "Peace Frog," which described "blood in the streets in the town of New Haven."

Like America itself, rock music in January 1975 was in a kind of malaise, the word Jimmy Carter would one day use to depict our mindset after he was elected president in 1976. Bruce Springsteen would not explode onto the scene until August 1975 with the release of his breakthrough album *Born to Run*. The punk era, bringing the rise of seminal bands such as the Ramones and the Clash, was yet to bust out. Disco music still filled the airwaves.

The big hits on the charts at the outset of 1975 included these awful ear worms: "Mandy" by Barry Manilow, a remake of "Please Mr. Postman" by the Carpenters (who were born in New Haven), "Laughter in the Rain" by Neil Sedaka, "Get Dancin' (Part I)" by Disco Tex and the Sex-O-Lettes, "Look in My Eyes Pretty Woman" by Tony Orlando and Dawn, "Morning Side of the Mountain" by Donny and Marie Osmond, "Angie Baby" by Helen Reddy, "Rock 'n' Roll (I Gave You the Best Years of My Life)" by Mac Davis, "Kung Fu Fighting" by Carl Douglas, "One Man Woman/One Woman Man" by Paul Anka and Odia Coates, and "Sweet Surrender" by John Denver.

You get the picture. We were primed for better music, something challenging and inspiring.

Enter Mike Spoerndle and his two buddies, Mike Korpas and Chuck Metzger, all out of Ohio. Spoerndle and Metzger had come to New Haven to enroll in the prestigious Culinary Institute of America; Korpas had a background in the bar business.

Spoerndle, who was called "Big Mike," was a burly, outgoing guy who loved to schmooze and party—the perfect personality for a restaurant or nightclub owner. We would become great friends, housemates, and business partners.

The promoter Jimmy Koplik, who with his business partner Shelly Finkel brought many of the country's biggest rock acts to Connecticut in the early seventies and beyond, recalled meeting Big Mike in 1977 when the young Toad's co-owner needed help getting national bands.

"My first impression was: *This guy is crazy!*" Koplik said. "He was larger than life: big, loud, heavy drinker, heavy drug taker. Everything about him was excessive. Everything! Remember, this was in the seventies."

"He was always a great friend," Koplik added. "His heart was as big as his body. But he never took care of himself. He just couldn't stop doing drugs."

Mike was the idea man and, as Koplik noted, would become "the soul of Toad's." But his over-the-top lifestyle and addictive nature would also lead to him having to leave Toad's after a twenty-year run of glory days and glory nights. And it would claim his life at the early age of fifty-nine.

Long before the drugs took over, Mike was an ambitious young chef, studying for a career in the restaurant business. After Mike and Metzger graduated from the culinary school, they hatched the plan of opening a restaurant with Korpas. But they didn't have much money; Mike had to borrow $11,000 from his mother to launch the venture. He was twenty-three years old.

The three old pals focused on a vacant property at 300 York Street, the former site of a laid-back eatery called Hungry Charlie's. It was a sandwiches and burgers joint with a pinball machine in the corner.

Oh yeah, I remember Hungry Charlie's—that was where I had my first beer! It was in 1973 while I was still a student at the University of New Haven. My buddy Lou Buccino and I went over to Charlie's to get burgers. This was the first time I set foot in the space that would totally change my life.

I ordered a beer to go with the burger; I didn't like the taste of that beer at all. But there was something happening to take my mind off my beer: Charlie's sometimes had live music, and that night they had an act called Roomful of Blues. I had never heard of them, but those guys, who came out of Providence, Rhode Island, had already been performing since the late sixties and would keep on trucking with different musicians for more than fifty years.

The waitress came over and told us, "Okay, you guys have to pay fifty cents each to stay for the show." I had like a quarter left in my pocket, as did Lou, so we asked the waitress, "How about fifty cents for the two of us?" She said okay, and we paid a quarter each to stay and hear Roomful of Blues. They were set up on a kind of makeshift stage with only a couple of speakers.

I didn't know much about music then, so the whole experience was totally new to me. But I kind of liked it even though I knew zilch about the blues.

When I was a kid growing up in New Haven and going to Catholic schools, all I listened to was whatever they put on AM radio. A friend of mine had a transistor radio, and we tuned into the local stations to hear Elvis Presley and then the Beatles. I didn't go to many concerts either. My cousin took me to see the Temptations and then the Byrds. Those were the only shows I saw.

My mother made me take guitar lessons when I was in eighth grade. I hated it! My fingers were always sore from the strings. After about six months my guitar teacher said, "You don't really want to do this, do you?" And that was the end. It just wasn't for me.

New Haven in the early seventies had a lively folk scene going and its center was The Exit Coffeehouse, near the New Haven Green. One of the musicians in that mix was Peter Menta, who played in the Blake Street Gut Band. Menta had a knack for using his connections to book other bands, and so he started doing that for Hungry Charlie's. He lured Roomful of Blues there, plus plenty of local bands.

When Mike Spoerndle and his two new business partners were getting ready to open their doors, they had to come up with a name for their restaurant. Mike told me they were sitting around one day and one of them noted that back in Ohio people who are couch potatoes are called "toads." If you were staying home, you would say, "I'm being a toad tonight." Mike said, "I like that! Let's call it Toad's Place!" All of a sudden they had a distinctive name; people would remember it. But the three partners didn't think that much about it. They didn't know Toad's was going to be there for forty-five or fifty years. They thought it would be this thing they would have for five years and then they would be on their way to something else.

After Hungry Charlie's closed because of lagging business and Mike's crew moved in there, Mike realized he needed live music to survive. Menta knew the music business; Mike and his partners didn't, so Menta stuck around for a couple of years as the Toad's Place talent scout and booking agent. This was before Mike got Koplik to help them out.

Menta, who as late as 2020 was still playing with Washboard Slim and the Blue Lights, remembers, "For Mike and his partners at the start, it was all about the food. Music was an afterthought. But their restaurant (with its shrimp baskets, chicken baskets, clam baskets, and buckets of steamers) wasn't doing much business." Creditors were circling in, demanding their money; United Illuminating briefly shut off the electricity.

Pat Healy, the first bartender at Toad's who would become a long-time mainstay and one of Mike's best friends, remembers the day in 1975 when Mike realized he needed to make a big change and then hit on how he could do it.

"Mike was standing out front on the sidewalk one day, looking around, watching all these college kids walking by," Healy recalled. "Remember, the drinking age then was eighteen. And Mike comes in and says, 'I got this figured out. What do college boys like?' Of course I told Mike, 'College girls.' Mike says, 'What do college boys and girls like to do?' Naturally I told Mike, 'Drink beer.' Mike asked, 'What else do they like? Music! Dancing!'"

Healy remembers Mike unleashing that big smile of his, the welcoming and mischievous smile everybody loved. And he just said, "Yep!"

Mike knew he needed to reconfigure and enlarge the space, making it more suitable for the bands. A thrown-together crew, including a teenager named Dave Plaskon and local musician David "Bobo" Lavorgna, whom Mike knew, brought in planks from a bowling alley to help build the bar and a bigger stage. Mike also got hold of a basketball court at a high school in Massachusetts and turned it into the dance floor. But the lights that hung over the stage were old coffee cans. These guys were making it up as they went along. They knew people would want pinball machines and a popcorn machine, so those were installed too.

According to Lavorgna, who seems to remember the mid-1970s better than the rest of us, the first live band to play at Toad's was a pick-up band that included Bobo on bass guitar and Menta on harp. Record keeping was sloppy in those days, so it's impossible to verify his story, but he said this happened in the summer of 1975, on successive Friday and Saturday nights. He recalls they played on the original small stage near the front door, with windows looking out onto York Street. At that time there were only a few seats and booths, but thanks to Mike's demo and remodeling crew, more seats were added, and the stage was moved farther back into the main room.

The local acts who played at Toad's in those early days included the folksinger Randy Burns, who had a deep, evocative voice and was also getting bookings in Greenwich Village clubs.

Another young New Haven–based singer was Michael Bolotin, who would soon change his last name to Bolton. It was a cooler stage name. Menta, who booked the rising young singer for Toad's, recalls him as "egotistical, but he always drew a big crowd because he had a good voice. You could tell he was destined for big things."

It's true, Michael Bolton has always had a big ego, but that was okay. It helped him get to where he was going, along with that voice. When he played shows at Toad's in the mid-seventies his following was picking up. Bolton was always trying to make the show a little better than what everybody else thought it could be. He wanted to bring it to a higher level. Early on he would jump through a hula hoop that was covered in paper. He did this as his entrance to his show, to make it more electrifying. And of course the women loved him, with that big hair and big voice.

The first big break for Toad's, what really got the club going, happened at the same time as the initial live shows, which were mostly bluegrass. Those bands played on Tuesday nights, and Mike hit on the idea of offering beers for twenty-five cents on Tuesdays. This was called "The Night of the Toad."

Bluegrass was popular in New Haven in those days, but Toad's offered a range of styles. Menta booked local bands such as the Helium Brothers, Jake and the Family Jewels, and the Simms Brothers Band. More and more people came in to drink cheap beer and dance to the music. Admission at the door was either a dollar or free, and word was getting out that Toad's Place was hopping.

While Mike Spoerndle came up with The Night of the Toad and was the idea guy, Chuck Metzger was the food guy and Mike Korpas was the bar guy who knew that part of the business. By the summer of '75, all three of them were realizing that music was starting to drive Toad's and make it financially successful. It wasn't the French food.

CHAPTER 2

Toad's Goes National

WHILE MIKE SPOERNDLE AND I STARTED TO BECOME FRIENDS, HE AND HIS TWO partners were fighting like cats over the bills and how to make more money to keep Toad's Place afloat. I didn't know it at the time (the summer of 1976), but things were beginning to line up for me and my future career.

I was using my free pass to come to Toad's more often, walking over from my karate school around the corner. As our friendship grew stronger, Mike, who was becoming almost like a big brother to me, began to tell me about the business.

When I stopped in one Tuesday for The Night of the Toad, Mike was at the door collecting the one-dollar admission fee. A guy started causing trouble about paying; Mike tried to talk him down, but the guy wouldn't stop. Mike, who couldn't afford to hire any security people and was on his own, grabbed him in a headlock and kept collecting money with his free hand.

When he spotted me in the line, Mike smiled and waved me up front. "Come on in!"

"Thanks," I told him. "If you need help, I'm here."

But Mike didn't need me. He had already called the cops and was holding onto the guy until they arrived.

One night not long after that, Mike told me, "I'm going to buy out my partners. When I do, and when you finish college, you can come in and work with me, be the manager. I'll teach you the ropes."

Because I liked Mike and it seemed like a fun place to work, I told him I'd do it. Plus at that age, your hormones are going and I knew a lot of women would be in there.

By the fall of 1976 I was working alongside Mike, who had reached a deal with his two partners to take over the business as the sole owner. They hung around until the end of the year, then they split. It was now Mike and me running the place. He encouraged me to consider it my own, and work with passion and dedication, the way he did. Mike showed me the ins and outs of the business. He introduced me to the whole bar scene mentality from the owner/manager point of view.

We kept Menta as the booking agent because he had so many contacts and knew the business. Menta also realized that some of the biggest blues players in the country were doing shows at a club called the Shaboo Inn in Willimantic, Connecticut. The Shaboo would have a good run from 1971 through 1982, and Menta knew that since the acts were already in the state, about an hour away from New Haven, he could probably get them to do a show at Toad's too. He went to work.

One of our first breakthroughs was getting Willie Dixon. I think we only paid him about $600, but he drew a big, enthusiastic crowd. Dixon was internationally known as a blues musician; he played upright bass and guitar. He was a great singer and a songwriter too. He had written "Hoochie Coochie Man," "I Just Want to Make Love to You," and "Little Red Rooster." Rock bands such as Cream, the Doors, the Rolling Stones, and Led Zeppelin had covered his songs. He was a bridge between blues and rock.

We also landed Bo Diddley, another blues legend and, like Dixon, a transitional figure from blues to rock music. He is considered one of the founders of rock 'n' roll because he popularized that syncopated beat later used by Buddy Holly (on "Not Fade Away"), the Who (on "Magic Bus"), and George Michael (on "Faith"). Bo was a real showman; he always dressed in black. He was a big guy carrying a square guitar. He took our stage and using his booming voice and that beat, got people going with his songs: "Bo Diddley," "Road Runner," and "Who Do You Love."

And then along came Muddy Waters! Here he was, this iconic bluesman who had written "I Can't Be Satisfied," "Mannish Boy," "Got My Mojo Working," and "Rollin' Stone." A certain British band who would appear at Toad's many years later took the title of that last song and used it to name themselves.

Menta had arranged to present Waters with a key to the city of New Haven. The rest of the band knew about it, but Waters didn't, so when Menta got up on stage to

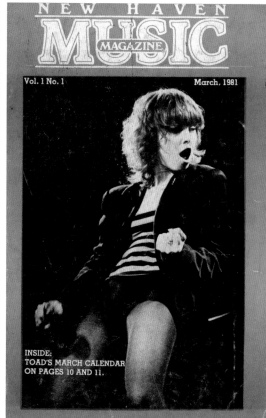

NEW HAVEN

MUSIC
MAGAZINE

Vol. 1 No. 1   March, 1981

INSIDE:
TOAD'S MARCH CALENDAR
ON PAGES 10 AND 11.

Clockwise from top left: Meat Loaf, Pat Benatar on the cover of *New Haven Music Magazine*, Ian Hunter (photo by Art Lehne), B.B. King, NRBQ, Tom Jones, Béla Fleck, Buddy Rich, Buddy Guy, and Joe Jackson.

do the honors, Waters was pissed at him for interrupting the set and almost punched him out.

Although we were all excited about having Waters in our club, Mike didn't have much money to pay him, and Waters always demanded cash. He also had to be supplied with a bottle of Piper Heidsiek champagne, or he wouldn't perform. At the end of the night, Mike only had some rolls of quarters left and that's how he paid Waters. But it worked out; Waters came back to Toad's many times.

For one of his performances, ticket sales were a little slow; maybe it was a late booking. I came up with a solution: We decided to do a flyer campaign around the Yale campus (there was no internet then). We charged only $2, with a Yale I.D. We absolutely plastered the campus. The promo worked and we got our capacity of 750 people. It was jammed. This was the largest audience we had for Muddy of all the times he performed at the club. It was mostly young Yalies with a ton of energy. The place went crazy.

There was so much buzz that Muddy got off his barstool and walked from one side of the stage to the other as he sang. He had those Yalies going. He even had them help him with the chorus lines. I had never seen him do that before.

Muddy was really pumped. When he got into the "Got My Mojo Workin'," he said, "Got my bbbbbbb working," and the crowd answered the same way. He made this sound by shaking his face back and forth at an impressive pace while uttering a guttural type of sound. People were laughing and crying at the same time.

There was another time when we tried to do something a little extra for Muddy. We had a Muppet handled by some professional NBC guys. I just knew in my gut we could make Muddy happy doing this. The Muppet was a puppet controlled by a ventriloquist. The Muppet sat on the guy's lap and they both sat next to Muddy. The Muppet started talking to Muddy and Muddy answered him. He started laughing.

At one point the Muppet said, "Fuck you," and Muddy came right back, saying, "Fuck you." Muddy started stomping his feet because he was so into it. The crowd was really digging it. The Muppet had Muddy laughing so hard he was crying. I said to myself, *My God, this is one historic moment that will never happen again.* Just being part of it and watching it defines why I have been in this business all these years.

Along with the big blues acts came some rockers in the early stages of their careers. Toad's was a launching pad for them. Meat Loaf was one such act.

Meat Loaf's debut album, *Bat Out of Hell*, was released in October 1977. Initially it didn't do much, but it would go on to become one of the best-selling rock albums of all time. More than forty-three million copies have been sold worldwide.

Shortly after that album came out, we booked Meat Loaf. The Toad's show was the first time he showcased those songs, such as "Paradise by the Dashboard Light," for a live audience. We had only about a hundred people there that night.

Ellen Foley, who had sung on the album, wasn't available for the tour, so Karla DeVito, a veteran of the national touring company of *Godspell*, filled in for her. Meat Loaf, with his big red scarf, was roaming around on the stage, sweating heavily, and doing his sexual back-and-forth with DeVito on "Paradise."

But the show almost didn't happen because of something bizarre that went down during the sound check. Meat Loaf was pacing around and lost track of where he was. We heard this big crash—he had fallen off the stage! There was a tense moment of silence while we all held our breaths. Then we heard this voice call out, "I'm okay!" He climbed right back up, the sound check continued, and that night he did a killer show. Years later, after he hit it big and still played at Toad's, he grabbed me backstage, got me in a headlock, rolled up his pants, and showed me a scar on his left leg. He told me, "You see that? This is from my first gig ever after releasing *Bat Out of Hell*. This is what I did! Right here at your club!"

"Okay," I said. "I'm sorry about that, big guy."

The following year, in August 1978, we booked Talking Heads. They had issued their first album, *Talking Heads: 77* a year earlier. When they came here, about 650 people showed up. At that time I wasn't that up on the punk scene because it was a new thing. I didn't understand the music; I didn't understand the fans. I saw guys coming in with leather motorcycle jackets and sneakers and I was getting nervous. They looked like bikers! *Is this going to be a tough crowd?* I wondered. But there was no trouble. They were there for the music and to check out the band's leader, David Byrne. I've got to admit, I didn't understand what he was singing about. "Psycho Killer" was one of their hits at the time, but some of it's in French. "Psycho killer, *qu'est-ce que c'est.* Fa-fa-fa-fa-fa-fa-fa-fa-fa-far better." And you could look up these other surreal lyrics:

"I'm tense and nervous and I can't relax. I can't sleep 'cause my bed's on fire; don't touch me, I'm a real live wire."

Everyone was just staring at David Byrne like he had a mental connection with all of them, like a Vulcan mind meld. I didn't see it coming. I didn't know they were going to be that big. Later he played here by himself, but that first night I dealt with the band's bass guitarist, Tina Weymouth, who was married to the band's drummer, Chris Frantz. She was the one I paid. She was very serious at the time, but later we became friends.

Another memorable act was Tom Waits, who played two sold-out shows at about the same time period, the late seventies. He was living in a hotel in Los Angeles and hanging out with Rickie Lee Jones, who would come to Toad's later on. Waits, then only twenty-nine, was working on a new album, *Heartattack and Vine*. He was a great piano player and had this distinctive guttural voice. He sang funny, ironic songs like "Better Off Without a Wife."

When Waits took the stage at Toad's in his faded black suit and black hat, he was backed by a jazz quartet and a drummer who banged away at a garbage can. Waits drank beer and chain-smoked through both shows. He was hanging onto the microphone like a wino on a lamppost.

One of the people in the crowd that night, Larry Dorfman, recalled that also on the stage, placed on a stool, was an old-fashioned cash register, replete with bells and whistles. Waits talked/sang some of his poetry while playing "lead" cash register. Some people in the crowd thought this was just too weird and booed him.

Randall Beach, who was reviewing that show for the *New Haven Register*, reported Waits also got heckled that night, but he knew how to handle the jerk. "That's my brother Roger," he said after a dude sounded off. "That's what happens when cousins marry. It starts in the home."

When he wasn't lurching around on the stage, Waits sat at the piano and played it with surprising tenderness. But he introduced "Waltzing Matilda" by saying, "I'd like to do a ballad about throwing up in a foreign country." His voice was reminiscent of Louis Armstrong.

Waits had a serious buzz on by the end of the night. He was still hanging around after the crowd left and he got talking with a drunk off-duty cop who had been there for the show. They just sat at the bar and kept drinking. Of course I let Waits hang out as long as he wanted to stay.

And to give you an idea how eclectic the bands were that came through Toad's at that time, how you never knew who you were going to see—we had the legendary banjo player Earl Scruggs, the former partner of bluegrass pioneer Bill Monroe and Lester Flatt, play one night. According to Randall Beach's review from that night, Scruggs, backed by his three sons and a brother-in-law, had the crowd whooping and hollering and stomping until 1:30 a.m. They heard the old master perform "The Ballad of Jed Clampett" (the theme from *The Beverly Hillbillies*) as well as "Foggy Mountain Breakdown" and "Orange Blossom Special."

"Thank you, it's a pleasure being with you folks," Scruggs told the mostly college-age crowd. After his second encore, he grinned out at everybody and said, "How sweet it is!"

For my first few years working at Toad's, I drank on the job, just like everybody else. I would do shots with some of the customers. But one night, I think it was New Year's Eve, I just said, "That's it, I'm done with the booze. When I'm working, I'm working." I just felt I wasn't sharp enough for those long nights. I couldn't do my job well enough if I was drunk. I was the hands-on guy. I figured the best way to make Toad's more successful was to be completely sober and focused at all times. Otherwise things will spiral down before you know it. This was an important step for me and for the betterment of my future.

But Mike wasn't of the same mind; he liked to indulge on a regular basis with whomever was in front of him. Mike would drink almost anything: a shot of Metaxa and German brandy was one of his favorites. Then he'd do shots with other people throughout the night. He graduated to Black Russians, sixteen-ounce cups. That's a strong drink, even though he was a big guy. He did go to AA meetings for a while but eventually he succumbed to alcoholism. He'd come in and drink non-stop until he left. He got caught up in it, unfortunately.

After working the shows at Toad's for a couple of years, I became a better manager. I began looking at things from the point of view of the customers. One of the things that was always important to me was trying to make sure everyone in the club had a good time. Even in the early days with local bands I would observe what people were

Lucy Sabini on Her Time at Toad's

Lucy Sabini, Toad's Place "talent buyer" (she booked the bands) from 1979 until 1985, remembers her years there as a time when the club was transforming itself from a venue for local bands to a nationally known outlet showcasing up-and-coming artists. This is her story:

I arrived at Toad's at the beginning of its legacy. Mike Spoerndle was the visionary; there wouldn't have been a Toad's Place without him. There was a magic about him. He was a huge music lover and he wanted to bring music into his club, to make it a place that not only the audience would enjoy coming to, but that the artists would enjoy too. He wanted people to be able to come see the stars of tomorrow.

I started working there after a friend of mine I'd worked with at WPLR (the New Haven–based rock station) called me and said, "I got you this job. Just show up Monday." So I went over there on a Monday morning, walked into the upstairs office, and I see three desks, two of them empty. I see this big, burly guy sitting at the other desk.

"Are you Lucy?" he asked.

"Yeah," I answered. "Are you Mike?"

He nodded, then pointed at a desk, and said, "Book me some bands." He was very sweet about it. I saw a Rolodex on the desk and I started going through it. That was the easiest job interview I ever had!

Mike had a charm about him that was infectious. He was smart too. He was attuned to all the acts. He'd say, "Let's get this band." So we called the agents for the bands. It was the perfect place between New York and Boston. It just blossomed.

It was hard work but it seemed effortless. You know that saying, "Do something you like and you'll never work a day in your life." It was like a family there, very much a team.

doing. I would see if everybody was upbeat and happy. As long as they were dancing, talking, smiling, and/or drinking, the club was active and generating positive vibes. When things were right, you could always feel it. When they were not, I would try to figure out some way to make it better. One of the things I oversaw was making sure the restrooms were in acceptable shape. The men's room got beat up on a regular basis.

When the big acts performed, I had developed a habit of scanning the crowd to see if people were excited and involved. If the performance progressed nicely with a

And Mike was very generous with everybody. He also used the club to do a lot of charity work. The organizations he helped included local Jewish groups and St. Bernadette's Church in New Haven, where the Five Satins recorded "In the Still of the Night."

Mike developed a relationship with the artists. He wanted them to have a great experience, and they did. You could tell by how many times they came back. The word spread.

I met the most wonderful people there. One of them was Huey Lewis. He played at Toad's three times. The first time there were only about twenty-five people in the club, but that afternoon during the sound check, I was up in the office and I said to somebody in the crew, "Tell Huey there's a big fan upstairs." Twenty minutes later Huey walks upstairs, carrying coffee!

"I hear you need some coffee," he said. "I'm told you're the reason we're here." He was so charming, so sweet, so much fun.

George Thorogood ("Bad to the Bone") was also very charming. He loved to have a good time and tell stories. It was about music and having fun. Talk about an artist rocking the floor! I mean, that floor was shaking! It was unbelievable. An incredible performer.

Another frenzied night was when Squeeze came in for a sold-out show. They had a hit out, "Pulling Mussels from the Shell."

The Pretenders drew a packed house too. Chrissie Hynde, their lead singer, was great; talk about a kick-ass woman! She was incredibly smart and really genuine, with no airs about her. But she was powerful and strong. That night, people were going crazy for them.

We were lucky enough to be a part of each artist's journey. It was a magical time, being there with all those amazing artists, some of them just starting out. I have always felt I was very lucky that I was there while it was history in the making. But when it's happening, you don't realize it; you're going with the flow. Later you look back and think, *Wow! That was an amazing time.*

slow but distinct build-up, I knew it would get people back in the club. At the end of a song with a long duration, if the band did it just right, and as the last note would play, the people would yell simultaneously. It would seem as though the crowd had synchronized with the performance. Whenever this happened, the show was a success.

When people throughout the entire club had smiles on their faces, I knew it was a moment they would remember as long as they lived. Helping to bring smiles to their faces and making them feel exhilarated—that's what the nightclub business is all about. Eventually the word spreads as to what a great time the customers had. This is what breeds success and longevity.

We also had promoter Jimmy Koplik helping us out more and more. Koplik had assisted a competing but short-lived New Haven club, the Oxford Ale House, book Elvis Costello. When Mike saw that happen (we never landed Costello), he called Koplik and asked him to help Toad's get national acts. Koplik liked Mike and said he would do it.

But luck helps too! One of the problems for the New Haven music scene had been that the New Haven Coliseum could hold only about 11,000 while the Hartford Civic Center had a capacity of 16,500. And so promoters would bypass New Haven for Hartford. But on January 18, 1978, Connecticut was hit by a heavy snowstorm. So much snow accumulated on the roof of the Civic Center that it collapsed! Fortunately, this occurred at about 4 a.m., so nobody was inside at the time and, subsequently, while the Civic Center was out of commission, the Coliseum got the big acts that came through the state. And sometimes Toad's got their late-night encores!

On September 16, 1978, Bob Seger and his Silver Bullet Band played a well-received show at the Coliseum. He was riding high; four months earlier he had released his tenth studio album, one of his best, *Stranger in Town*. There were so many hits on it that it went platinum in less than a month. The cuts included "Hollywood Nights," "We've Got Tonight," "Still the Same," "Feel Like a Number," and "Old Time Rock 'n' Roll."

For the Coliseum show, Seger did two encores, one of which was "Night Moves." But he was just getting warmed up. He left the Coliseum and came directly to Toad's to play some more. He gave the smaller but just as excited second crowd "Old Time Rock 'n' Roll" and the classic hit by Van Morrison's Them, "Gloria."

On August 25, 1978, one month before Seger, the Coliseum delivered another gem for us, a performer who was in his prime: Bruce Springsteen.

This was exactly three years after Springsteen broke through with his now-legendary five-night, ten-show performances at The Bottom Line in New York City. Those shows were part of his tour to promote his third album, *Born to Run*, which was released one week after the blockbuster Bottom Line run. And that fall, in October 1975, he was on the cover of *Time* and *Newsweek* in the same week. But it all got started for him at The Bottom Line, which unfortunately closed in 2004. The point is, The Boss loved to play in clubs whenever he got the chance.

Springsteen and his E Street Band were so hot in the summer of 1978 that they sold out the Coliseum almost as soon as the ticket sales were announced. Some fans set up tents outside the arena to make sure they got those tickets. When Springsteen came to New Haven, he was on the heels of a three-night stand, every night sold out, at Madison Square Garden.

The Coliseum show, a three-and-a-half-hour treat, highlighted the band's new hit album *Darkness on the Edge of Town*. The Boss leaped into the crowd during "Spirits in the Night." His already legendary saxophone player Clarence Clemons jumped in too. Springsteen kept going past midnight, with "Rosalita" and "Born to Run."

But was he tired? No way. Fortunately for us, that same night we had booked Beaver Brown. They were a bunch of local guys from Rhode Island who modeled themselves after Springsteen and his band. John Cafferty, the charismatic and determined leader of Beaver Brown, got the idea of going down to the Coliseum to invite Springsteen to jam with Cafferty's band after the Coliseum performance. During the sound check before the Coliseum show, Cafferty got the nerve to walk up to Springsteen and ask him if wanted to stop by Toad's later. Springsteen's glorious response was, "Yes!"

Late that night Springsteen left the Coliseum, got into the bus with Clemons and "Miami Steve" Van Zandt, and made the five-minute ride to Toad's. We brought them down an alleyway outside, through the basement, and up onto the stage. Before anybody knew it, Bruce, in a white sleeveless T-shirt, Clarence, "Miami Steve," and Cafferty's bandmates were rocking the stage! People went crazy. They couldn't believe it! The guys jammed for about half an hour. They played the oldie classics "Double Shot of My Baby's Love," and "You Can't Sit Down" and, for the second time that night in New Haven, "Rosalita." Those who were lucky enough to be there will never forget the night Springsteen hit the Toad's stage. And we were lucky that the Hartford Civic Center roof had fallen in because that enabled the smaller New Haven Coliseum to book him and for Springsteen to be in town.

This was the first superstar act to hit Toad's. Little did we know that it was the first of many to come. Toad's Place was now "on the map." And we were just getting warmed up!

CHAPTER 3

Billy Joel, U2, and Much More

ONE DAY IN JULY 1980 PROMOTER JIMMY KOPLIK, WHO WAS BECOMING A GOOD FRIEND of ours, got a startling phone call. Billy Joel wanted to play at a club for a live album (*Songs in the Attic*) he was making. Koplik came through for us, telling Joel's guy that Toad's was where Joel should do the show.

At that time Joel was known around the world for his catchy songs, evocative lyrics, and dynamic performances. He had had his breakthrough in 1973 with his *Piano Man* album, featuring the title track and "Captain Jack." He followed it with *Streetlife Serenade* the next year, then *The Stranger* in 1977 and *52nd Street* in 1978. *The Stranger* had four hit songs: "She's Always a Woman," "Just the Way You Are," "Movin' Out (Anthony's Song)," and "Only the Good Die Young."

But in the summer of 1980, he decided he wanted to record a live album in a variety of venues, ranging from Madison Square Garden to intimate clubs such as ours. In his liner notes for that album, Joel wrote that it was "a presentation of older material in a concert setting, which I have always referred to as 'songs in the attic.' Some songs were recorded in 300-seat clubs. Ambience was essential in capturing the original spirit. It puts us in close, personal contact with a small but intense group of people."

Koplik knew Toad's could give Joel that "small but intense group of people."

We also lucked out because that summer Joel was scheduled to be in Connecticut to do two shows at the Hartford Civic Center, whose caved-in roof had been repaired by then. Both of the shows quickly sold out; about thirty-three thousand people moved fast to buy tickets. Those performances were going to be on a Friday and Saturday, so we scheduled the initially secret performances to happen on the following Wednesday and Thursday (July 9 and 10).

We advertised the band for those shows as The Dakota Five in order to keep the lid on this for a few days. That whole week was very stressful. We were all nervous about the Piano Man coming, and just about anything going wrong. Was there anything we hadn't thought of?

Joel got into New Haven on Monday, July 7. He came to Toad's that night to see a show we had booked with Manhattan Transfer, a sell-out. Joel was a fan of that band and he went down to the dressing room to speak with some of them.

After he was done downstairs, he wanted to get back to his hotel in downtown New Haven. I offered to give him a ride and he jumped into my car. Joel was beside me in the passenger seat, his security guys were seated behind us. I was a little nervous, so I made small talk by pointing out some of the Yale landmarks.

"I'll enjoy working with you," he said.

I knew he was going to be around for a second day, so I asked him if he wanted to do anything while he was in New Haven. He said no, he was all set.

Although we had booked one of the hottest performers of the day, we had a problem with ticket sales for the Joel shows. Mike simply could not keep a secret. I could hear him on the phone.

"Don't tell anyone," he said. "This is top secret. No one knows—Billy Joel is coming to Toad's!" He probably told fifty people or more, and you know those fifty people told all of their close friends. I'll let Koplik jump in here.

"Those shows almost got cancelled because of Mike," he explains. "We hadn't initially said it was Billy Joel; it was going to be announced on WPLR. But when I got there outside Toad's on the morning of the first show, there was a line of about a hundred people out on the sidewalk. I went upstairs and I asked Brian and Mike, 'Why are they on line?' Brian said, 'I don't know.' Mike said, 'I don't know.' So I went back down to the sidewalk and I asked the people, 'Who are you here to buy tickets for?' And they all said, 'Billy Joel.' And I said, 'Who told you?' They all said, 'Mike told me.' I went back upstairs and said, 'Mike, I love you, but your friends aren't all going to buy tickets before the general public; that's not right.' So we told everybody on the sidewalk to go home and we set up a new ticket site at a trailer near Long Wharf (in New Haven's harbor area a couple of miles away) and they did the ticket sales."

Clockwise from top left: Jim Koplik, Little Feat, Big Al/NRBQ, Chick Corea, Extreme, John Entwistle, Yngwie Malmsteen, Chuck Mangione, and U2.

We then put the Koplik Plan B into action. WPLR announced Billy Joel was going to play two shows at Toad's and you could get tickets only at that trailer. Everybody raced down to Long Wharf and of course both shows sold out almost immediately. The people who scored those tickets acted like they had won the lottery. We sold only 460 tickets for each night. Right away those who had gotten tickets for the first night came right back to the sidewalk outside Toad's to wait for the doors to open.

A crew we sometimes used from A Team Security was brought in to surround Joel. The bouncers patrolling outside were wearing buttons that said, "It's not rock 'n' roll, it's a big hassle." And it sure was a hassle for anybody in line who tried to get inside with a recording device or a camera. Photographers who had been assigned to cover the show for the *New Haven Register* and other media outlets were forced to smuggle in their equipment, strapping lenses and other apparatus around their legs and stomachs. But after they got in and started shooting, they were yanked from the crowd by those security guys, and their film was confiscated. As the *Register* reported, "Billy Joel doesn't like having his picture taken." The newspaper ended up using an old publicity shot.

Randall Beach, the *New Haven Register's* rock 'n' roll reviewer, reported on that first night, "Scalpers added to the fun, offering to sell $7.50 tickets for $50. Groupies in cowboy boots and shiny tight pants anxiously awaited outside a side door, which accepted only VIPs and roadies. Cops wandered up and down the line of ticket holders, announcing through megaphones, 'Don't push forward. You'll crush everybody ahead of you.'"

Here's more from Beach's review: "At 9:45 p.m. the band came out and Joel followed, smoking a cigarette and bouncing around the stage in his trademark sport coat, jeans and tie. Already cranked up, the crowd erupted as Joel tore into his new hit single, 'You May Be Right.'"

Joel, then thirty-one, who had been a boxer as a teenager, was bobbing and weaving as he performed. This was the great thing about having Joel at Toad's and why it was such a treat for that lucky audience: You saw everything, up close. As Beach noted, "After seeing Joel in his usual BIG arena venues, it's a revelation to watch him from only a few feet away. You can see the defiant expressions on his face, the sloppy grins, the sweat on his brow. The guy sweated up such a storm that he needed to wipe it away with a towel after every song. His entire face put out like Dick Nixon's upper lip."

The crowd was loving it. But there were some hassles, as the bouncers' buttons had warned, during those shows, spurred on by those zealous security guys and Joel. During "Big Shot" Joel popped his Molson like he was uncorking a bottle of champagne and it sprayed all over the stage. A wise guy in the crowd decided to do the same thing with his beer bottle, and he got immediately thrown out by one of those A Team dudes. The security guy just wasn't in the mood and it was the end of the night for that unfortunate fan who thought it would be funny to imitate his idol.

Another tense moment came after the crowd had exuberantly sung along with "Piano Man," Joel's autobiographical remembrance of performing in California cocktail lounges. Shortly afterward some idiot yelled out, "Piano Man!" Joel stopped the show, looked around, got off his piano stool, and walked over to the edge of the stage, toward that poor fool. Joel looked at him and said, "We already did that song! Where were you? Did you go out to take a piss or something?" Then he walked back to his stool and continued the set. But this showed you something: our club's intimacy could bite you in the ass if you did something stupid.

During the first show there was a glitch with the sound system. When Joel lit into "The Entertainer," static hit the Moog synthesizer; Joel stopped the song, cursed and started the song all over again.

Although Joel was at the peak of his career, you could tell he had a chip on his shoulder when it came to rock critics. A writer for *Rolling Stone* had dissed him as "a particularly obnoxious frat boy who's hoisted a few too many while trying to put the make on an airline stewardess." And so Joel reminded the Toad's crowd that his album *Glass Houses* was number one in America. Then he said in a deadpan tone, "Thank you, *Rolling Stone*."

Joel covered several rock 'n' roll classics during those two nights that would never make it onto that live album, including "Mustang Sally," "Hold On, I'm Comin'," "In the Midnight Hour," and a somewhat obscure Beatles' song, "I'll Cry Instead." The crowd played ball with it, but they were there to hear Joel originals. They got really excited when he pulled out his big hits: "My Life," "Big Shot," and "It's Still Rock 'n' Roll to Me." Between those numbers, the crowd yelled, "Billy! Billy! Billy!"

Those shows clocked in at about two hours and fifteen minutes. From Beach's review of the first night: "The encores lasted until midnight, when he slapped all extended hands, shouted, 'Don't take any shit from anybody,' grabbed his beer, and dashed off stage."

The song from those shows that made it onto *Songs in the Attic* (produced by Phil Ramone) was the little-known "Los Angelenos." But there it was, the fourth cut on side one, with the notation: "Recorded July 1980, Toad's Place, New Haven, CT." When it begins, you hear the low expectant hum of our crowd, then the people coming alive as the band kicks in and Joel sings, "Los Angelenos all come from somewhere . . ."

Five months later—on December 14, 1980—a band came into our club that would go on to become superstars of the same magnitude as Billy Joel. But at that time virtually nobody outside of Ireland or England knew about a young band out of Dublin called U2.

They weren't even our lead act! They were the openers for a band called Barooga. I know what you're asking: "Who??"

This was only the eighth show U2 had ever done in North America. They were promoting their first album, *Boy*, which was new and almost unknown in America. "Boy" indeed. They were so young that two of them (the drummer Larry Mullen and lead guitarist David Howell Evans, also known as the Edge) were still teenagers. They were nineteen years old. Bassist Adam Clayton and lead singer Bono (Paul David Hewson) were twenty. If they had walked in off the street, we would have carded them before serving them a beer.

When U2 came into Toad's, the world, especially the musical world, was in shock. John Lennon had been assassinated the week before in New York. England was in mourning for its native son and America was shattered that an icon who had moved to the US had been killed here.

Either people were too depressed to go out to hear rock music or U2 was too obscure, but whatever the reason, only about a hundred people showed up on the first night we had them.

Koplik, who was involved with booking the show, said he paid the band $100. U2 was supposed to perform at the Arcadia Ballroom, located about a mile down the road from Toad's and a competitor of ours in the seventies and early eighties before it went out of business. But their booking fell through.

Bono wasn't in a good mood that first time we had him. First he got into an altercation with one of the Barooga guys. They almost had a fist fight before we could get them under control. And then, during the show, when Bono counted out for "11 O'Clock Tick Tock," Mullen didn't come in because he was on the floor trying to re-position his drums, which had slid forward. Bono got upset and threw part of the drum kit into the crowd.

Bono clearly felt guilty about this for a long time. Three years later, in an interview with Beach for the *New Haven Register* before U2 did a sell-out show at the New Haven Coliseum, he said he still felt ashamed about what had happened. "I lost my voice and things went very wrong on stage," he said. "Then I threw the drum kit into the audience. The energy level got a bit out of hand."

"I didn't sleep well that night," Bono continued. "The next morning I walked around the university (Yale), talking to people who'd seen the show and apologizing. Sometimes when you try to break through the barrier between yourself and the audience, you fall into the audience! Music should break down barriers, not build them."

When U2 returned to Toad's on May 27, 1981, they still weren't well known in America. For that show they drew only a couple hundred people. The band played seventeen songs, starting with "The Ocean" and ending with "Twilight," "I Will Follow," "A Day Without Me," and "Fire" as encores.

Six months later, on November 15, 1981, when U2 came back for their third and final show at Toad's, word had gotten out that they were something special. We were filled to capacity, 750 people. This time they performed fifteen songs, ending with a reprise encore of "I Will Follow."

U2 rolled back into New Haven in May 1983, but we lost out to Yale. The band performed at the domed and historic Woolsey Hall, which had earlier hosted shows by Janis Joplin and Jimi Hendrix. Koplik, who booked that U2 performance, recalled, "I told Bono, 'Don't stand on the box or we're all dead; that's America's largest pipe organ.' So on the first song he dances on the pipe organ with his big boots! That was one of the worst moments of my life. Later that night, after the show, Yale maintenance people checked it out. Thankfully, it wasn't broken."

One month after the Yale show, U2 was in New Haven yet again, but this time they were performing at the New Haven Coliseum. They had moved beyond the club circuit but we had bragging rights: We got them first and not just once, but three times!

A few years after those U2 shows, the band, now easily filling arenas, came back to Connecticut to play at the Hartford Civic Center. After one of their songs, Bono asked the crowd, "Does anybody know Toad's?" and people let out a big roar of approval. That was a Toad's shout-out I'll always remember.

Koplik, whose Cross Country Concerts was booking all the major acts at the New Haven Coliseum and the Hartford Civic Center, was also becoming a key connection for us. Koplik said it worked like this: "Ninety-nine percent of the shows at Toad's were booked by Toad's; Katherine (Blossom) and Lucy (Sabini) were their bookers. It's impressive the 'girl power' the club had back in the seventies and eighties. I would bring in my level of artists: Billy Joel, Dylan, the Stones. It was such a great club. Mike and Brian taught me about quality. Mike would replace the floor every couple of years. I told him, 'Mike, you don't need to do that.' But he said, 'You've got to do it every few years or it becomes a stale club.' And he was right."

Whatever we were doing seemed to be working. We were pulling in some interesting acts. One of our early shows in the 1980s, on March 26, 1980, was an up-and-coming band that would soon hit it big: the Pretenders. This was four months after their first album, *The Pretenders*, was released in America. (They were a British-American band). That album had some hits on it: "Brass in Pocket" and a cover of the Kinks's song "Stop Your Sobbing." But our ticket sales for that show were only so-so and we decided to offer admission for about $2 to anybody with a Yale I.D. Once we did that, we packed the place, with 715 bodies. Lead singer Chrissie Hynde was wearing a Dallas Cowboys shirt. With the energy from all the Yalies in the crowd, the band got into it and put on a memorable performance.

Three months after the Pretenders we had a well-known veteran band; John Kay and Steppenwolf came in for the first of several appearances. They of course played "Born to Be Wild" and "Magic Carpet Ride" and people were loving it. This was a fun summer show.

Katherine Blossom on Her Time at Toad's

I was hired as a receptionist and office person at Toad's after some of the local bands I was in had played there. I was assisting Lucy Sabini. When she left in the early eighties, I took over promotion and advertising and then booking the bands, as Big Mike became less involved with that. I negotiated what we would pay each band. I learned to be very flexible with their needs because every band was different. Sinead O'Connor almost didn't go on stage because we didn't have a tea kettle for her. We had to run out to an apartment around the corner and borrow one!

I met my future husband Peter Blossom at Toad's. He painted many of the signs that hung in the club. He also did lighting for some of the shows and played in local bands, opening for B.B. King, NRBQ, and others. Many people met at Toad's and got married!

I'm a shy person and it wasn't my role to talk with the musicians anyway. But sometimes I had interactions with them. Johnny Cash was charming and gracious and lovely. When David Bowie was at Toad's with Tin Machine, he walked past me on the way to the stage, smiled, and said, "Hi! How are you doing?" He was jaunty and happy. When U2 came in the first time, I interviewed them for a fanzine. They were really sweet, pretty humble, young, and eager. More people turned up to see them the second time they came. You had an inkling they were going to hit it big.

When we were booking Dizzy Gillespie, I had to check off what he wanted in his dressing room. I called a contact number and I was surprised when a man answered the phone and said, "This is Dizzy." I said, "Really? I'm talking to Dizzy?" And he said, "Listen . . ." Then a trumpet started playing to prove it was him. He was playing for me over the phone!

There were times when we spoke with agents for bands and we didn't know how popular they would become. One time an agent told me, "I've got this band who I think will be big. You should book them. Katherine, I urge you!" The band wanted $1,000 and we had to make sure we could sell tickets. We decided to trust the agent's word and book them—it was the Dave Matthews Band!"

Toad's became a jewel in the music industry, nationally and internationally because of the music we were able to bring. There was something for everybody.

As fall rolled around, we booked a band that didn't have much of a following yet. Huey Lewis and the News came to Toad's in September of that year. We might have had all of fifty to a hundred people at the start of their show, and when they finished there were four people left, sitting at the same table! It was kind of sad. And so I went downstairs to the dressing room and gave Huey and the guys a pep talk.

"Don't worry about it," I said. "You guys played great. This happens sometimes. Soon you'll be on an upward swing." It turned out I was right: within a year they were playing to a sell-out crowd at the Hartford Civic Center. And Huey didn't forget us. He came back to Toad's after they had started doing the arena shows.

Not all the acts we booked went on to make it big, but we made it a point to book a wide variety of performers. You never knew what you might encounter when you walked into Toad's. One of our strangest dudes was Captain Beefheart, originally named Don Van Vliet. Why did he change his name? "I have a beef in my heart against the world," he said.

Beefheart and his Magic Band came into Toad's on a cold Sunday night in December of 1980. Beach, who was there that night covering the show, reported Beefheart kept the crowd waiting for longer than usual, holding them hostage with "a recording of what sounded like a pack of wild dogs and Confucius singing in the shower."

When Beefheart finally walked onto the stage, dressed in a black suit, black hat, black shirt, and with a long orange scarf draped around his neck, he was carrying a bag full of harmonicas. Between songs he meticulously combed a fireman's hat, explaining, "I'm trying to keep up with the 'New Wave.'"

For ninety minutes he and his band delivered demented poetry, oddball songs such as "Making Love to a Vampire with a Monkey on My Knee" and "Ashtray Heart." Many people in the crowd were getting into it, bobbing around and swaying to the weird rhythms. But somebody was overheard saying, "What are they clapping for? I don't understand."

Beefheart was so ornery that he insulted one of our lighting guys. "Out! Out! That red light's too damn hot! Turn that damn light out! Did you go to college?" Then he went back to banging the gongs he'd brought with him.

"I'm speechless," said a member of the audience at the end of the night.

A lot of us shared that reaction. But we all got a night we would never forget. We still have an autographed photo of Beefheart. In addition to his signature, he wrote this message, "There are forty people in the world and twenty of them are hamburgers." I never knew what the hell he meant.

Yep, 1980 was an odd year, coming on the heels of the far-out seventies. In April of that year we brought in Flo and Eddie, the remnants of the Turtles ("Happy Together" and "It Ain't Me Babe"). Howard Kaylan (Eddie) and Mark Volman (Flo) arrived without a band but backed by a booming sound system that delivered the theme song to the movie *King of Kings*. Their stage act combined comedy, bizarre music, and a Turtles slide show. Somehow it worked. The crowd recognized *King of Kings* and applauded it. During the encore, with that song blaring, Flo and Eddie stood in comic reverence, holding guitars and stuffed animals over their heads. Quoting Kaylan, "It's a lot safer working with stuffed animals than stuffed musicians."

The crowd was not so receptive to the poet–punk musician Jim Carroll, who brought his band to Toad's in March 1981. We took a chance with that booking, knowing he had a single, "People Who Died" off the album *Catholic Boy* that was getting some airplay. But our crowd didn't dig him and he got booed.

And then we got Iggy Pop! The punk legend came to us for the first time on August 9, 1981. He and the band tore through fourteen songs, starting with "Raw Power," going on to do "Lust for Life," "Search and Destroy," and ending with "Dog Food" and a cover of the seminal Them song "Gloria." The crowd was eating it up.

Iggy returned on October 18, 1982, a month after releasing his album *Zombie Birdhouse*. He bellowed, "I feel like a horse!" as he introduced "The Horse Song" from that album. From Beach's review of that show: "The Popheads in the audience, in chains and leather, were slam dancing into one another by evening's end. Pop leered over them, taunting, spitting, sweating and parading back and forth in black tunic and pink tights."

He was thirty-five by then, old for a punk rocker, but still there were scratch marks on his chest and hickeys on his arm. Iggy crawled around the stage while singing "Watching the News," another new cut from his album. "I wanna be known!" he shouted. "I wanna be on the news!"

During the encore, as Iggy performed "Bang Bang," a few of his devotees tried to climb up onto the stage; roadies pushed them back into the crowd. Iggy, who had donned a turquoise chenille bathrobe with red trim for the finale, giggled and swaggered as he watched his wasted and fervent fans.

The month after Iggy Pop's first show with us, we landed Joan Jett, also her first time with us. She fit in perfectly with our rock 'n' roll image; her big song "I Love Rock 'n' Roll" was exactly the way everyone at Toad's felt. But Jett was one of those performers who hadn't yet been discovered, so we had only 380 people there for that fun show.

In the middle of acts such as Iggy Pop and Joan Jett, we brought in Buddy Rich, one of the most famous drummers of all time. Rich was closer to being a jazz musician than a rocker, but his talent transcended genres. Mike and I had talked about booking him when we saw he was out on the road and we figured, "Yeah, let's do it. This guy's a classic. So what if it's not rock 'n' roll?" The drummers in the audience wanted to kiss his feet. This was the only show my father ever came to see at Toad's.

Two months later, in October 1981, we booked another legendary old schooler: Dizzy Gillespie. The audience was treated to his jazzy horn sound. The way his cheeks blew up with every note like a blowfish was amazing.

When the show was over and the band gathered downstairs, I got a clue as to maybe why they called him Dizzy. I don't think they had a tour manager. They were trying to figure out how they were going to get to their next show, which was in Chattanooga, Tennessee. It quickly became clear they had no idea how to do it. Nobody seemed to know who was leading the way. They were all just looking at each other. I decided to step in and give them a hand with the navigation. I got them train tickets and later I heard they made it to Chattanooga.

Later the following year, in September of 1982, we were able to bring in another revered performer from the Big Band era: renowned jazz pianist Count Basie and his orchestra. We did two shows and both sold out. We offered about six hundred tickets for each performance. The Count, whose bandmates called him Holy Man or simply Holy, was in a wheelchair and couldn't stand at that point. We had to install a ramp to get him on stage. Decades later, people are still talking about that show. The Count died less than two years later, on April 26, 1984.

Sometimes we would be able to book acclaimed members of big groups that had broken up. In February 1981 we had Roger McGuinn and Chris Hillman, formerly of the Byrds. McGuinn had a huge grin during the Sunday night show when the crowd roared its approval for the opening song, "Don't You Write Her Off," from his new album. But inevitably the audience saved its biggest reception for Byrds oldies: "Turn! Turn! Turn!" as well as "Mr. Spaceman," "Mr. Tambourine Man," "Eight Miles High," and "So You Wanna Be a Rock 'n' Roll Star."

Two months later, we had another former Byrd: David Crosby. He strolled on stage alone on that Tuesday night, carrying an acoustic guitar. Hearing an affectionate ovation, he grinned and said, "You guys must've been having a good time before I even got here."

That was an intimate and revealing evening. "I'm always nervous when I first come out," he said. "I'm never sure if I'm gonna be able to do that (guitar) lick." Several times before he started a song, we could hear him mutter to himself, "Good luck, Dave."

He grumbled that his record company, Capitol, wouldn't put out his latest album titled *You Might as Well Have a Good Time.* "They don't like it because it isn't enough like Devo or Elvis Costello," he told the audience. "It isn't the music of the eighties."

Still he performed several tunes from that album. But he also pleased the crowd by doing Crosby, Stills, Nash, and Young standards, including "Wooden Ships," "Déjà Vu," and "Guinevere." As Beach said in his review, those were the highlights of the show. Crosby was so pleased by the applause that he reacted like a struggling newbie, saying, "You liked it!"

Crosby also marveled at the audience's rapt attention during his songs and at the respectful silence between some of the numbers.

"Wow!" he said. "A quiet spot where nobody yelled 'Boogie!' or 'Where's Neil?'" He was seeing that a Toad's crowd is something special.

But after he left the stage Crosby reminded us he can be moody and stubborn. He refused to come back for an encore despite a prolonged, tumultuous plea from the crowd. He remained downstairs, his door shut and guarded by one of our security guys.

When he refused to speak to reporters, one of Crosby's associates explained, "David's going through some personal problems right now."

That spring of 1982 was also memorable because the English progressive rock band King Crimson came in to do three shows in the space of two days. All of them sold out. The band, led by Robert Fripp, was best known for its 1969 debut album, *In the Court of the Crimson King.* The song list for March 4, with fourteen numbers, began with "Frippertronics" and ended with "Larks' Tongues in Aspic, Part Two." These aren't well known in popular culture circles, but the cultists who were there are still talking about that Toad's visit.

Fripp came back in March 1983 for a solo show. He was an oddball. I said hello to him and he just stared at me. Then we were told, "Don't talk to him; he doesn't want to talk to anybody." He also didn't want any cameras in the club. He put that in the rider of his contract about twenty times. Despite all that, he was a master on stage with his guitar workmanship. He was a genius. We just said, "Okay, you're above us; not a problem." Anyway, very few clubs can say they had the full band of King Crimson.

While we never did have the Doors (band member Jim Morrison died in a bathtub in Paris in 1971 from what was believed to be a drug overdose), we did get Robbie Krieger, who had been the Doors's lead guitarist, in 1982. He had a positive attitude about being a keeper of the Doors's flame and he was a good sport when it came to the constant, inevitable questions about Morrison, along with demands to play old Doors music rather than his own, newer material.

After the sound check that day Krieger sat down with Beach for an interview. Kreiger was enjoying some slices from New Haven's famed Sally's Apizza (we know the Sally's owners, so musicians who come to Toad's got those pies rather than the fare from rival Pepe's) and explaining that he "couldn't be happier" about the ongoing and revived interest in the Doors. "It's amazing that the stuff holds up today the way it used to."

But Krieger also noted during that interview that, "Nobody really knows I wrote most of the hits ('Light My Fire,' 'Touch Me,' 'Love Her Madly,' 'Love Me Two Times'), but I guess eventually they'll find out." Sorry, Robbie, that hasn't happened yet, but we hope this helps!

Krieger also had to address the Doors's weird and notorious history in New Haven. As I noted earlier, in December 1967 at the New Haven Arena, Morrison had a run-in with some New Haven cops that ended up with him being busted and the show cut way short. Kreiger entertained our crowd between songs by telling the story of what happened on that crazy December night. "Jim was backstage necking with a girl in a shower when a policeman mistook him for some hippie. He tried to kick him out and Jim wouldn't stand for that. He ended up with Mace in his eyes. We went on stage and in the middle of a song ('Back Door Man') Jim told the story of what had happened. The cops didn't like that, so they busted him on stage. It was written up in *Life* magazine."

Krieger then launched into "Back Door Man," and the crowd really got into it. That was another cool and unforgettable moment on the Toad's stage.

The crowd had been a bit antsy at first because Krieger wasn't doing Doors's songs, but people went nuts when Krieger and his band played "Love Me Two Times" and, in the encore, "Roadhouse Blues." It didn't matter that he didn't have a great voice; this was the closest the people there would ever get to being at a Doors concert.

We also booked Frankie Valli and the Four Seasons that year. We caught a break with them because in September 1982 there weren't many venues in which they could play (Connecticut's Foxwoods and Mohegan Sun casinos didn't open until the nineties), but we could accommodate them. Valli still had a fantastic voice and could hit every note. He and his band had a deep connection with an older audience, and so the place was packed. There was just one bad moment—somebody called out for "Sherry Baby" and Valli replied, "I'm gonna do that later! And if you open your mouth again, I'm not gonna do it!"

One of the good-times bands we hosted many times was George Thorogood and the Delaware Destroyers. Crowds loved it whenever he did "Bad to the Bone," "Move It on Over," and "One Bourbon, One Scotch, One Beer" (this song was originally done by John Lee Hooker). For one of his tours, Thorogood decided he was going to do fifty shows in all fifty states, one night after another! And he was doing those long rides in a Checker cab. It was an amazing feat.

Our long-term bartender Pat Healy remembers seeing Thorogood as he rolled up in that cab to do his Toad's show during the marathon tour. "I said, 'George, you don't look very well. This tour is really kicking your ass.' He said, 'Come here' and he took me over to a mirror. And he said, 'You don't look so good either! What's your excuse? I'm driving around in a Checker cab!'"

Commander Cody was another character who did plenty of shows with us. His one song that made it big on the radio was "Hot Rod Lincoln," and he was pissed that his other stuff never got recognized. He was also mad at his record company for not promoting him. When Beach interviewed him backstage, the Commander was in an ornery mood. "I'm not mad," he said. "I'm . . . stoned." He went on to explain, "My writing's getting better, my piano playing's getting better, my singing's getting better, my band's getting better, but I'm not making any money."

Four hours later he walked on stage, introduced as "the duke of disgusting." He took a swig from his beer and remarked, "This is the number-one health food in the world. It goes very well with triple-cheeseburgers." The crowd, 90 percent male, laughed and saluted him with their own beer bottles. Then Cody and the band played "Two Triple-Cheese-Side-Order-of-Fries."

While performing the Hank Williams classic "Smoke, Smoke, Smoke that Cigarette," Cody loaded up his mouth with multiple cigarettes. It was a hoot. He pulled a Jerry Lee Lewis by playing part of that song with the heel of his foot on the piano.

Cody and his band (no longer the Lost Planet Airmen) kept the joint rocking with "Riot in Cell Block No. 9," "Red Cadillac with Jukebox Drive," "Too Much Fun," and of course "Hot Rod Lincoln." Then they knocked out the drunken beer bottlers with an encore of "Lost in the Ozone Again."

Another of our regulars was Jeff Lorber, the keyboardist of the band Jeff Lorber Fusion, who latched onto that name because they played jazz fusion. One day while he was with us, we got hit with a snowstorm. Jeff spent the whole day working on a new song, an instrumental. He called it "Toad's Place." A nice tribute. One of the guys in his band was a saxophonist named Kenny Gorelick—better known as Kenny G. He would go on to have a spectacularly successful career.

The group that would become our unofficial "house band" was NRBQ, which stood for the New Rhythm and Blues Quartet. Their fans, however, called them "the Q," and always looked forward to a rollicking fun time on a Friday or Saturday night when they came to Toad's. When "the Q" came to town we knew we'd have a good party weekend and people would leave with smiles on their faces. The band delivered this irresistible mix of rock, pop, blues, and levity. When we had them, starting in the early eighties, the line-up was keyboardist Terry Adams, guitarist Al Anderson, bass player Joey Spampinato, and drummer Tom Adrolino. They played for us maybe a hundred times. We were bummed when Anderson left the band.

Anderson, speaking over the phone with Randall Beach in November 2020, said of Toad's, "It's a great club. I have fond memories all around. We always loved playing there. It had a great sound; it's all wood." Alluding to one of the famous New Haven touchstones, Anderson added, "Another great thing was they always had Sally's pizza!" He then went on to say, "I thought we played there too much, but we always sold out."

During NRBQ's heyday, when they were often at our club, Anderson told *Connecticut's Finest* magazine, "Some clubs treat you like cattle. At Toad's, though, you can always count on being treated like a human being. Their hospitality is great. I think Toad's is one of the best clubs—maybe even the best—in the nation. And I've played them all."

The guys in NRBQ were our friends and we were always happy to host them. The audience was always happy too. NRBQ fed off the crowd. The show would build into a frenzy, leading up to their big songs, including "R.C. Cola and a Moon Pie," and "Ridin' in My Car." They would play them, one after another, and the crowd would go crazy, screaming as loud as they could. Terry and Al asked to have electric fans blowing in their faces because they would be sweating so much. And their contract always specified they wanted Mexican food, just like the Ramones wanted their Yoo-hoo chocolate milk.

Paul McCartney was a huge fan of NRBQ. He was going to jam with them at Toad's the night before he did a show at the Yale Bowl in the summer of 1990. We were going to have a Beatle on our stage! We had a secret game plan; we were getting it all set up. But unfortunately some people who lived around the Yale Bowl started complaining that the McCartney fans were going to come into their neighborhood and urinate on their lawns and bushes. They got the politicians all stirred up and it became a drawn-out controversy. Eventually McCartney's people heard about it and he said, "If they don't want me to play, I'm not coming." He pulled out of the Yale Bowl gig, so we lost him too. That one really, really hurt.

Remember Clarence Clemons, who joined Bruce Springsteen for that wonderful surprise show in 1978? He came back without Bruce but with his Red Bank Rockers in January and July of 1982. Clemons, who we all loved as the sax player with the E Street Band, was called the Big Man. He was looking for what he called extra "fuel" to give him more energy. "Fuel" was high-grade coke, the pure stuff. But we don't supply that at Toad's. I don't know if he found anybody who could fulfill his needs, but I do remember he put on a great show.

Another artist we always enjoyed who did well for us was Arlo Guthrie. He's a great guy and told stories between his songs. He was the perfect club performer. He heard the video games going and he called out, "You'll be drafted if you get too many points on your score!" Of course he sang "Alice's Restaurant Massacree," his epic account of getting arrested for littering and then singing, "You can get anything you want at Alice's Restaurant" when he was called in to get drafted. (They didn't take him.) It was sad to hear him announce in October 2020 that he had suffered multiple strokes and could no longer perform in public.

One of the nuttiest nights at Toad's was when Rickie Lee Jones came in. This was in the summer of 1982; she was thirty-seven, still riding along on her one hit, "Chuck E.'s in Love." We booked her for two shows that night, not knowing what we were in for. Both shows sold out, which was good for us, but we were providing her with Bushmills Irish Whiskey, her liquor of choice. With her low body weight, she was shot pretty quickly.

As Beach reported in his review, during the first show she swore at the audience and called them babies. She threatened to walk out if the crowd wasn't absolutely silent. That just wasn't going to happen with hundreds of sweaty bodies pressed up against each other and up against the stage. The song she wanted silence for was a ballad she dedicated to her father. She was sitting at the piano, shouting, "Listen! Listen for two fucking minutes! This is to my father; it's very dear to me."

The crowd kept quiet for most of that song but when she sat back down at the piano later in the set, she heard too much talking. "Listen, babies, listen! I'm gonna say it one more time," she scolded. "I'm here workin'. I'm doing my best. And if you continue to talk, I'm leavin'."

"We're listening, Rickie!" a fan called out. "Don't leave," somebody else shouted. "You're beautiful!" yelled a third.

She got through that first show, delivering "Chuck E.'s in Love," "The Last Chance Texaco," and a finale of "Danny's All-Star Joint." She had a superb nine-piece band backing her.

By the time she got into her second show, she was well into her second bottle of Bushmills and was getting even more pissed off at the crowd. For some reason Rickie thought we had pool tables in the club, inside the main room where the show was happening. She ordered the crowd to stop playing pool or she was going to end the concert. She yelled at the baffled audience, "I'm gonna count to four and if the pool doesn't stop, I'm outta here!" She counted off, "1-2-3-4" and then she screamed, "I am out of here, out of this place! I'm not gonna stand for what's going on." One of her crew helped get her off the stage and downstairs. They put her in a limo and got her back to her hotel.

One of the people shaking his head in the crowd was John Griffin, the WPLR program director and DJ known as the Wigmaster. He was a big fan of Jones, but he recalled thinking, *Whoa! She's crazy! Damn!*

A few years later she heard about what had happened and that we had had buttons made that read, "I played pool with Rickie Lee." She came back to Toad's and put on an impeccable performance. She stayed sober as a judge. After the show she went back into our game room, which at that time did have a pool table. She played a game while people took pictures. Rickie was a good sport about the whole thing and to this day we are all still huge fans of hers.

During that same summer of '82, we booked John Prine, one of the great American songwriters. The mass media couldn't tell you who he was then, but those who showed up were treated to a fabulous night of Dylanesque lyrics and country instrumentation right up there with Willie Nelson. Here's what Beach reported about that Thursday night: "They made the club sound like an Irish beer hall as they stood and stomped and shouted out the wonderful lyrics to 'Illegal Smile': 'And you may see me tonight with an illegal smile; it don't cost very much but it last a long while; won't you please tell the man I didn't kill anyone; no, I'm just trying to have me some fun.'"

Our crowd sure had some fun that night, as did Prine, though he was shaking off his disappointment at not being able to eat a hamburger earlier at Louis' Lunch, which lays claim to being the inventor of that American classic; Louis' was closed that day. Everybody who was at our club that night and everybody in the Toad's community as well as his fans worldwide went into mourning when Prine died from COVID-19 in the spring of 2020.

Two other well-respected singer-songwriters came to Toad's within a couple weeks of each other in August 1982: Steve Forbert and Joe Jackson. Forbert had scored with "Romeo's Tune" in 1979. His writing was so good that the *Village Voice* saddled him with the label "the new Dylan." Our audience loved him; the show was highlighted by "Goin' Down to Laurel," about a "dirty stinkin' town" in his native Mississippi.

Joe Jackson, who had hit it big with "Is She Really Going Out with Him?" and "Steppin' Out" as well as "It's Different for Girls," played to a sold-out crowd. The fans knew the words to just about every song. They loved every minute. We were lucky to get him.

We also had Jerry Jeff Walker, and we got him more than once. His most popular songs were then and remain "Mr. Bojangles," which he wrote based on his experience in a jail in Austin, Texas; Guy Clark's "L.A. Freeway," and Ray Wylie Hubbard's "Up Against the Wall Redneck Mother." That last one is a great bar song and guaranteed to get the crowd hooting along. Jerry Jeff was another popular singer-songwriter who died in 2020, like Prine. Walker, who had a distinctively gruff voice, succumbed to throat cancer.

Another real character was Warren Zevon, who came to Toad's five times. When he rolled in on September 21, 1982, he was well-known for "Werewolves of London" and "Excitable Boy." He played for two hours and the crowd kept calling him back for more. "I love you, rock 'n' roll!" he shouted as he left the stage.

At that time, Zevon had gone off the bottle. In an interview with Beach backstage after the show, Zevon sipped coffee and admitted, "I had a terrible drinking problem. I've deliberately set out to de-bunk the drunken artist theory. I don't think drunks are funny. I don't think I've ever done anything funny when I was drunk. Certainly I've never written anything funny while drunk."

Zevon said he had been bothered by all the drinking among the Toad's crowd but had learned to deal with it. "Tonight someone raised a bottle in front of me all night long. On my last tour I'd have wrenched it out of his hand. But now I know I don't have that right. That's too judgmental."

But Zevon did have a temper. Before one of his shows during the sound check there was a problem with the microphone on his piano. Our sound man, Keith Dupke, could see that Zevon was struggling and he went up on the stage and tried to help him install the mic. It was a tedious job. Zevon stepped back and watched. Unfortunately Keith dropped one of the mics into the piano. Zevon told him, "I got it, asshole." Keith said, "Okay, no problem" and went back to the soundboard.

Anthony "Tank" Dunbar, our head of security, witnessed this and said, "We didn't know what he was doing; we couldn't make heads nor tails of him. After acts like that go crazy on stage, they come off and say, 'Can you find me something?' And I wanna say, 'Find you what? A psychiatrist?'"

We also had a problem before one of Zevon's later shows. A story in the *New Haven Register* (not by Beach) had a misquote from Zevon, saying he didn't like his guitarist David Lindley. Zevon read it and it really pissed him off. We told him we had had nothing to do with the article, but that didn't matter to Zevon. He blamed us for it and he never played Toad's again.

In October 1982 we landed R.E.M. for the first of what would be several shows over the years. They had only been together for two years but I already could tell they were headed for the top. Many times through the years, as I moved through the building listening to the bands and making sure the ship was sailing smoothly, I paid attention to what I was hearing. On that particular night I stopped dead in my tracks and just took in the sound of R.E.M.: guitarist Peter Buck, bassist Mike Mills, drummer Bill Berry, and lead vocalist Michael Stipe. It almost knocked me over how tight those guys were. I knew something had to happen with that band because they were just too good. It was great being on the ground floor with them, knowing they were headed for superstardom.

But then there were those acts who were headed in the opposite direction. Sometimes we'd book somebody who had previously been selling out arenas but then couldn't pack them in anymore. Case in point: Peter Frampton. He had been so big with his *Frampton Comes Alive!* album and tour in 1976. He managed to sell out when we had him on October 19, 1982, and he put on a fantastic show. But it had to be kind of a letdown for him, playing for 750 people instead of 10,000. Afterward I went downstairs and thanked him for coming. I gave him my usual rap, "It's a great honor to have you here tonight." I didn't want to go on too long or screw it up or accidentally say something that gets you into trouble, like a politician.

A week before Frampton, we had a new guy we thought would be worth the gamble. His name was Billy Idol. We could see there was promotional money and push behind him. He had that distinctive blond hair and a tremendous amount of energy on stage. He brought the roof down; it was an amazing evening. He was another one we landed early who was headed for greatness.

We also caught Bonnie Raitt when she was slowly building up her reputation as a wonderful singer and guitarist who mixed blues, rock, folk, and country. Her first album came out in 1971 and in 1977 she scored a hit with her cover of Del Shannon's "Runaway." But she wouldn't have a breakthrough album until *Nick of Time* in 1989. We booked her several times before that and before she started winning an avalanche of Grammy Awards.

In December of 1985 we had another up-and-coming band, 'Til Tuesday, with lead singer and bass guitarist Aimee Mann. Earlier that year they had the hit single "Voices Carry." This band was part of the "new wave" movement of alternative rock. Aimee was loaded with stage presence and she delivered for a sell-out audience. Later on in her solo career she returned to Toad's, accompanied by Sean Penn's brother, singer-songwriter and guitarist Michael Penn, and Mann's future husband.

In August 1986 we brought in Simply Red, a British soul and pop band led by singer Mick "Red" Hucknall. They had scored with two singles, "Money's Too Tight (to Mention)" and "Holding Back the Years," so our crowd was pumped to see them. The performance was superb.

Sometimes you get lucky; other times it's your instincts. One day in the early eighties we got a call from an agent who said he had a rising all-female band: the Go-Go's. We already had a band booked for the night the agent wanted, a local group out of Bridgeport called Uncle Chick. They had a good following in Connecticut and we had to decide whether or not to blow them off. Fortunately we decided to go with the Go-Go's, thinking they could end up being something big. Soon afterward they were doing big arenas, with lead singer Belinda Carlisle doing their hits "Our Lips Are Sealed" and "We Got the Beat." For that night we guessed right, and in 2021 they were elected to the Rock & Roll Hall of Fame!

Sometimes you don't, and you get an act that gives you nothing but trouble. In September 1982 we booked Jimmy Cliff and Peter Tosh into our Waterbury Toad's outlet, a short-lived experiment on a second venue that just didn't work out for us.

We hung in with Waterbury for three and a half years in the early eighties, but it was a long slog. It seemed the people of Waterbury preferred to leave the area on weekends. It was not the right city for a nightclub. Then their management team got involved in drugs and started to steal, so we had to shut it down. But before we did, we got Gregg Allman, Johnny Winter, and Ian Hunter to play there.

Cliff, the Jamaican reggae star, didn't dig the Waterbury club either. Before the show his tour manager said, "We don't like the vibe here, mon." Meanwhile, Cliff was backstage talking with Beach, the room heavy with the smell of dope and sweat. "I used to play in bars," he told Beach, "but at this point it is really pointless to play in a place this size."

We had booked the band to play two shows that night, and Cliff kept the crowd for the first show waiting for nearly two hours as he pouted and smoked. Finally I told the manager, "If you don't play, you're not getting your equipment back."

"You're holding us hostage, mon!" he replied.

Cliff told Beach his affection for "the people" was the only reason he decided to go ahead with his performances. When he did go out there, he quickly mellowed the angry and impatient crowd by walking up to the mic and singing, "You Can Get It If You Really Want," from the film *The Harder They Come*. The people started moving with the rhythm and everything was cool.

"Tell the world you know you are special," he sang, and the crowd yelled back, "Special! Special!" Later he had the audience shouting African chants with him.

The crowd for the second show also had to suffer in the wake of Cliff's antics. Because of the delay with the first show, those with tickets for show number two were kept waiting outside in the rain for more than an hour.

Reggae bands are unpredictable, but one thing you know for sure: your club is going to reek of pot the whole day and night. That's what it was like when Ziggy Marley, Bob Marley's son, came to Toad's. There's no controlling it; they all do it. This is the way they live. Some bands drink gallons of beer; reggae bands smoke prodigious amount of weed. As soon as I got there that day for the sound check at 4 p.m., I could smell weed. They were high and they were going to stay high. They want their own version of reality through marijuana; the stronger, the better. But everybody's happy, nobody's fighting.

Before the casinos came to Connecticut in the 1990s and started taking away some of our mainstream regulars, we were able to have Kris Kristofferson with us for multiple gigs. Of course he was also a movie star (*A Star Is Born*) with those killer good looks. Middle-aged women would arrive on our sidewalk as early as 6 a.m., setting themselves up on chaise lounge chairs so they could get close to the stage for that night's show. Beach, in the *New Haven Journal-Courier* (the *Register*'s sister paper) on June 22, 1983, reported seeing this: "He was besieged by hordes of women. They screamed and sighed long into the night as he performed two sets, then had to make his way through the eager women waiting outside his dressing room as well as those surrounding his tour bus."

Tank Dunbar, who was overseeing security at the time, remembered Kristofferson as being "a chick magnet." "The women wanted him but he didn't want them," remembered Tank. "He was just a friendly (married) guy who signed autographs after the show until the line was done. A husband who was dropping off his wife for one of those shows said to her: 'Just don't come home pregnant.' And I'm wondering, *Why is he bringing her here?* I told her, 'I don't think you're going to get pregnant tonight.'"

But Kristofferson was happy to charm the ladies through his music. He sang "Help Me Make it Through the Night," "Sunday Morning Coming Down," and "Me and Bobby McGee," which he wrote but Janis Joplin turned into a mega-hit.

From Beach's review: "They loved him when he smiled, when he took off his black leather jacket, when he sang his ballads. Women of all ages swooned as he crooned, 'Lay your warm and tender body next to mine.'"

As erotic as this all was, Kristofferson told Beach he had stopped drinking and taking drugs. "I've got my life back together!" he said. He had also found religion; the last thing he said to that hysterical crowd was, "God bless you."

Another memorable show was on July 25, 1983, when Stevie Ray Vaughan and Double Trouble hit the stage. Stevie was one of the greatest guitarists we ever had at Toad's. (No, we never got Eric Clapton). Earlier that year he had played on David Bowie's *Let's Dance* album and that June, Vaughan's album *Texas Flood* was released. We got him shortly after he wowed the crowd at The Bottom Line in New York. Then he blew the roof off our club. People were frantic watching him play. Seven years later he died in a helicopter crash in East Troy, Wisconsin. He's in the Rock & Roll Hall of Fame.

On certain nights we've been willing to host humorous, oddball acts. And that's why we invited "Weird Al" Yankovic and Dr. Demento, the cult DJ, into our place in May 1983. Yankovic was then only twenty-three, but was riding the charts with his song parodies. And, unleashing his accordion, he sure played them at Toad's: "My Bologna" (to the tune of the Knack's "My Sharona"), "Another One Rides the Bus" (from Queen's "Another One Bites the Dust"), and "Ricky" (a take-off on Toni Basil's "Mickey").

It was fitting that these two were touring together, as Yankovic got his early inspiration by listening to Demento's radio show when he was a teenager hunkered down in his bedroom in the suburbs of Los Angeles. Demento played tapes of some of his favorites at Toad's: "They're Coming to Take Me Away, HA-HAAA" by Napoleon XIV, "The Monster Mash" by Bobby "Boris" Pickett, "Hello Muddah, Hello Fadduh" by Allan Sherman, and "Harry's Jockstrap" by Dickie Goodman.

How did the crowd react? From Beach's review of that show: "These two characters performed their craft for an amused, occasionally befuddled audience. There's never been a show quite like this one."

While chomping on a pizza backstage before his performance, Yankovic told Beach, "I'm only doing what most high school kids do—make up your own words as you sing along with the radio. I just decided to continue with it. I never grew up, I guess."

And he's still doing it! In April 2020 the *New York Times Sunday Magazine* devoted a long story to "Weird Al," calling him "a completely ridiculous national treasure, an absurd living legend." And our audience got to see him when he was just getting started.

When Cyndi Lauper first came to Toad's on December 2, 1983, she too was just getting recognized but she wasn't on the radio as much as "Weird Al." Two months earlier she had released her first album, *She's So Unusual*, which included "Girls Just Want to Have Fun," "She Bop," and "Time after Time." But those songs took a while to get traction, and so when she arrived at our place there were barely a hundred people on hand to see her. By the end of her show there was hardly anybody left. But we treated her well; we could see her record company was really pushing her. I showed her our shirts and sweatshirts and told her, "Take anything you want." She took an armful of swag. I had no idea she was going to be as big as she got.

Four months later she was back, in front of a sell-out crowd! "A lot has happened since I saw you last," she told the audience. Beach described the scene: "She immediately took over the place. She was a skirt-twirling whirling dervish. People were riveted by her appearance. She wore sunglasses along with an old-fashioned man's hat, a long dress, a bullet-spangled belt, mega-earrings, all kinds of bracelets, bright lipstick, very heavy on the make-up. Her hair: flaming red."

She climbed all over the speakers and skipped around the stage, talking to the crowd between songs in a breathless Betty Boop voice. She climbed back onto the speakers to do "Girls Just Want to Have Fun" and the room went bonkers.

She returned to Toad's after that as well, when she was playing at much larger venues. Maybe she was remembering how nice we had been to her during that deserted first show. This time she played shows on a Monday and Tuesday night; both of them sold out. On that Monday, Cyndi's tour manager said they wanted to go out and get a nice meal.

"Why don't we go next door to Mory's (the historic restaurant favored by its Yale members)," I said. "You can eat at a place that has a tremendous amount of history in the Yale world." We walked over there and met Wayne Nuhn, the head waiter, who was a Toad's friend and a big rock music fan. Even though Cyndi and her manager were dressed like bikers, Nuhn gave us the complete red-carpet treatment, bringing us up to the second floor and into a private dining room.

It so happened that every Monday night the Whiffenpoofs, the famous Yale singing group, performed for Mory's customers. They came into our room in their white tuxedoes, surrounded our table and sang two songs; the second was Cyndi's "Time After Time." Cyndi was crying as they sang her song. They were loving it too. She was so moved that she invited them to sing it with her on stage the next night. And so on Tuesday, Cyndi's second night at Toad's, she and the Whiffs sang "Time After Time" together and a couple of other songs. The audience really ate it up, especially the Yalies. It was a great night in Toad's history.

In January 1980 we had another female rocker in the early stage of her career: Pat Benatar. At that time she had already scored on the charts with "Heartbreaker" and "Hit Me with Your Best Shot," but she still wasn't that big a star. And so for that first outing with us she was the opening act for the Laughing Dogs, a favorite band of Koplik's.

Benatar came in for her afternoon sound check and all was in order. It was still a few hours before the show and we needed to get her back to her hotel, which was nearby. In those days few bands had the luxury of traveling in a motor coach, so the tour manager asked me the best way to get her to the hotel. After I found out the cab would be delayed, I said, "Hey, let me give you guys a ride." We all piled into the car: Benatar, the manager, and a couple of the guys in her band. She squeezed in next to me in the front seat, with her manager on her other side.

"Oh boy!" I blurted out, trying to make a joke. "I get to sit next to Pat."

She gave me the look of death. I swallowed hard and tried to smile. After that I kept pretty quiet. Sometimes you step in it, no matter how hard you try to be cool.

Benatar and her band put on a great show that night. She wore a very sexy outfit and sang, danced, and moved like a panther. She did return to Toad's but then went on to selling out arenas all over the country. When she did an interview with *People* magazine, she was wearing her Toad's Place t-shirt! When we saw that, we knew Pat Benatar was a true member of the Toad's family.

Some of the acts we brought in never became part of our family. In April 1983 we had John Lydon, earlier known as Johnny Rotten when he was with the notorious British punkers the Sex Pistols. They had only lasted from 1975 to 1978 but had shaken up the music world with snarling ditties such as "God Save the Queen," including the added line, "She ain't no human being!" After they broke up, their bass player Sid Vicious died of a heroin overdose. Lydon formed a new band, Public Image Ltd.

That was a weird and unsettling night for us. Beach reported for the *New Haven Journal-Courier* that when he arrived outside, the first thing he saw was a leather-clad youth with blood streaming down his face. Inside there were lots of other tough guys dressed in leather, many of them with Mohawk haircuts.

When the band finally came out at 11:35 p.m., the crowd surged toward the stage. Beach wrote, "A giant wad of spit sailed from amongst them and hit Lydon square in the face. He wiped it off, shook his head in disgust, and sneered, 'All right, I'm leaving!' But he remained. Lurching across the stage, spitting out the words, he shrieked, 'Wish I could die! Wish I could die!' The punks were pogoing, Mohawk-haired dudes ricocheting off each other in tribal slam dancing. The club's bouncers sought to dissuade them."

People kept spitting on Lydon and calling out insults such as "Hey Johnny! Nice career!" Finally he asked for the house lights to be turned on so he could see his tormentors. "Oh! Ugly!" he shouted. He spent most of the rest of the show with his back turned toward the crowd. They responded by lifting one of the punks up and passing him over their heads until he somersaulted onto the stage. A bouncer threw him back into the crowd.

After an hour of this, Lydon stomped off the stage, showered by more abuse and spit. He did one short number for an encore, then left, screaming, "Bye bye folks—I don't believe in spoiling you!" This drew more obscenities from the crowd. He just smiled and took off.

Another difficult act was Sinead O'Connor. She was the Irish singer-songwriter who was very outspoken on organized religion, women's rights, war, and child abuse. I had no problem with her political views, but she was pretty crude. She spat on the stage during the sound check and was barking out orders. I stayed away from her; I didn't want her in my face. I just wanted the show over with, to give her whatever the hell she wanted, no matter if it was in the contract or not. I wanted to get the night done, so we didn't have an incident.

We had a much better time with Debbie Harry of Blondie, who had had hits with "Rapture," "The Tide is High," and a few other songs. She played at Toad's at least two or three times. Each show was better than the last. Debbie was really friendly. She came to my office just to hang out and talk.

We had another memorable show on July 21, 1986 when the Allman Brothers Band came to town. By that time they had broken into two parts. We got lucky; first we booked the Gregg Allman Band and then we were able to add the Dickey Betts Band as a separate act on the same night.

The original band had broken up in 1976, five years after Duane Allman died in a motorcycle accident. We did a full show of music by each band on that beautiful summer night; it was sold out and everybody loved it. As a surprise bonus for the crowd, at the end of the night the bands had a jam session together, so the audience wound up getting a full-fledged Allman Brothers show.

Gregg Allman loved Toad's; he played here a lot. One night he was playing at the Palace Theater a few blocks away from us and he decided to stop in and see us. When he came in, he went straight up to the bar, slammed his fist down and said, "I want some Jack Daniels and I want some pussy!" There were a lot of groupies hanging around, so he had no problem. He could get laid any time he wanted to. He came to my office and I gave him a Toad's jacket. He put it on right away. He hung out for a few more hours and had more than a few drinks, then left in his car. Unfortunately, he got pulled over by a New Haven policeman. Gregg told the cop he had just left Toad's. The officer saw the Toad's jacket and recognized him, so he escorted Gregg to his hotel. The cop later told me what had happened. In 2017 Gregg died of liver cancer; the world lost a great musician and Toad's lost a friend.

Because musicians liked hanging out at our club, they would sometimes just swing by, like Allman did that night, even if they didn't want to play anything. One night after Van Halen played at the New Haven Coliseum, Eddie Van Halen came in and sat at the bar. I don't think he wanted to perform. When we booked John Entwistle of the Who, Pete Townshend came in to see the show. He did a lot of drinking with Big Mike. Well, ol' Mike got wasted, but so did Townshend, so it worked out. But Townshend never got on our stage.

Everybody in the club seemed to drink plenty of beer whenever the Marshall Tucker Band came in to play. One night we sold more than two hundred cases of Budweiser alone. The stacks of empty beer cases reached the ceiling. This remarkable total tied for our all-time bar sales record with the night John Valby, "the prince of porn," came in. His dirty songs and X-rated jokes have always drawn a rowdy, beer-swilling crowd. Valby has been doing a Christmas show for us for many years; more than five hundred people show up every time. I guess Valby's antics get them in the Christmas spirit. In an email message sent to Toad's in 2020, Valby wrote: "The Xmas shows!!— OMG—the energy in that crowd is inspiring."

Southside Johnny, with the Asbury Jukes, was also a perennial good-time crowd pleaser who helped us with our bar sales. But one night he lost his voice after only about one song and couldn't get it back. He was plenty pissed, but there was nothing anybody could do about it. The band played a few more songs and tried to keep the crowd as happy as possible. Sometimes stuff like that just happens; you can't predict it or plan for it. We had to provide some refunds, which made Mike mad. He had one of our staffers write Johnny a nasty letter, saying we wanted our money back. That's when things were going bad with Mike, as his substance abuse was becoming an issue. When Johnny got the letter, he was furious. I had to step in and write him a letter of apology.

We always booked our bands with an eye toward sales. Sometimes we would get a band that was on the cutting edge of stardom but we would book them on a Tuesday for the Night of the Toad. This meant twenty-five-cent beers from 8 to 11 p.m. In July 1982 we had the Stray Cats for one of those nights. The Cats, a rockabilly act led by Brian Setzer, were getting a lot of press then and definitely were on the upswing. It was a sell-out show. People had a fine time drinking beers for a quarter and dancing to great rockabilly.

Budd Tunick, the drummer for the Simms Brothers Band who played many shows for us, was at that time doing bookings for Toad's. He remembers hearing Mike on the phone in our office, saying, "Who the hell are the Stray Cats?"

"Mike, give me the phone!" Budd said. He had seen them on the TV show *Fridays* and was blown away. Thanks to Budd, we got them for only $750. After the encore, Setzer said to the crowd, "That's all we've got!"

We also were able to bring in the Red Hot Chili Peppers in November 1985, just one year after they released their first album. This was a group that would go on to become one of the best-selling bands of all time; they performed during halftime at the Super Bowl in 2014. But timing is everything and we got them early, when we could afford them. They did an encore for us in October 1987.

They were always energetic and put on a great show. When they came back on stage for their encores, they were totally naked except for a sock covering their genitals!

And then there were the rising acts we didn't get, even when we had a chance. We almost had Madonna before she hit it big. But she wanted $3,500 for a Saturday dance party and we were doing huge money those nights. She was going to do only four or five songs and bring three dancers with her, no band, just pre-recorded music. She had just one song out then and hardly anybody had heard of her. Mike, Jimmy Koplik, and I were on the phone with her agent. We offered $2,500 to have her come in, but they wouldn't agree to that price. She said no, so the show didn't come off. Not long afterward, when she had become a superstar with "Like a Virgin," one of our crew members got a job working with her and mentioned he had worked at Toad's. She got out a brochure and wrote on it, "Sorry you passed me up." We could've had her, and we blew it! That would have been a huge feather in our cap. You're always haunted by the ones that got away.

We never got the Grateful Dead either, no Jerry Garcia at Toad's. But several times we brought in Bob Weir, a founding member of the Dead and their rhythm guitarist and vocalist. He toured with his band, Bobby and the Midnites. You can bet those shows sold out, sometimes with back-to-back performances on the same night.

The drummer for the Midnites was Billy Cobham, also a legend in the music world. He had played with Miles Davis. Cobham was built like Arnold Schwarzenegger; his arms were immense! The crew had to bring in a lot of extra drumsticks because he broke so many during a show. All the drummers in the crowd were awestruck.

We landed Santana for two shows on July 21, 1987. This was eighteen years after their breakthrough performance at Woodstock, highlighted by "Soul Sacrifice." Both of our shows sold out as soon as the tickets went on sale. The tour was playing in much larger venues, so it was a coup that we got these guys. They played eighteen songs for the first show, encoring with "By the Pool," "Europa," and "Right Now." There were fifteen songs in the second show, including "Samba Pa Ti," a slow-dance favorite showcasing a mood-setting solo by Carlos Santana, as the encore. They did their big hits, "Black Magic Woman/Gypsy Queen," "Oye Como Va," and "Evil Ways" in both sets.

The crowd was entranced. The only problem with that night was their suspicious bean-counting tour manager. He kept double checking the ticket counts. Finally we had to grab the box with the collected tickets at the front door and count them in front of him. He wanted to make sure they were getting every nickel that was coming to them.

Nights of Jaw-Dropping Music

Thom Duffy is a former rock music reviewer for the *New Haven Register* and is now senior editor for *Billboard* magazine. He spent a lot of time at Toad's in the day. This is his recollection.

For most of my years as a reporter at the *Register*, from December 1980 through March 1986, Toad's Place was my second home. Indeed, during my first job interview at the *Register*, when asked why I wanted to come to New Haven, I blurted, "Because it has the best rock club between New York and Boston!"

Since I was vying for a job covering the planning and zoning board in Milford, the editor interviewing me didn't quite see the relevance. But I was hired as a suburban reporter and soon began covering shows at Toad's for the *Register* (and later the morning *Journal-Courier*) on the side.

I came to the Elm City a few months too late to see one of that year's most notable shows at Toad's: the two-night stand by Billy Joel, who had already reached arena-packing status with *The Stranger* album three years earlier.

In 1980 I was also too oblivious to take in another act that made its inauspicious debut at the club that December: U2. The Irish foursome came to town, billed in a newspaper ad as "U-II," and played only a handful of songs as an opening act to a sparse crowd.

The following year brought U2 back to Toad's Place twice. (Inexplicably, I still didn't catch the soon-to-be massively popular band until they played the New Haven Coliseum on the War Tour of 1983). But 1981 also gave us the Brooklyn-bred rock 'n' soul of Garland Jeffreys, a sweaty summer night with the pure punk of bare-chested Iggy Pop, and a winter evening with the growling blues of George Thorogood.

Often I'd come to the club in the late afternoon or early evening, perhaps for an interview with an artist during the load-in of his equipment or just to hang out in the office upstairs with Mike Spoerndle, talent buyer extraordinaire Lucy Sabini, her successor Katherine Blossom, and artist Charlie Hunter, whose portraits of performers grace the walls of the club.

And what performers! I wrote countless reviews for the *New Haven Register* and *Journal-Courier* in the former newsroom on Sargent Drive. But a review of internet listings for shows at Toad's during my years in New Haven brings back a flood of memories.

Peter Frampton, Joe Jackson, the Stray Cats, John Mayall and the Bluesbreakers, Marshall Crenshaw, Dave Edmunds, R.E.M., NRBQ, Renaissance, and the first headlining show by an act better known as a sideman—Clarence Clemons and his band the Red Bank Rockers. And those were just highlights of 1982.

My nights at Toad's Place fell into a familiar routine. I would drive into the center of the city, searching for a free parking spot for my green Volkswagen bug on Grove Street, reluctantly opting for the paid lot on Broadway, or later stashing my Honda motorcycle in the alleyway beside the club. I'd arrive early enough for dinner (I believe I hold a record for the most eggplant parmigiana grinders ordered during those years from Yorkside Pizza, next door to Toad's).

The summer of '83 introduced New Haven audiences to the Blasters, one of the greatest bands to emerge from the L.A. punk scene, led by brothers Dave and Phil Alvin. July brought R.E.M. back to Toad's, en route to the band's status as one of the biggest American rock acts of the next decade. That month also saw the Toad's Place stage all but set afire by the blistering, soulful Texas blues of Stevie Ray Vaughan; I recall his performance to this day as jaw-dropping.

It's easier to see now, looking back, that the early to mid-eighties was a golden era for rock clubs nationwide, including Toad's Place. FM rock radio stations like New Haven's WPLR introduced their listeners to acts who then headed out on tour to build their audiences, night after night, city after city. This explains U2 playing Toad's three times in 1980 and 1981 before graduating to the New Haven Coliseum, then the Hartford Civic Center, then to stadiums worldwide. Jimmy Koplik, with partner Shelly Finkel of Cross Country Concerts (Koplik is now a regional president of Live Nation), brought many artists to Toad's as part of the artist development path that led to the larger venues they booked. During my years at Toad's, Mike Spoerndle expanded the seating area around the sound board to comfortably host VIPs, including record company executives who traveled up I-95 to New Haven to show support for their priority artists on tour.

What we couldn't see coming then was a new promotional path to massive popularity for artists, which edged into national awareness in 1981. It would first complement, then detour around, the national showcase rock club circuit. It was called MTV.

Yet in the mid-eighties, even MTV stars still toured through New Haven, and I recall some unforgettable nights on York Street. Cyndi Lauper played Toad's one month before arriving at Radio City Music Hall as the most nominated artist at the first MTV Music Video Awards in 1984. The quirky Wall of Voodoo, whose hit "Mexican Radio" got a boost from MTV, gave one of the most memorable shows of that era at the club. Huey Lewis and the News, who would later become an MTV staple, gave performances at Toad's Place in 1982 (and later at the Agora, about a mile away) that led me to predict in a *New Haven Register* review that they would become "one of the biggest bands of the eighties." (I was very seldom that prescient).

National artists grabbed most of the attention at Toad's Place. But attention also must be paid to the remarkable talent of local and regional artists who played regularly in the club, including the Simms Brothers Band (whose drummer Budd Tunick joined the Toad's staff in the upstairs office); the Helium Brothers' Andy "A.J." Gundell, who went on to an Emmy-winning streak as a television musical director; and John Cafferty and the Beaver Brown Band from Rhode Island, whose muscular and lyrical rock 'n' roll reached No. 7 on the Billboard Hot 100 in 1984 with "On the Dark Side," after the song was featured in the film *Eddie and the Cruisers*. (That band also welcomed musical soulmate Bruce Springsteen onstage at Toad's years earlier, in August of 1978, after Springsteen played the New Haven Coliseum).

For all the artists famous or now obscure that I recall from my years at Toad's Place, other names from the era must be recalled. In 1984 Rob Light had just begun his career as a booking agent, placing tours by rising acts into clubs like Toad's. Today he is a partner and managing director at the powerhouse Creative Artists Agency and he has run CAA's music division for the past two decades. In the mid-eighties, among Light's many competitors booking shows at Toad's was Joel Peresman who, two decades later, became president and CEO of the Rock and Roll Foundation.

I think most fondly now of other superstars at Toad's Place who never got the spotlight. Security man Anthony "Tank" Dunbar and his counterpart Bill Walkauskas ("Whiskey") welcomed me every night at the door. Sound man Keith Dupke greeted me when I snuck into the VIP seating area. Waitress Ann Marie Gursky served me gin and tonics, my drink of choice in those days. (What was I thinking?). In his dapper Toad's Place "uniform" of white shirt and black vest, co-manager Kevin Meehan kept watch over the crowd from behind the front bar. Downstairs in his office or checking in on artists in the adjacent dressing room, I always knew Brian Phelps had everything under control.

It's been nearly thirty-five years since I left New Haven. In August 1989 I received a phone call from dearly missed Mike Spoerndle, inviting me to that "birthday party" for Jimmy Koplik. My grandmother had just died, I explained to Mike, so I couldn't make it to Koplik's "party." Mike didn't tell me what band would make a surprise appearance that night, so I missed returning for the Rolling Stones' set that kicked off the band's Steel Wheels Tour.

But the following January I traveled back to the Elm City to witness Bob Dylan's now legendary marathon performance at Toad's. Among the highlights of that night: a truly loose Dylan responding to a fan's shouted request, covering Springsteen's "Dancing in the Dark."

For the past three decades I've been a writer and editor for *Billboard* magazine. I've had the opportunity to travel the globe covering rock 'n' roll and the music business. But I owe my start as a music journalist to my *New Haven Register* colleagues, Mike Spoerndle, Jimmy Koplik, and Brian Phelps—and "the best rock club between New York and Boston."

You couldn't ask for a sweeter group of performers than the Roches (sisters Maggie, Terre, and Suzzy), who were with us on multiple occasions and always got an affectionate response from their cult followers. During their show in the last week of November 1989, reviewed by Randall Beach for *Billboard* magazine, they drew applause and laughter for "Big Nuthin,'" their sardonic song about an appearance on *Saturday Night Live* that didn't exactly launch them to superstar status. The Roches also gave our crowd a cover version of the Four Seasons's "Dawn (Go Away)." Then they strutted their harmonic power on "The Hallelujah Chorus" as the Toad's Christmas tree twinkled nearby.

In that same month, November 1989, we had Joe Strummer of the Clash. His seminal band had broken up but those Clash classics retained their power. Beach, again at Toad's to review the show, but this time for *Billboard*, reported that when

Strummer's new band tore into "London Calling," "The dance-along crowd at Toad's erupted and sang with him, fists aloft." On that night Strummer also delivered the Clash hits "The Magnificent Seven," "Brand New Cadillac," and their cover of Bobby Fuller's "I Fought the Law." During that song, which was the encore, Beach recalled, "The crowd offered up some thrashing male bodies above the throng and heaved them up on the stage like sacks of potatoes. Strummer, who has seen all this before, kept on singing and strumming."

A few weeks later on December 3, 1989, we brought in two-thirds of another legendary British band, Cream. Jack Bruce and Ginger Baker, who had partnered with Eric Clapton during Cream's glorious run from 1966 to '68, patched up their long-running feud well enough to be on the same stage at Toad's.

John Dubuque, an independent booker of rock shows who for a few years had an office at our club and also watched over our front door, recalls the anxious wait for drummer Baker that night.

"I was at the door, looking for him," he remembers. "We were all wondering, *Where is he? When is he going to show up?* I turned around for a moment and there he was. I noticed he had a pair of slippers on from his nearby hotel, and he said, 'Can anybody direct me to the dressing room, please?'"

Dubuque, a fan of Cream, recalls them performing "White Room" and "Sunshine of Your Love." "It was just awesome," he said.

One of the weirdest nights was when Roy Buchanan came in for a show. He was known throughout the blues world as one of the top guitarists anywhere. But he was an odd dude and traveled without a tour manager. One night in the early eighties he was supposed to do two sets. After the first set he banged on the door to my office and asked if he could get paid. I observed he had a little buzz on.

I put my hand on his shoulder and said, "Did you know we have planned for two sets tonight? We're doing a live radio broadcast on WPLR and it's been advertised for two sets." I was trying to speak extra soft and friendly because I didn't want him to fly off into a rage.

Fortunately he said, "I do? No problem. I believe you. I will get up there and do another set."

And so he did that second set, then came back to my office to get his money. I think I paid him about $2,500. I handed it all to him in cash and he put it into his pocket without counting it. He said he trusted me.

Then he sat down and I got him another drink. He was getting mighty comfortable; he said he had a story for me.

"Brian, we met a long time ago," he began. "It was not in this life. We met in a past life. We were riding horseback on a dirty, dusty road in the Old West. We met at a crossroad and talked for a bit. Then you went on your way and I went on mine. We made a connection that transpired all the way to this life."

I decided to roll with it, so I told him, "I do feel we have this connection, and it's been pivotal to our lives. I am so happy you brought this to my attention."

Then he said, "Do you realize that you are really Judge Roy Bean?" I knew Bean as the hanging judge from movies I'd seen. I just said, "Okay, I can feel that."

We had a few more cocktails together. He went on to tell me his claim that just before John Lennon was shot, Roy was at the recording studio where Lennon and Yoko Ono were working on what would turn out to be their last album, *Double Fantasy*. Roy said he knocked on their door; Yoko came out and he told her, "I know something bad is going to happen to John." According to Roy, she replied, "He loves you."

And then there are some bands that just become special. For us it was the Ramones. They stopped off at Toad's for almost every one of their tours, starting in the late seventies. Most of their shows sold out. They liked bright lights and high volume. Their songs were short and electric: "Blitzkrieg Bop," "Cretin Hop," "Teenage Lobotomy," "I Wanna Be Sedated," "The KKK Took My Baby Away," "Rock 'n' Roll High School." They wore motorcycle jackets and sneakers, as did most of their fans. At a carefully planned point during each show, they would have a guy hold up a sign that read, "Gabba gabba hey!" This was a refrain from their song "Pinhead." This dude would walk back and forth behind the band as they played.

We at Toad's consider the Ramones to be the greatest rock 'n' roll punk band of all time. This was their line-up: Joey Ramone as lead singer, Dee Dee Ramone on bass guitar, Johnny Ramone on guitar, and Tommy Ramone on drums (he left in 1978, replaced by Marc Bell, who then switched his name to Marky Ramone). None of them were really from the Ramone family; it didn't exist. They weren't related, they all just used that name.

On their final performance with us on February 23, 1996, as part of what they called their "farewell tour," we got a huge cake for them as a send-off. We thought that was the way to go because none of them drank alcohol. They always wanted Yoo-hoo chocolate milk in their dressing room.

Rick Allison, a DJ who was program director at WPLR from 1981 to 1983, recalls that when the Ramones were starting out, "This was a band that was 'dangerous'—people were afraid of them. They were punks. They were dirty! They would start a song and it was 1, 2, 3, bang! Go!"

Many years later, in February 2015, Marky Ramone came back to Toad's. But his appearance was upstairs in what we call Lilly's Pad, a small adjunct performance space. He came there to promote his book, *Punk Rock Blitzkrieg: My Life as a Ramone*. The room with filled with eager fans, but there was an undercurrent of sadness: He was the only Ramone still alive.

When I introduced Marky that night, I told the audience that the first time the Ramones rolled in to Toad's I was kind of afraid of them, as Allison said. We had had some trouble with bikers, and when I saw photos of the band, I wondered, *Should I get extra security for this? What's going on?* But then they walked in, all of them were wearing sneakers! So were their followers. Marky told us during his talk in 2015 that the band members just wore what they had always worn back in Queens. But for me it was a sign it was going to be okay; they were harmless.

When Marky was asked how it feels to be the only Ramone left standing, he said, "It sucks. We were like brothers. They died too young."

CHAPTER 4

The Stones Roll In

IN THE SUMMER OF 1989 THE ROLLING STONES WERE PREPARING TO GO ON TOUR for the first time in eight years. They had not played in front of a live audience for that entire period, a noteworthy absence for what was still the greatest rock 'n' roll band in the world.

Mick Jagger and Keith Richards had patched up their relationship after some verbal dueling over the merits of their solo albums during the previous years. Along with Charlie Watts, Ronnie Wood, and Bill Wyman, they had gone back into the studio to record *Steel Wheels*, their twenty-first studio album. This would turn out to be a comeback for them after the tepid response to their previous effort, *Dirty Work*, from 1986.

Steel Wheels wouldn't be released until August 29, 1989, and the first concert of the Stones' worldwide tour wasn't scheduled to happen until two days after that, at Veterans Stadium in Philadelphia.

The band needed a quiet, secluded place to rehearse after all those years off the road. Richards, who lived in Connecticut's Fairfield County (and has remained there for decades), found a suitable site at the former Wykeham Rise girls' school in the tiny town of Washington in the northwest hills of Connecticut.

After rehearsing for a few weeks, the Stones, nervous about playing for a live audience after close to a decade of not doing so, started looking for a small club where they could show off their classics like "Brown Sugar" and introduce a couple of songs from their new album, including "Mixed Emotions," which would become a hit after its August 17 release, and "Sad Sad Sad."

Koplik got the phone call from the band's representative on July 28. The question was this: "Where can they play?"

Koplik's reply: "There's only one place, and that's Toad's."

Koplik would later explain, "I told them it had to be Toad's because it was the best club in Connecticut and one of the best in America. Although it had one of the ugliest dressing rooms I had ever seen! And the bathrooms were ugly too. Yet the artists and agents knew it was a great club in which to play, with its fabulous sound system and receptive audience and that Brian and Mike knew what they were doing."

Originally the Stones wanted to hit different clubs each Wednesday night in August, a plan that was later scrapped because the Stones kept postponing the shows. They were thinking they weren't ready to play live after their lengthy lay-off. But Koplik started working the phones to set up places within an hour's drive of their temporary digs at that former girls' school. Hartford's CitiLites was on Koplik's list, but they didn't return his phone calls. And the people Koplik phoned at Water Street Station in Torrington, Connecticut, quickly figured out he was calling about the Stones, so they too got scratched off the list; loose lips could be a problem. Koplik was also considering Gemini's in Simsbury, Connecticut, but Toad's was always at the top of his list.

Koplik spent six weeks ironing out the details with the band's people, all while working carefully to keep the plan a secret. With the show about two weeks off, we met with the Stones' stage crew. They went through the entire PA system and lighting to make sure it was up to their needs. We also had to expand the stage.

Initially we were told we were going to have the Stones on Saturday, August 5, but four days before that, as we were continuing to prepare, Koplik got another call from their representative: Mick felt the band wasn't ready. And so everything was put on hold for a week. But somebody associated with the Stones obviously had told a few people about the original August 5 date because we had a ton of extra people come in for our DJ dance night. They kept asking us about the Stones playing and we told them it wasn't happening. They didn't believe us and so they stayed until we closed, drinking plenty of beer while they hung around. It was a nice, unexpected windfall for us!

We didn't get the green light until August 9, three days before that big Saturday night.

But still it wasn't a sure thing. The band's people made it clear that if word got out the band was playing at Toad's and the Stones saw thousands of people on York Street, the bus would just keep on going; there would be no show.

Clockwise from top left: John Cafferty and Bruce Springsteen; Bob Geldof, The Rolling Stones, Debbie Harry of Blondie, J. Geils, The Simms Brothers Band (photo by Budd Tunick), and The Ramones 1978 (photo by Tom Hearn).

How could we possibly keep this a secret? It helped greatly that this was before social media and cell phones. But still, people talk! Could those few people in the know keep quiet about it? Especially big mouth Big Mike?

Koplik remembers being really worried about this. "The problem, I felt, was Mike opening his extremely big mouth," Koplik said. "He was a very bad person to tell a secret to, as we had learned with the Billy Joel shows. Mike wanted to tell everybody he had the Stones coming in. I told him, 'If this gets out, it doesn't happen.' And so he managed to keep his mouth shut." (Mike did come close to blowing it when he told Phil Gallo, the rock music critic for the *New Haven Register* a few weeks before the show that something big was brewing—"the kind of thing that makes your hair rise and gives you goose pimples.")

Meanwhile, Koplik had to see to another detail. "I needed to make sure all of the pay phones were disabled so that anybody who came in the door and figured out what was happening couldn't call a friend and tip them off. There were no cell phones back then, thank God. There's no way you could pull this off today."

In addition to taping down the phones, we had to put duct tape over all of the Stones' equipment, which had been brought in earlier that day. We needed to make sure everything that said "Rolling Stones" was covered over.

We also needed a cover story for what was going to happen that night, so we told a few hundred people to "Come down to Toad's for Jimmy Koplik's fortieth birthday party." (His birthday was actually August 11, but close enough.)

"It was somewhat humiliating to tell people to come to my birthday party," Koplik remembers. "But I didn't want them to miss the show. People brought me presents! I got a lot of belts."

We billed the night as a dance party, our usual set-up for a Saturday night. But before the dancing got going, there would be a band: The Sons of Bob. This was a local group out of the small suburban town of North Branford, Connecticut (See the sidebar at the end of this chapter).

The admission price to see the Sons of Bob and celebrate Koplik's birthday was $3.01.

Thank God Mike managed to stifle himself and not tell people the Stones were coming. But of course there were a few exceptions. Wayne Nuhn, who was a good friend of Mike's and the head waiter of Mory's, the Yale-connected dining club next door, recalls what happened on the morning of August 12.

"I missed my trash pick-up at my home in North Haven. I just didn't get it out to the curb in time. But then I realized I could bring my trash to Mory's, so I drove down there. And I see Mike in front of Toad's; he's unloading equipment from a truck. And I'm thinking, *Why is Mike doing this? What about the roadies?* I walked over and I said, 'Hi Mike.' He said, 'Hi Wayne.' He had a strange look on his face, like he was hiding something. Then he said, 'Wayne, I'm going to tell you something I've only told my wife and my priest: I've got the Rolling Stones coming here tonight.' I said, 'Sure, tell me another one.' But then I saw he was serious. And he said, 'Why don't you bring your wife and your sons down tonight? The Stones go on at 10 o'clock. We're gonna lock the doors.' Well, we got down there that night and we were twenty feet from the stage at the center of the room. What a wonderful night! Just think, if it wasn't for my trash problem, I would've missed the Stones!"

Dean Falcone, a local musician who was working at Cutler's Records around the corner, also noticed something unusual happening at Toad's that day.

"We had heard the rumor for a few days that the Stones might play Toad's for a tour warm-up," he remembers. "I took a walk and sure enough, I saw a van unloading road cases into Toad's. Then I saw it: their lips/tongue logo! I ran back to Cutler's and called my closest friends. I was one of the first three people in the club, at about 5 or 6 p.m.; there was no line. When I found out the phones were taped up I had to go next door to Yorkside Pizza and use their phone to try to find a replacement for my gig that night. Nobody was supposed to leave once entering Toad's but I knew the guy at the door, told him about my predicament with the gig, and promised not to call anybody. Well, I couldn't get anybody to fill in for me. I went back to Toad's, paid the $3.01 again, but then I had to leave thirty minutes before the show started to get to that cover show at the Steak & Sword in Milford. This was a weekly gig for me, so it would have been a bad one to cancel."

Tank Dunbar, who originally had been told he was going to have that night off from his job working security for us, can still remember the phone call he got from me on that Saturday afternoon.

"Brian called me and said, 'We need you to work tonight.' And I said, 'Doing what, Brian?' He told me, 'Doing your job.' That didn't sound right. But anyway I came down. When I walked in the front door an English guy comes up to me and says, 'You the head of security here, mate? How many security people have you got?' I said, 'Four or five.' And he said, 'Oh no, I don't think so.'

"Then I see a guy from A-Team Security (a local company). He tells me, 'I've got twelve or thirteen guys.' They had people up on the roof and all over the place. We all worked together."

Tank remembers that soon after he arrived, I came up to him and asked, "Tank, you know what's going on here?"

"No, what's happening?" he said.

"The Rolling Stones are playing here tonight."

"What?" he asked, disbelieving. "You got me good!"

But then I told him again and he saw I wasn't kidding around. Tank knew he needed to get ready for his most challenging night.

We had an incredible number of details to take care of in order to make sure the show went smoothly and in accordance with the Stones' specifications. One of the key matters I had to oversee was having somebody pick up a bottle of Rebel Yell for Keith Richards at the Quality Wine Shop around the corner. It happened that there was a guy in the store who knew everything about the Stones and had heard the rumor they might be playing at Toad's. Seeing our bar helper buy that bottle of Rebel Yell was the smoking gun for that fan. He alerted a few of his friends and they saw the show they would never forget.

Jerry Zajac, who was Koplik's assistant and notes he had been "involved from the get-go" with pulling off the show, recalls Richards didn't finish all of his Rebel Yell.

"I went down to their dressing room later that night and saw he had left the bottle," he recalls. "I took a real good swig out of it!"

Katherine Blossom, who was handling our bookings and promotion, recalls, "I knew about the show for weeks, and I couldn't tell a soul. Finally, the night before, Jimmy told me, 'Okay, you can tell your parents now. They can come.' My mother did, but my dad didn't. He's always regretted it."

Katherine was as nervous as the rest of us that the secret would be blown and the Stones would back out. She remembers, "During the sound check, one of the Stones' crew did the opening of 'Start Me Up' and I cringed! I was terrified that people out on York Street would recognize that unmistakable sound."

As incredible as it sounds in retrospect, we were having a problem drawing a good crowd!

"I had kept it too quiet," recalls Koplik. "We had trouble getting people off the street to come inside. It was supposed to be a dance night and those didn't start until 11 p.m. But the Stones wanted to start playing at about 10:30. At 8:30 or 9 o'clock we only had a couple hundred people, and many of those were record company executives."

Koplik's friends were there for the "birthday party," but some other people had shown up because they had been tipped off about what was really about to happen. Gradually the crowd inside started to build as more people heard the rumor about the Stones and ran down to see if it could possibly be true.

Two special guests who had gotten the word were Daryl Hall of Hall & Oates and Joey Ramone. Hall had some kind of stupid argument with one of our waitresses about paying for his drinks.

"I haven't paid for a drink in over ten years!" he told her.

Finally Hall's manager said, "All right, all right, I'll pay for the drinks." We really needed stuff like that happening that night.

John Griffin, who used the radio name "the Wigmaster" for WPLR, where he was a DJ and program director, remembers seeing two angry young women outside the ladies' bathroom early that evening.

"They were saying, 'I thought this was supposed to be a dance party! But some band, the Sons of Bob, is playing. We're getting out of here!' I could have told them not to leave, but I just figured, 'No, let them suffer.'"

At 9:15 the Sons of Bob began their six-song, thirty-minute set. They were under strict instructions not to play for more than thirty minutes. The crowd gave the band a warm reception; many people in the room had found out by then that the Stones were on deck, so everybody was in a good mood and getting more and more excited.

But before the Sons of Bob played, we still hadn't received the green light from the Stones. Koplik, who was going to be the one to give the "go" signal, was pacing

"The Night We Got 'Stoned' at Toad's Place"

(Randall Beach's *New Haven Register* column © New Haven Register/Hearst Connecticut Newspapers)

The call came at about 6:30 p.m. Saturday. Fifteen minutes later I came home, turned on my telephone answering machine and heard this: "There's a real good chance that the Stones are playing at Toad's tonight."

After I picked myself up from the kitchen floor, I listened to the rest of the message, "Just thought you oughta know. Don't tell anybody where you heard this. You can call me—Deep Throat."

My guardian angel had come through. My wife and I had just enough time to run down to Toad's Place to catch what has already become a legendary night in our town's rock 'n' roll history.

Just a couple of hours earlier, I had said to my wife, "Look, today's your birthday. Whadya wanna do tonight?"

She sighed and replied, "I wish there was a place we could go dance." But when we scanned the club listings, we found nothing that appealed to us. New Haven, we concluded, was boring.

Little did we know that later that night we would be dancing to "Brown Sugar" and "Jumpin' Jack Flash" performed live, ten feet away from us, by THE GREATEST ROCK 'N' ROLL BAND IN THE WORLD, MAN!

So how much did it cost to see the Rolling Stones live at Toad's Place? Three bucks, plus a penny. That was part of the just-another-night ruse ("Stones? What Stones?") being played by the poker-faced security people at the club's door.

There was no line to get in. When I asked who was playing that night, the Toad's employee taking the money said, "Sons of Bob" without even winking. (In fact, that band was the opening act.) We shrugged, paid our $3.01 each, and went inside.

around inside, making sure things were still cool and communicating with the Stones entourage over a walkie-talkie.

"Their bus was coming in from that girls' school in Washington," Koplik recalls. "When I gave the okay, the bus came right up to the sidewalk near the club. We had security people block off the area and the Stones came in the side door, going straight downstairs to the dressing room."

It was already crowded, far too crowded for 7:45 p.m. (But no more than seven hundred people at the most would make it inside). The place was crawling with reporters and disc jockeys and record company executives. I bumped into a *Hartford Courant* reporter who said he'd heard the rumor nearby at Atticus Books.

Then I spotted a WPLR disc jockey I know and asked him, "Is it true?" He smiled and whispered into my ear, "Ten o'clock. Twelve-song set." (Their song "Dead Flowers" was on the setlist but the Stones decided not to play that one, so they actually did eleven songs.)

I rushed to the line-up of telephones to tell my friends to proceed directly to Toad's. But guess what, all the phones in the club were sealed with masking tape and marked "Out of order." And you couldn't leave if you wanted to get back in.

Another clue: The downstairs corridor was blocked off by a black curtain and guarded by two hefty security guys. A third security guard waved his flashlight down the stairway to a lingering female and yelled, "I want her OUT OF THERE!"

At 10:40 p.m., rumor became reality. Toad's owner Mike Spoerndle and rock promoter Jimmy Koplik came up to the microphone. Spoerndle said, "Ladies and gentlemen" and Koplik said, "Please welcome the Rolling Stones!"

The crowd went stone nuts. There they were, on stage—unbelievable!—Keith Richards, Bill Wyman, Charlie Watts, Ronnie Wood—and then Mick Jagger. He wore a T-shirt adorned with tongues, the official jersey of their upcoming national tour.

Jagger jumped as the band launched into "Start Me Up."

The next 55 minutes were loud, hot, sweaty and mind-bombing. Nobody sat down. Mick, who is 46, and "the boys" still look great and sound great. Never had any of us been this close to them, nor will we ever be again.

As he arrived and as he departed, Jagger slapped hands with the fans standing at the edge of the stage. "You're too kind," he said. "You're just too kind . . . my goodness."

My goodness indeed. Ten minutes later—after we'd staggered outside and waded through a gauntlet of fans who'd heard the show in the street—we retreated to the Elm City Diner, our ears still ringing. A New Haven cop burst in there and shouted to the wide-eyed waiters and waitresses, "I just saw the Stones!"

Katherine Blossom remembers, "I was going to be the liaison with the Stones. I had been told they'd call when they were two blocks away. The call never came. Somebody came into my office and said, 'Oh, they're here.' I said, 'What do you mean? They can't be!' I was taken down to the dressing room to see them, to prove to me they were really there. The guy who brought me down pretended he'd got me there to check out the air conditioning. When I got into the dressing room and saw them, I was sort of in a daze. They looked almost like cardboard cut-outs. They were so famous."

She said virtually nothing to them, even though Mick and the boys might have felt welcomed by her native British accent. "It was ingrained in me not to speak to the artists unless I was spoken to. We respected their privacy," said Blossom. "We never acted like groupies."

WPLR DJ Mike Lapitino recalls, "I was standing outside the dressing room and I saw the Stones come in. What struck me was how short they all were, especially Bill Wyman. You think they're bigger than life." Lapitino recalls hearing Keith Richards say, "This reminds me of the times we played in small clubs."

"It was surreal to stand there next to the Stones and be that close," Lapitino said. "They also had three back-up singers and Chuck Leavell, the keyboard player, but I just remember thinking, *God, this is fucking unreal! The Rolling Stones!*"

Koplik remembers being in that dressing room with the Stones for only about two minutes as they were getting ready to do the show. "Mick wanted me to introduce them," he said. "But I couldn't do that to Mike. I said, 'How about if Mike and I share the announcement?' Mick said, 'Okay, as long as you don't screw it up. You have to say this: 'Ladies and gentlemen, please welcome the Rolling Stones.'"

Koplik recalls pulling Mike aside and explaining, "Mike, it's very simple. All you have to say is, 'Ladies and gentlemen' and I'll say the rest."

At 10:40 p.m., Mike and Koplik had one of the biggest moments of their lives. Mike managed to get out his "Ladies and gentlemen" and Koplik finished with, "Please welcome the Rolling Stones!" And then, unbelievably, there they were! On stage! Right in front of us, the greatest rock 'n' roll band in the world!

Keith hit the opening riff of "Start Me Up" and the room lit up.

"When I heard those guitar lines," said Koplik, I thought, *Oh my God, they're really here!*"

WPLR DJ Rick Allison looks back on it decades later and says, "Holy shit! To see the Stones in that kind of native environment; oh my God!"

Roger Catlin, reviewing the performance for the *Hartford Courant* captured that moment perfectly: "People were rubbing their eyes to see if it was true."

Jagger, wearing a T-shirt with multiple reproductions of the Rolling Stones' logo with the big lips and tongue, was then forty-six but had no trouble jumping and prancing just as he had when the band hit it big in 1964. He took his first jump at the outset of "Start Me Up." Later he called out, "Everybody doin' alright?" Keith grinned out at the crowd as he traded licks with Wood. These were the intimate details you could never see from way back at a stadium seat.

Although all of the club's phones were taped down, somehow the word had gotten out. We must have had about three thousand people on the sidewalk and in the street. They too were going wild. New Haven cops had set up barricades and, with the help of our security team, held the crowd back. Eventually we decided to throw open the doors so everybody could at least hear the show.

Earlier that evening I had let in a guy who had Associated Press credentials. This turned out to be a great move because the AP story and photo made it into almost every newspaper in the country and beyond, including in China. It was like we had hit the biggest lottery that ever existed.

WPLR's Griffin had brought his son Zach; it was the kid's sixteenth birthday. "He was right on the edge of the stage, next to Keith Richards," said Griffin. "Afterward Zach said, 'Dad, that was the best birthday ever!'"

"When you think the Rolling Stones," Griffin notes, "you're seeing them on a screen in a stadium, little figures dancing on a stage. But here right in front of us were the Stones! You could touch them. It took a couple of days for it to sink in. My God, yes!"

The Stones had decided they would play eleven songs, which would take just under an hour (they were on stage for fifty-five minutes). The line-up went like this: "Start Me Up," "Bitch," "Tumbling Dice," "Sad Sad Sad," "Miss You," "Little Red Rooster," (originally by Willie Dixon), "Honky Tonk Women," "Mixed Emotions," "It's Only Rock 'n' Roll (But I Like It)," "Brown Sugar," and "Jumpin' Jack Flash." There would be no encore. What do you expect for $3.01?

"This is the first time we're playing this song in public," Jagger said as he introduced "Mixed Emotions." "So please be kind." He appeared to be anxious about whether those new ones would go over well and was visibly pleased by the crowd's warm response.

A Gig of a Lifetime

Who were the Sons of Bob and how did they wind up opening for the Stones?

More than thirty years after his band had the great luck to be chosen as the opening act for the Rolling Stones at Toad's, bass guitarist Ted Canning continues to process how it happened.

"I'm still shaking my head in disbelief. It was absurdly amazing; beyond anything you would even dream about," he said. "We were just an eager little rock and roll band."

They called themselves the Sons of Bob because all four of them really did have fathers named Bob (Robert). They were a local band out of the suburban towns of North Branford and Branford, about ten miles from New Haven. The members included Rob Guadagno on guitar and keyboards; James "Mertz" Polisky on drums; and James "Crash" Beatty on guitar and keyboards. Canning was the lead vocalist, backed by Guadagno and Beatty.

During interviews with Randall Beach in 2020, Canning and Polisky described the lead-up to their performance, the Stones' set, and what it was like meeting their idols backstage.

Polisky, who went on to be a graphic designer and artist in Providence, Rhode Island, said the Sons of Bob had a crucial inside connection with Toad's Place because his father had developed a friendship with Mike Spoerndle.

Canning, who would become a social worker for the state of Connecticut, said Polisky's dad mentioned to Spoerndle, "My kid's got a band." Spoerndle asked him for a cassette of their music and after listening to it, said, "Hey, they're not bad! I'll get them in on a local bands night and give them a shot."

Spoerndle kept his promise and the Sons of Bob played at Toad's for the first time in 1988. After the show, Spoerndle told them, "I love what you guys are doing. You remind me of U2. I'd love to get you opening for bigger acts."

But nobody, not even Spoerndle, could have imagined who that "bigger act" would turn out to be.

Two or three days before that August 12, 1989, surprise show by the Stones, Polisky and Canning were sitting around the house they shared with the other band members in West Haven when Polisky got a call from Spoerndle.

"What are you guys doing Saturday night?" Spoerndle asked. "I've got a gig for you guys."

Spoerndle used the same ruse he was telling other people in an effort to get a few hundred bodies to Toad's, saying that this was a fortieth birthday party for Jimmy Koplik.

"We had a show already booked for that night," Polisky recalled. "But it was a shitty gig at a little dirty hole (127 West Club) near Southern Connecticut State University. So I told Mike, 'Let us think about it. Can I call you back?'"

Spoerndle told Polisky, "You've got twenty minutes. You'd better call back by then or I'm giving the gig to somebody else."

Polisky and Canning didn't need twenty minutes to make up their minds. Canning recalled, "We said to each other, 'What the hell are we debating here? Why would we not take this gig?'"

"We figured, 'Let's play Toad's. It's Jimmy Koplik's birthday, he's a huge dude,'" remembers Polisky. "So I called Mike back in less than five minutes. But we could've blown the whole thing!"

The Sons had no idea they were going to be opening for the Rolling Stones. But Polisky noted, "There were these rumors flying around that the Stones might play somewhere around here." (People knew the band was rehearsing for its tour in Washington, Connecticut.)

The night before the big gig, Polisky went out for pizza with his dad, who told him he had heard from Spoerndle that "something really cool" was possibly going to happen at Toad's. Polisky said his dad kept it "very gray" in terms of what this meant, but Polisky had a "strong hunch" what he was trying to tell him.

Canning said that on the morning of August 12, "Rob and Jim woke me up and Jim said, 'My dad is saying Mike told him we might be opening for the Rolling Stones!' I immediately called my girlfriend, now my wife, and told her she had to come down to see our show, that we might be opening for the Rolling Stones. She said, 'You're insane!' She also said she wasn't feeling well and wanted to stay home. I told her, 'You really need to get down here. There's a serious rumor going around that we might be opening for the Stones.' Fortunately, she did come down."

Canning recalled the Sons of Bob's arrival at Toad's that afternoon. "When we got there the Toad's people came out and started unloading our gear. Never before had that happened. And when I walked in and looked at the enlarged stage and I saw the quality of the amps and the other gear, I knew then and there it was going to happen. The gear screamed Rolling Stones."

Polisky was having the same reaction. "When I didn't have to carry my drum set in, I thought What's this all about? That was a huge indicator. And the stage was longer, coming out into the crowd. There was also a giant black curtain extending from the bar, covering the whole left side of the club. There was this weird buzz going on."

"A few minutes later," Polisky said, "Mike and Jimmy Koplik came over to us. Mike was grinning like I'd never seen a human being smile."

Canning recalled, "Mike said to us, 'Do you know who you're going to be opening for tonight? You're opening for—the Rolling Stones!' We were kind of speechless but buzzing with excitement at the enormity of what was happening. It felt like a dream. I was thinking, *This is too ridiculous to be real*. That whole day and night had a surreal feeling."

Polisky remembered Spoerndle told them something else. "There's a lot that could go wrong. It could be shut down. Here's the deal: You can't use the [pay] phones and you can't leave the club." (Remember, in those days there were no cell phones).

Since it was only about 4 or 5 p.m., the Sons of Bob had lots of time to set up and think about what almost certainly was going to be happening that night.

"The Toad's people took us downstairs to a closet-type space, like a boiler room," said Polisky. "They said, 'This is your dressing room.' But they brought down a case of Heinekens for us."

Polisky said when he was setting up his drum set, "I was right next to Charlie Watts's drums. I put my hand on his bass drum and I thought, *Holy fuck! This is really happening!*"

"We were told, 'You guys will have a half-hour; that's your window to play, boys,'" said Polisky. "So we scribbled out a song list and just got up to play."

"When we hit the stage," Canning said. "I was almost paralyzed with the enormity of it for about twenty seconds. I asked myself, *Are you gonna freeze up?* But we pushed through. We all figured we'd do our set and do the best we can."

"We squeezed in six or seven songs," Canning said. "We didn't get booed off. By then, people were pretty aware of what was going on. We were just happy they put up with us."

"The tempo was probably faster than it should have been," admitted Polisky on the drums. "I was feeling the adrenaline!"

The Sons finished their thirty-minute set (no encore; forget about it!) and went downstairs.

"I'm standing there and I fucking hear Mick Jagger's voice!" remembers Polisky. "He was coming down the stairs from the side entrance. I turn around and he's standing right next to me. I said, 'Yo Mick.' He turns around and sticks out his hand. I'm shaking hands with Mick Jagger! Then the rest of the band comes bounding down the staircase, except for Charlie Watts. I never saw him. I'm shaking Keith's hand, and Bill Wyman's! We're saying, 'Hey, Keith. Hey, Bill,' like we're old friends. It was crazy. We chatted for a few minutes, small talk, then they went into their dressing room. We were saying, 'Holy shit! We just met the Rolling Stones!'"

Canning said he missed seeing Jagger because he was using the bathroom. "But I saw Keith come down the stairs. Rob said to him, 'Keith, we just opened for you guys. You missed us!' And Keith smiled and said, 'Aw, shit!' It was beautiful. We were all laughing, all hanging out backstage, joking with the Rolling Stones. We were kids! I was twenty-four. Imagine this happening to a twenty-four-year-old!"

Canning said that he and the other Sons got to hang out for a few minutes near the stairway with Wyman and guitarist Ronnie Wood. "Ronnie was nervous as hell. They hadn't played live in eight years. He asked us, 'What's the crowd like? How'd it go out there?' Then he said, 'Do you think they're going to be into it? Do you think the crowd will like us?' And I said, 'Are you kidding? They're gonna tear the fucking roof off this place!' Ronnie chuckled, took a drag off his cigarette and said, 'Good, good.' He was almost relieved."

Polisky said that a few minutes later, "One of the Toad's guys said to us, 'You guys can come upstairs.' They brought us up and said, 'You guys can stand here.' We were just to the left of the stage in a roped-off section, velvet rope. You couldn't get any closer to the band unless you were on stage. I could have touched them."

Canning chose to watch the show slightly apart from his future bride and the other Sons. "I stood opposite the middle of the stage," he said. "I wanted to get a good sound mix. It was a nice vantage point. I was smack in the middle, right in front of Mick."

In a 2011 write-up by Troy Church for his *Bigfoot Diaries* blog, Guadagno said, "The crowd seemed electric for the whole night. But once the Stones hit the stage, the place erupted into a frenzy of cheers. That was the first time the crowd realized the Stones were in the building, and they were sure of it. Everyone applauded, screamed, and sang along throughout the whole set."

Guadagno added, "Opening for the Stones that night was the single most incredible thing that ever happened to me in my life. It still seems like it was a dream. But really it was a dream come true."

At the end of his interview with Beach, Polisky said, "To have this in your back pocket, it's always cool for us to carry forward. I still have a chunk of wood from Charlie Watts's drum riser. It's always this really cool badge of honor: We're one of the bands that opened for the Rolling Stones."

On the following Monday morning, Canning, still high on the experience and wanting to thank the Toad's staff, bought a dozen roses and brought them to the club's office. Canning said he presented the flowers to a "beaming" Spoerndle, who was "radiating joy over what had happened. We were all still gasping in disbelief."

"Mike said to me, 'On your way out, go see Brian. He has your money.' But I thought it just seemed ridiculous to ask for money, the usual hundred bucks for a local band to do that gig. I just waltzed out the front door onto York Street with a wide grin on my face."

The Sons of Bob broke up several years later. While Polisky pursued his graphic design career in Rhode Island and Canning did his social work for the state of Connecticut, Rob Guadagno became a designer for Reebok footwear in Vietnam. James "Crash" Beatty became a lineman for a utility company in New Hampshire.

The only perceptible glitch came during "Bitch." In the second verse Jagger stopped singing, then found his place as the rest of the band continued to rip through it.

"We've been playing for about six weeks ourselves," Jagger said near the end of the show. "It's great to get some people to play for, you know."

When they wrapped it up, basking in the rabid applause, Jagger slapped hands with the people at the edge of the stage. "You're too kind," he told them. "My goodness!"

Then the Stones ran downstairs and went back into the dressing room for just a few minutes.

"They invited me in," said Koplik. "Clearly they were all very pleased with how the show went. They said, 'We have a birthday present for you' and handed me a check for $10,000! I split it with Mike."

The Stones wanted to get going, but they went out the front door, into the teeth of the hyped-up crowd! Why?

"Mick likes crowds," Koplik explains.

"Before the Stones hit the street," recalls Tank Dunbar, "Mick asked me, 'You in charge of security? Hey man, thanks a lot!'"

When asked how the band had dealt with all the stress and tension of that night, Tank added, "The Stones were as cool as the other side of the pillow."

But the crowd outside was not so cool.

"We had to do a human chain to get them to their bus," remembers Tank. "There were people banging on the windows, running around the sides."

As for me, I was a nervous wreck that whole day and night, up until the moment the police escorted the bus off of York Street. There were so many things that could have gone wrong. But it all worked as we had hoped it would.

When the people who had seen the show started to walk out the door, the people outside were drooling as they watched them, as if they were seeing diners who had been treated to a sumptuous feast. It was like the folks outside were starving, and all they wanted was a crumb by touching one of "the chosen." And the people who were coming out were yelling and pumping their fists. They still couldn't believe what they had seen; it was something out of a dream, the show of a lifetime, something only a very few lucky people were able to see. They would have a story they could live on for the rest of their lives.

Decades later, the legacy of that unbelievable night lives on. People who were there are telling their children or grandchildren about it. Those who missed it roll out their explanations for why they couldn't get there. Randall Beach's wife, Jennifer Kaylin, talked about seeing that show one night as she sat in a New Haven restaurant. A guy nearby overheard her, walked over, and asked, "Did you really see the Stones that night? Could I touch you?"

CHAPTER 5

Bob Dylan, All Night Long

EXACTLY FIVE MONTHS AFTER WE HAD THE STONES, WE GOT BOB DYLAN—FOR A mind-blowing four hours and twenty minutes. He gave the crowd fifty songs.

This remains the longest show Dylan has ever done.

And it was his first club date in many years. Not since 1975, when Dylan performed at New York City's Folk City to open his Rolling Thunder Revue tour, had he played for a club audience.

He called his night with us "a practice session," a rehearsal for his upcoming world tour. But for the lucky people who were at Toad's that night, it was a gift from a God, a night never to be forgotten.

Once again it was Jimmy Koplik who made it happen for us. He recalls, "I had been friendly with Dylan's manager for a number of years and he called me with the thought of Bob doing a warm-up show for his upcoming tour. Since it was only a few months after the Stones' show at Toad's, my suggestion for Toad's was met with much enthusiasm."

We designated our friends at New Haven's WPLR to announce the show. On Wednesday, January 10, 1990, two days before it happened, WPLR broke the news at 2:22 p.m., eight minutes before we opened our box office. That was the only place fans could buy a ticket.

Moments later people were streaming toward Toad's. They were double-parking and triple-parking outside on York Street to get in line. "Go ahead and tow my car!" fans were yelling. "I don't care!"

Eighteen minutes after we began selling tickets, they were gone. Only 750 people would be allowed in. Tickets cost $18.50 each, but nobody (including us) had a clue how long Dylan would perform.

Mike later told the *New Haven Register,* "I never expected this in a million years." He said we had thought Dylan would play one set, starting at about 8 or 8:30 p.m., after which we would hold our usual Friday night dance party. Instead people were dancing to Dylan way past midnight.

"It was a magical night," Spoerndle said. "I don't think it can ever be duplicated." And he was right.

It wasn't just the sheer length of the performance that made it special. On this night, for whatever reason, the often-reclusive Dylan was in a great mood. He joked with the crowd. He even took requests.

"I never saw him smile before!" long-time Dylan fan Joel Evans told the *New Haven Register.*

Keeping things loose and casual, Dylan brought in with him a small, tight band consisting of G.E. Smith, a New Haven native who was then a regular on the band for *Saturday Night Live,* along with Tony Garnier and Christopher Parker.

The crowd never knew what to expect or what was coming next, which was part of the fun. When the band came on stage at 8:45 p.m., they opened with an old Joe South hit from the seventies, "Walk a Mile in My Shoes." This was followed by the first Dylan songs of the night, "One More Cup of Coffee" and "Rainy Day Women #12 & 35."

Dylan pulled a slew of his other numbers out of his hat, but some were obscure, including "Lenny Bruce" from 1981, "I Dreamed I Saw St. Augustine" from his 1967 country album *John Wesley Harding,* and "(I Heard That) Lonesome Whistle," from his coffeehouse days in Greenwich Village.

Dylan finished his first set at 9:40 p.m. We all figured, *Okay, Bob, thanks. See you down the road sometime.* But then he asked us if he could play another set. We told him, *Sure, go for it.* And so he delighted the crowd by coming back on stage at 10 p.m. and performing "Watching the River Flow," the only time during the marathon that Dylan picked up an acoustic guitar. The second set also included "Across the Borderline," a John Hiatt/Ry Cooder/Jim Dickinson song.

Just before 11 p.m. Dylan finished the second set with "All Along the Watchtower." Again we thought, *That's it. Wonderful show, Bob.* But once again he asked if he could keep going. Why would we say no?

Clockwise from top left: Bob Dylan (photo by Peter Tobia), Gregg Allman, Village People, Tower of Power Gold Record, Marshall Tucker Band signed promo, Rickie Lee Jones, Joan Jett, and Eddie Money.

And so there he was, back on the stage at 11:15 p.m. Nobody knew it, but he was just getting warmed up. That third set went on for an hour and fifteen minutes. For the second time the band played "Political World," his latest single. They would do it a third time that night, adding new verses each time.

After the end of "Been All Around This World" didn't come out just right, Dylan cheerfully told us, "We're just working on the endings tonight." He and his bandmates sometimes huddled between songs, apparently working out what to play next.

Talk about free form! When a voice from the front row called out for Dylan to play "Congratulations" from the Traveling Wilburys' album, Dylan grinned and turned his back to the crowd to show his bandmates the chords. They happily fulfilled the request.

Dylan abided by another shouted request for "Joey," his tribute to the gangster Joe Gallo. Initially Dylan resisted, saying, "We'll be here all night if I sing that one." But then he relented after noting, "I ought to do it. God knows we don't have many heroes left these days."

And how about this for a cover song? Also by request, Dylan delivered his own version of Bruce Springsteen's "Dancing in the Dark." He followed that with another cover, Kris Kristofferson's "Help Me Make It Through the Night."

I went down to his dressing room during yet another intermission and asked Dylan what everybody else was wondering, "How ya doing? Where are we going from here?"

"Can we play another set?" he asked.

"Yep, not a problem," I told him. "We'll take care of it on our end." I didn't say anything else because I didn't want to say the wrong thing. I was kind of afraid to talk to him.

I don't think Dylan and the band had planned it this way; they just wanted to get ready for their tour. At one point Dylan was walking back upstairs with his band and said to one of them, "I can't believe they are actually paying for this practice session." But to his fans it was a gourmet meal made in heaven.

The fourth and final set began at 1 a.m. and lasted until 2:20 a.m. We had to close the bar at 2 a.m. because of the state law, but we didn't have to shut the club down entirely because we had the top brass from the New Haven Police Department on hand, enjoying the show along with the rest of us. Nobody was going to bust us. We just had to collect all the drinks from the crowd.

Dylan's Complete Setlist from His Night at Toad's

"Walk a Mile in My Shoes"

"One More Cup of Coffee"

"Rainy Day Women #12 & 35"

"Trouble No More" (Muddy Waters cover)

"Been All Around This World"

"Political World"

"Where Teardrops Fall"

"Tears of Rage" (The Band cover)

"I Dreamed I Saw St. Augustine"

"It Takes a Lot to Laugh, It Takes a Train to Cry"

"Everybody's Movin'" (Glen Glenn cover)

"Watching the River Flow"

"What Was It You Wanted"

"Oh Babe, It Ain't No Lie" (Elizabeth Cotten cover)

"Lenny Bruce"

"I Believe in You"

"Man of Peace"

"Across the Borderline" (John Hiatt, Ry Cooder, and Jim Dickinson cover)

"Leopard-Skin Pill-Box Hat"

"All Along the Watchtower"

"Tight Connection to My Heart (Has Anybody Seen My Love)"

"Political World"

"What Good Am I"

"Wiggle Wiggle"

"Stuck Inside of Mobile with the Memphis Blues Again"

"Paid the Price" (Moon Martin cover)

"Help Me Make It Through the Night" (Kris Kristofferson cover)

"Man in the Long Black Coat"

"Congratulations"

"Dancing in the Dark" (Bruce Springsteen cover)

"(I Heard That) Lonesome Whistle" (Hank Williams cover)

"Confidential" (Sonny Knight cover)

"In the Garden"

"Everything is Broken"

"So Long, Good Luck and Goodbye" (Weldon Rogers cover)

"Where Teardrops Fall"

"Political World"

"Peggy-O"

"I'll Remember You"

"Key to the Highway" (Charles Segar cover)

"Joey"

"Lay Lady Lay"

"I Don't Believe You (She Acts Like We Never Have Met)"

"When Did You Leave Heaven?" (Jimmy Scott cover)

"Maggie's Farm"

"Been All Around This World"

"In the Pines"

"Highway 61 Revisited"

"Precious Memories" (John Wright cover)

"Like a Rolling Stone"

Koplik, who, like me, had expected Dylan would play just one set that night, was sitting in the sky box V.I.P. seats with his family as the show began. "I never expected a four-set show that lasted so many hours," he remembers. "I left during the third set because my kids were fast asleep. With Brian there, I knew Dylan and his team were in good hands."

Mike Lapitino, WPLR's afternoon drive DJ, recalls, "It was great, because he sounded like Bob Dylan, like what you'd hear on his records. He doesn't usually sing that way in his concerts. And the way he was joking around! You realized this guy's funny! He's got that New York Jewish sense of humor."

But Lapitino adds the show went on for so long that many people, including Lapitino himself, left before Dylan finished. "I probably stayed around until about midnight. That was the witching hour for me. I had kids and my wife had to leave for work early the next day."

Dylan's final song was "Like a Rolling Stone." Alan Light of *Rolling Stone* magazine wrote, "Though his voice was starting to show signs of fatigue from its arduous workout, and the audience was exhausted, it was a final, exultant moment."

As Dylan departed, he threw his harmonica into the crowd and even slapped hands with folks in the front row.

Light noted Dylan was a year away from his fiftieth birthday. "Here he was, in close contact with his fans once again. It was an awe-inspiring performance, as close to a comprehensive retrospective as Dylan is ever likely to offer onstage."

CHAPTER 6

Bowie, Johnny Cash, Little Richard, and More

AFTER BEGINNING THE NINETIES WITH THE UNFORGETTABLE DYLAN MARATHON, we continued to bring in national acts who either were well-established or headed for stardom.

We did , however, begin to face competition from two wealthy casinos, operated by Native Americans still in Connecticut: Foxwoods, which opened in 1992, and Mohegan Sun, which opened in 1996. We simply couldn't afford to pay bands what the casinos offered.

But occasionally we still were able to land superstars, despite our small size. Having Jimmy Koplik as a connection was key to those coups. A prime example occurred on November 19, 1991, when we brought in David Bowie and his band Tin Machine. The show sold out almost immediately. Bowie had long impressed music critics and fans for his talent and ability to keep changing his sound. Bowie's first single on the British charts was "Space Oddity" in 1969, later a hit in America. His popular albums ranged from *The Rise and Fall of Ziggy Stardust and the Spiders from Mars* in 1972 to *Let's Dance* in 1983. Five years later, wanting to rejuvenate his career, Bowie assembled Tin Machine. Oddly enough, two members of the band were the sons of comedian Soupy Sales: bass guitarist Tony Fox Sales and drummer Hunt Sales. (In 1965 Soupy released a horrible dance record, "The Mouse," which somehow became a hit.) Another member of Tin Machine, Reeves Gabriels, played guitar and helped Bowie with the vocals, as did the Sales brothers. Bowie played a twelve-string guitar and saxophone during his show at Toad's.

Roger Catlin, the rock critic for the *Hartford Courant*, reviewed the show, which he noted was the band's fourth stop on their US tour. Catlin also wrote that Toad's was

Clockwise from top left: Johnny Cash, The Black Crowes, David Bowie, Rick James, Victor, John Kay of Steppenwolf (photo by Ray Cote), and Kris Kristofferson.

"probably the smallest club [Bowie] has played since he started out in rock a quarter-century ago."

"The sold-out audience was thrilled by the many aspects they've grown to love from Bowie: his melodicism, his still-strong vocal authority and his very theatrical presentation that makes him, even at forty-four, a thoroughly compelling performer," Catlin wrote.

Bowie and the band played songs from Tin Machine's two albums, which Catlin said were, "infused with a roller-coaster screech of experimental guitar." They also surprised the crowd with cover versions of "Go Now" from the Moody Blues and "Debaser" from the Pixies.

"Flanked by huge banks of speakers encased in chicken wire and safety lights, the band played unfancily on a stage lit by stark white or moody blue lights," Catlin wrote. "Hunt and Tony Sales provided a strong backing throughout. And though their occasional lead vocals lent a change of pace, they were also plainly inferior to lead singer Bowie."

This was another special night in the history of Toad's Place. Twenty-five years later there was shock and widespread mourning when Bowie died of liver cancer, two days after his sixty-ninth birthday.

In the summer of 1990 we got a phone call telling us that Johnny Cash, one of the biggest and most beloved country artists in the world, had an open date on his tour schedule and wanted to play in a club. We immediately booked him for two shows on August 2, 1990.

We had to pay Cash $20,000, the most we had ever paid an artist. But this was Johnny Cash. Both shows sold out within a few days.

WPLR's program director and DJ John "the Wigmaster" Griffin, will always remember that night. "Johnny Cash, oh my God!" he said. "That was on my bucket list. I got to see both shows. They were spectacular. The whole group was there: June Carter Cash [his wife] and John Carter Cash [his son]."

Cash had a tradition of starting his shows by saying, "Hi. I'm Johnny Cash." And he carried on that tradition at Toad's. He then began a setlist that included "Ring of Fire," "Folsom Prison Blues," a cover of Kris Kristofferson's "Sunday Morning Coming Down" (which Kristofferson sang when he was at Toad's), "Get Rhythm," "A Boy

Named Sue," the old standard "Riders in the Sky" (originally done by Stan Jones and His Death Valley Rangers), a cover of Tim Hardin's "If I Were a Carpenter," and "I Walk the Line."

Another legendary name graced our stage in November 1995: Little Richard. He hadn't played a show in Connecticut for decades, but he was back on the road the week before his sixty-third birthday, and we got him.

He was introduced that night as "the originator, the innovator, the architect of rock 'n' roll."

Catlin of the *Hartford Courant* wrote in his review: "Little Richard emerged resplendent in spangly suit, thick pancake makeup and poodly black wig-hat." He had an eight-piece band backing him, including two horn players.

"He sat at his grand piano like a relaxed king," Catlin continued. "Pumping out runs between songs to tease the audience. Breaking into a laugh or another good-natured boast, he was clearly having fun, and the fun was infectious."

Little Richard delivered an eighty-five-minute show, beginning with "Good Golly, Miss Molly," then launching into Fats Domino's "Blueberry Hill," Larry Williams's "Bony Moronie," the Beatles's "I Saw Her Standing There," and Hank Williams's "I'm So Lonesome I Could Cry."

The crowd was also treated to the singer's originals: "Lucille," "Rip it Up," and, at the end, "Long Tall Sally."

Catlin noted Little Richard even offered some vaudeville, "with a sing-along of 'Baby Face' that had him getting up from his piano to step gingerly from one side of the stage to the other." He also sang parts of "Itsy Bitsy Spider."

Truly an American original. As Catlin wrote, "Toad's Place can add another feather in its cap."

Throughout the nineties we were still bringing in artists who were on the cusp of making it big. In March 1990 we booked Lenny Kravitz, then a budding singer-songwriter whose debut album *Let Love Rule*, released in 1989, blended rock, blues, soul, jazz, reggae, folk, and funk. The show was a near sellout. Kravitz went on to become a world-renowned star.

One of our last shows in 1990 was by the revered blues guitarist and singer Buddy Guy. As Beach noted in a freelance review for the *Hartford Courant*, Guy had toured with the Rolling Stones, jammed with Eric Clapton, and played with Muddy Waters at Chess Records in the sixties.

"From the moment he walked on stage at Toad's Place," wrote Beach, "Buddy Guy had almost complete devotion from the sweaty crowd, which was seeking heat on a cold winter's night."

Attired in gray sweatpants and a sweatshirt, Guy played for nearly two hours. The show's highlights included "I Just Want to Make Love to You," the Eddie Floyd hit "Knock on Wood," and "Hoochie Koochie Man."

For the encore, Guy performed "Money," getting the crowd singing, "That's what I want!"

We had B.B. King at Toad's several times, but his February 1991 show stands out because it marked an amazing weekend when we hosted three Grammy Award winners. On that Friday night we had King, who played two sold-out shows. During his performance, the Kentucky Headhunters, the country rock/Southern rock band who had just won a Grammy, came in to watch, so we set them up in the sky box. In the middle of his set, King announced, "We have some Grammy winners here!" and pointed straight to the band. The Headhunters waved while the crowd cheered. King hung out with them after his show.

The following night the Headhunters did a fabulous show for us. They returned King's favor by telling the crowd that he had performed at Toad's the night before. Then on Sunday night we had another Grammy winner, the jazz artist Mark Isham. It was a beautiful weekend, something we couldn't have dreamed about when Toad's was just getting started.

When Phish was beginning to break out beyond its devoted fan base in Vermont, we had them for two shows, in March and May 1990. As the world now knows, the Phish members were inspired by the Grateful Dead and known for long jams. But when I first heard them, I didn't get it, nor did the general public at that time. For their first show they drew only about a hundred people. Our club was slow and empty. Nobody had any idea who they were, except the people who showed up.

After that first show I asked Katherine Blossom, who booked them for us, "Why did you book that band?" And when she brought them back two months later, drawing about the same one hundred people, I asked her, "Them again?" For the second show

I didn't even come in; I took the night off. I wish I'd been there and taken them out to dinner. That's the thing about rock 'n' roll: You never know. You ask yourself, *How did that band get so big?*

In November 1990 we booked the Black Crowes, who earlier that year had released their debut album, *Shake Your Money Maker*. It included two singles, a cover of Otis Redding's "Hard to Handle," and an acoustic ballad, "She Talks to Angels." They played two shows for us on the same night; both sold out. Everybody there was pumped up, including Kate Hudson, Goldie Hawn's daughter, who that year married the band's lead singer Chris Robinson.

On the Monday night after the Black Crowes we had booked .38 Special and the tickets just weren't selling. After we had sold only a couple of dozen tickets, we were thinking, *Holy shit! We're gonna take a bath on this!* But I had a brainstorm: We gave everybody coming into the Crowes show a four-pack of free tickets to the .38 Special gig. On Monday night we were packed! And we made out at the bar because many fans of .38 Special were big drinkers. However, I had to tell the .38 Special tour manager that these were comp tickets and I wasn't able to pay him what he had expected. I'm not sure he believed me. He gave me this look and it wasn't a happy face. He knew he would have to tell the band.

In May 1991 we had Eric Burdon, who had long before that left the Animals and his later band War. When he played at Toad's he disappointed our crowd because he wasn't up for playing many Animals' oldies. But he did lead off with "Don't Bring Me Down" and finished with "House of the Rising Sun." He introduced it by saying, "I hate this fucking song. I've been singing it for twenty-five years!"

Burdon was in a foul mood that night. From Beach's review for the *Hartford Courant*: "During a wild and willfully ragged two-hour exhibition, Burdon repeatedly swore at the lighting man, the sound man, and the crowd and delivered several bitter political tirades."

"Wearing shades and a headband," Beach continued, "Burdon roamed the stage, banging on a cowbell, and making everybody wonder what he would do next. 'Everybody here's having fun but me,' he yelled as his anger mounted about the sound system. 'Gimme a break, guys. I got into this business because I wanted to have a fucking good time! I should be fucking dead by now, but I'm not—so I live with it.'"

But Beach wrote that Burdon seemed to cheer up when he sang his old War hit, "Spill the Wine." Beach observed that during this song Burdon "shared what appeared to be a marijuana cigarette with the band."

Burdon might also have been pissed because only several hundred people showed up to take in his ranting performance.

We had a much more mellow evening in August 1991 with good old Randy Newman. Sitting at his piano for two hours, he performed thirty songs, ranging from his earlier work ("Yellow Man," "Louisiana 1927") to "I Love L.A." and of course his sardonic hit "Short People." *Connecticut* magazine named this one of the top ten shows of the year.

We were never able to lure the Eagles to Toad's because they had made it big very fast, and did so before we opened. But we did manage to snag Joe Walsh in March 1990. The Eagles were on a break, so Walsh decided to go out on his own. He did two shows that night and both sold out almost immediately. Joe had a nice buzz going; maybe it was marijuana. It sure didn't hamper his performance. It was an honor to have him. Any time you've got somebody from the Eagles, it's prestigious.

We were also proud to host the Kinks. The well-respected band was with us on May 3, 1993. Check out some of the highlights from this setlist: "Come Dancing," "Til the End of the Day," "Lola," "All Day and All of the Night," "You Really Got Me," and "Celluloid Heroes."

The odd thing about the Kinks was this: brothers Ray and Dave Davies were so estranged that they wouldn't even talk to each other. They required separate dressing rooms. This was not an issue in October 1995 when Ray Davies returned for a solo show. Kinks fans were treated to his acoustic guitar renditions of gems such as "Stop Your Sobbing," "Days," "Victoria," "Well Respected Man," and once again, "Lola." Occasionally he read passages from his autobiography, *X-Ray*. He was on our stage for two and a half hours.

We've had John Hiatt in for several shows and he always drew a good crowd. In 1993 the opener for him was Sheryl Crow, before she was well known. She did an acoustic set of about forty minutes. I had a lot of things to coordinate that night, so I didn't make it down to her dressing room to shake her hand and thank her, as I always try to do for opening acts, even if I've never heard of them. You never know if they'll become big names and you'll want to get them to come back. And guess what? Eight months later I heard her on the radio as her career was taking off. She got too big too fast for us to ever bring her back as a headliner.

In October 1992 we brought in Bon Jovi, led of course by singer Jon Bon Jovi. They were already well-established; four months later they would play at the Hartford Civic Center. For our show their opening song was a tip of the hat to the Beatles: "With a Little Help From My Friends." A highlight that night was "Born to Be My Baby" and they encored with "Livin' on a Prayer," "Wanted Dead or Alive," and "Keep the Faith."

We had Eddie Money on our stage several times, including in 1992 and 1995. He had scored big in the seventies with "Two Tickets to Paradise" and "Baby Hold On." During Eddie's third visit with us, while he was waiting for a sound check he was standing near the wine coolers and asked a bartender if he could have one of them. When the bartender handed it to him, Eddie drank the whole thing down in one gulp, then asked, "Was there any alcohol in that?"

I've called NRBQ our house band, but there's a contender for that title: Tower of Power. This group is based in Oakland, California, but they hold the Toad's record for the most sell-outs (thirty-two sold-out shows). We used to have them twice a year and they would always sell out. Always! They became legends in Connecticut. People love their rhythm and blues funk sound, backed by a great horn section. They started more than fifty years ago, in 1968, when Emilio Castillo, a saxophonist, met Stephen "Doc" Kupka, who played baritone sax. Kupka is called "the funky doctor." He usually wears a fedora and a vest. During one of their times here I did six or seven shots with him, which I rarely do with any musicians. I made an exception to my rule when it came to Kupka and that band we knew so well.

Their hits included, fittingly, "Down to the Nightclub." They also scored with "Don't Change Horses in the Middle of a Stream" and "What is Hip?" In one of their biggest hits, "You're Still a Young Man," when Lenny Williams crooned, "I'm down on my knees," everybody in the horn section sank to their knees and the crowd screamed.

If you check out the testimonials at the start of this book you can read Castillo saying Toad's "has been a Tower of Power favorite for over four decades. We played there too many times to count and always loved it. We became personal friends with the owners over the years and have many, many friends that we met at Toad's Place still to this day."

Castillo added, "The gigs were always really exciting 'cuz the place was packed to the brim and the crowd was super energetic and loud. We got several encores every time. Afterward in the dressing room, the owners would have a huge stack of Sally's pizzas waiting for us."

Castillo said Toad's "set the bar for all other rock nightclubs." He added, "If those walls could talk, we'd all be in big trouble!"

One of our most memorable nights was when Joe Cocker came in to do a warm-up for his performance at Woodstock II in the summer of 1994. He had made his name at the first Woodstock in 1969, especially when he sang "With a Little Help From My Friends" by the Beatles.

I will never forget the roar from the crowd when Cocker walked out on our stage. They knew they were seeing a god of rock music. And his voice was still so on cue! A lot of those guys can't sing after a while because of the cigarettes and booze. But he was right there. Absolutely beautiful.

We hosted another amazing vocalist in August 1993: Tom Jones. He was looking for a small venue where he could be filmed for the ABC show *20/20*, and we served his needs perfectly. We didn't quite sell out, which surprised me. The 650 or so folks who were there got to see and hear something special. Jones, then fifty-one, was decked out in Edwardian ruffles and a black vest, which got the ladies screaming. He opened with covers of two Otis Redding songs, "I Can't Turn You Loose" and "Hard to Handle." Later that night he sang a third Redding hit, "Try a Little Tenderness." Another cover was quite the surprise: Prince's "Purple Rain." But he also gave the crowd his hits, including "It's Not Unusual," "Delilah," "Help Yourself," and "What's New Pussycat?" Jones delivered one of the most professional shows I have ever seen. His band, his horn section, his back-up singers were so tight!

Once we got into the early nineties we occasionally needed to adapt to new acts performing rap or hip-hop music, a trend that accelerated after 2000. They sometimes draw an excitable crowd, which can be challenging for our security crew. But those acts sell a lot of tickets. One night, in January 1992, Naughty by Nature came in. They had hit it big with the song "O.P.P," which stood for "Other People's Pussy/Penis/

Property." We paid them $7,000 and their contract called for them to perform for sixty to ninety minutes.

This was an all-ages show and so Randall Beach's nephew Johnny Beach, who was only eleven but a hip kid into the music scene, came to New Haven from his home in Bedford, New York, to see it. (Johnny went on to become a booking agent for the Mercury Lounge and then the Bowery Ballroom in New York City). When Beach got to Toad's that night, he quickly realized that Johnny and his schoolmate couldn't see over anybody in the crowd. He used his Toad's connections to get the entourage up into the sky box, which has twenty-four seats for V.I.P.s.

From Beach's column in the *New Haven Advocate*: "At 8:45 p.m., here they come, the Naughty ones, strutting around the stage. One of them's shouting, 'Check this shit out!' He's wearing a T-shirt that says 'Bo Knows Racism.' The people in the crowd immediately sway their arms as if choreographed, and jump, jump, jump.

"'Do that shit!' yells the lead man [Treach], backed by a half-dozen male dancers and two guys at turntables. 'Make some mother-fucking noise!' Between songs the lead man flips the bird at the crowd and shouts, 'How many guys here like to get drunk as shit? How many ladies here enjoy a nice wet slippery tongue?' After grabbing their crotches and more swearing and shouting, the Naughty boys go away. They've been on stage for no more than 25 minutes."

Beach gave them too much credit; they were done in twenty minutes. Then they were just out the door. They blew out really fast. It was a total rip-off. People had paid $15.50 in advance or $17 at the door to see that. But most of the crowd hung around for the dance party.

In December 1992 we got a kind of pay back when we brought in another hip-hop group, Public Enemy, and they delivered a generous two-hour set. Their front man Chuck D. was remarkably courteous, telling our crowd, "We want to thank y'all for your support over the years." Acknowledging that hip-hop acts have a notorious reputation for splitting early, he added, "This may not be the best rap show you've ever seen but it sure as hell is the longest." He and Flavor Flav and Terminator X performed "Public Enemy No. 1," "Bring the Noise," "Rebel Without a Pause," and some James Brown covers.

When Ice Cube performed, things didn't work out so well. We had a big crowd, nearly a sell-out. But shortly after Ice Cube (O'Shea Jackson) walked onto the stage, a huge brawl broke out. It looked as if everybody on the dance floor was fighting. A few people jumped over the bar to try to get to a safe place. One of them was a woman, who punched our female bartender after she told the jumper, "You can't come back here." A couple of our other bartenders also got whacked. We had a huge security staff and we'd hired six cops, but it still wasn't enough to control the fight. Another dozen cops had to be called in.

Following that big rumble I was more nervous about upcoming shows that might become aggressive. We had the rapper Ice-T scheduled for the following week and we had sold almost all the tickets. But we decided to cancel it.

One of our wildest and most memorable nights had nothing to do with music. On June 17, 1994, we were settling in for a show by Blackfoot, a Southern rock band out of Florida, who was popular enough to fill our club. The opening acts were Diamondback and Steel Rodeo, and they did their usual sets. But three thousand miles away in Los Angeles, suddenly there was breaking news: O.J. Simpson, who was supposed to turn himself in to the L.A.P.D. on charges of murdering his ex-wife Nicole Brown Simpson and her friend Ronald Goldman, had fled and was a fugitive from justice. O.J., "the Juice," was at large. At 6:45 p.m. California time (9:45 p.m. for us in New Haven) a cop spotted O.J.'s white Ford Bronco SUV on an L.A. freeway. (This could get you to singing "L.A. Freeway," written by Guy Clark and sung at Toad's by Jerry Jeff Walker: "If I can just get off of this L.A. freeway without gettin' killed or caught!")

The chase was on. Soon that Bronco, driven by O.J.'s buddy Al Cowlings, who was sitting alongside the distraught and suicidal O.J., holding a gun up against his head, was being followed by about twenty police cruisers and ten TV news helicopters. All the major networks cut away from their usual programs to cover it live. The whole country was watching it, transfixed. Californians gathered on highway overpasses to chant, "Go O.J., go O.J.!"

When we got word about what was happening, we quickly lowered our big fifteen-foot screen from the ceiling and a camera on our catwalk picked up the broadcast. Soon just about everybody in Toad's was also yelling, "Go O.J, go O.J.!" The guys in

Blackfoot were getting into it too. They were hanging out at the edge of the stage, watching it with everyone else. People were loving it.

The chase continued for about an hour, until the Bronco turned around and went back to Simpson's home in Brentwood, where cops surrounded the vehicle and eventually talked O.J. into getting out and surrendering. As soon as it was resolved we said, "Okay, let's get the show going." Blackfoot put on a great performance, and everybody who was at Toad's will always remember that bizarre night.

Two months before "the O.J. show" we had New Kids on the Block, the boy band that had been so hot in the late eighties, selling more than seventy million records. By the time they came to Toad's they had peaked and could no longer fill stadiums; we had to work to sell out their show with us. But we didn't want to pass them up, so we stayed open on Easter Sunday to accommodate their schedule. Although they were no longer "the new kids" (they were then ages twenty-one to twenty-four), a lot of screaming girls filled Toad's that night.

We had an easier go with Radiohead, a band we were able to score just as it was catching the wave. This group played at Toad's in May 1995 while on tour to promote a second album, *The Bends*, featuring the single "Creep." The crowd was pumped up because those fans knew the band's songs. This British alternative rock group, led by singer-songwriter Thom Yorke, went on to win six Grammy Awards. We were lucky to get them; after they were with us, they quickly began filling much larger venues.

Toad's has always been known for the diversity of the bands we book. Although rap was dominating the music scene more and more, we still made time for excellent singer-songwriter-guitarists. Three who graced our stage during the nineties were Dave Edmunds, Graham Parker, and Marshall Crenshaw.

Edmunds performed for us five times. His last visit came in September 1994, when he played from about midnight until 1:15 a.m. The *Hartford Courant*'s Roger Catlin noted Edmunds opened with one of his best-known songs, "I Knew the Bride (When She Used to Rock 'n' Roll)." When he broke a guitar string during "Chutes and Ladders," he used the brief time out to remark, "It's still nice to be back at Toad's."

Parker gave the audience an unforgettably intimate show in November 1993: a ninety-minute, twenty-four-song retrospective of his career, including "Back in Time" and "Strong Winds." Only a few hundred people were there, comfortably seated in chairs at tables. Parker, performing solo, used three guitars and two harmonicas.

Crenshaw has been with us ten times, the final show coming in 1995. He has a loyal following and had a Top-40 hit "Someday, Someway."

We also landed Hootie & the Blowfish for shows in April 1998 and September 2004. They had performed for us earlier in the nineties, but in July 1995 they paid us a spontaneous visit that unfortunately didn't lead to any surprise stage time. The band was in New Haven to play before a massive crowd at the Yale Bowl for the opening ceremonies of the Special Olympics World Games. Afterward they decided to head over to Toad's. Unfortunately, we had a Saturday dance party that night, so the band couldn't get on stage and jam as planned. We gave them some drinks and some of our new Toad's T-shirts and they left happy. Two days later I was thrilled to see them on *Good Morning America*, all of them wearing their Toad's shirts for the world to see.

Their 1998 show was a set of nearly two and a half hours, with four encores. They did a lot of cover songs that night, including Led Zeppelin's "Hey Hey What Can I Do," Bad Company's "Feel Like Makin' Love," and the Surfaris' "Wipeout."

We also caught the Dave Matthews Band at the right time, in October 1994. Their debut album, *Under the Table and Dreaming*, came out that same year and brought them worldwide recognition. But they were still catching on when we booked them; we didn't sell out the show until the day of the event. The encore included their own version of Dylan's "All Along the Watchtower."

During that same month we brought in Beck for an hour-long show. The crowd was younger than we usually saw because he was big on MTV. The kids dug his khaki bell-bottoms and sneakers, along with his hit song "Loser." But Beck didn't dig the youngsters' idea of crowd surfing during his acoustic songs. He asked them, "Can't you come back tomorrow and do that?"

One of our more bizarre performers was Marilyn Manson, befitting his image. He had come up with his name and his band's name by juxtaposing Charlie Manson and Marilyn Monroe, so we knew this night in November 1995 would be different. Sure enough, he told all of our security guys to put on trash can liners with eye holes and to stand in front of the stage. Then, in the middle of his set, he told everybody in the crowd to spit on him. But of course some of that spittle was landing on our guys wearing the trash can liners. They weren't too happy about it. I was thinking, *Just get this part of the show over.* It was one of the strangest things I have ever seen.

When Queen Latifah came to Toad's in 1994 she was twenty-four, but already well-established as an actress and a rapper who focused on issues of domestic violence, sexual harassment, and fighting for the dignity of black women. Her album at that time, *Black Reign*, included a song scolding men who treated her as a sex object: "U.N.I.T.Y." She highlighted it during her hour-long set for us. The Queen also sang "Ladies First" and "Latifah's Had it Up 2 Here." We had a fight start to break out at her show too but she quickly said, "Come on guys, let's not do this," and things quieted down. (We were pleased to see her score the lead role in a new CBS series *The Equalizer* in 2021).

We had a good crowd one night in December 1996 for Weezer, a rock band out of L.A. The people in the audience didn't seem to mind that the band's leader, Rivers Cuomo, never spoke a word to them, not even a thank you. But Weezer played for seventy-five minutes and the crowd especially enjoyed "Say It Ain't So," "My Name Is Jonas," and "Buddy Holly."

There are nights in the club business when I just have to ride out arguments with band representatives, and that was the situation when Bobby Brown came to Toad's. I had worked out a reasonable percentage deal with his tour manager (I agreed to pay him about $10,000), but it turned out the guy had a wicked attitude. He arranged to have some of his people counting heads as patrons came in, but his guys weren't doing it accurately. When it was time to settle up, our number didn't match their number.

"Our people counted another 150 coming in," he said. I tried explaining the difference to him, but the manager was really pissing me off; we had a loud discussion. I called a cop into my office because I didn't know what this manager might do. He was all over me. At one point he said, "We've got Whitney Houston (Brown's wife) coming down! You've got to pay for our hotel rooms!" I knew he was bullshitting me about Houston. Finally we got the deal done and got him out of the office. I was so stressed I couldn't sleep that night.

We also had to learn to play ball with the excessive drinking habits of certain band members. Danny Joe Brown, the lead singer of the Southern rock band Molly Hatchet, was a wild man who drank bourbon like it was water. His hospitality rider in the contract was of the utmost importance because it contained his liquor requirements. On one particular night, as we prepared for a sell-out crowd, we heard there was a snowstorm coming in. We needed to make the band aware of it so they could make it to their next venue. But when Brown arrived that afternoon, all he cared about was making sure he got his usual pitcher of White Russians. This consisted of a large quantity of vodka, Kahlua, and cream, shaken vigorously. The reason he needed it so early in the day was to coat his stomach in preparation for the real booze he would be consuming throughout the night: Jim Beam. He would suck down the pitcher of White Russians in several large gulps and then get started on his two bottles of Jim Beam. If he finished those off before the show, we had to make sure he had another bottle to get him through his last song. Sometimes when the band came out, we had to enlist our lead security man Tank Dunbar to help get Brown onto the stage.

After that night's show he was pretty wasted as he sat in the dressing room, but that was the usual situation with him. I walked in and told his tour manager a blizzard was moving quickly toward us and the band should get rolling. Danny was sitting there taking this in; you could see by his eyes that he was starting to get mighty stressed. He jumped up and said, "Hold on a minute! I need you to double check and make sure we've got plenty of Jim Beam for the ride! A lot of bottles or at least a case. We might get stuck in the snow!" And so we saw to it that he was well supplied. They made it safely to their next destination.

CHAPTER 7

Playing into the Twenty-First Century

When we rolled into a new century we had to adapt to changing times: the rising popularity of hip-hop, along with its unpredictable rapping performers and audiences. We never knew what might happen on any given night. But the new music gave us a chance to introduce riveting, rhythmic artists such as Cardi B and Snoop Dogg to our audiences.

The music industry had become more fragmented. There wasn't the ongoing supply of emerging rock bands on which we had relied for so many years. But we still had the dance parties and the latest crop of college students who wanted to have a good time and hook up.

The entire country had to roll with the punches as much as we did. The first major shock of that era came on September 11, 2001.

On that horrible and tragic day of the terrorist attacks on the World Trade Center and the Pentagon we had booked the Jamaican reggae singer Buju Banton. America came to a standstill but we decided to stay open on that Tuesday night because Banton and his band were already in town (as was the opening act, Slightly Stupid) and we had sold 425 advance tickets. We got virtually no walk-up sales; too many people were in shock to go anywhere.

For Friday of that week we had scheduled Oysterhead, composed of Trey Anastasio, the lead singer for Phish; Les Claypool, the bassist for Primus; and Stewart Copeland, the drummer for the Police. (We were never able to lure the Police to Toad's; they quickly got to the arena level.) Oysterhead was so hot that we sold all the tickets from our club in an effort to curb scalpers. The show sold out almost immediately. However, in the wake of 9/11 the members of Oysterhead cancelled their show. I think they

Clockwise from top left: Bow Wow Wow (photo by Claude Bell), Snoop Dogg (photo by Buddy Mention), Living Colour, Chi Ching Ching (photo by DJ Buck), Dave Matthews Band, Manchester Orchestra (photo by Benji Wagner), Edie Brickell, Bon Jovi, and Faith No More.

were simply too depressed to perform, as were many bands at that time. We had to refund most of the tickets; some people held onto them as souvenirs. The show was never rescheduled.

The comic X-rated act of singer John Valby, "the prince of porn," who was a perennial favorite, drew an unusually small crowd on the Thursday of that sad week. People just weren't ready to go out and they sure weren't in the mood for rowdy laughs. Instead Valby went off on the terrorists with a torrent of profanities.

And then, as if that week wasn't already enough of a horror show, on the day after 9/11 we got raided by the New Haven police and state Liquor Control agents. There were about a dozen cops and twelve to fourteen agents. They found eight people with fake IDs out of a crowd of several hundred people who had come in for one of our dance parties. We were ordered to close for a week, which we did a few months later. After that, we tightened up our screening of IDs.

But we maintained our tradition of offering new talent on the cusp of superstardom. In March 2004 we booked Kanye West. That year he had released his first album, *The College Dropout*. West has since then won acclaim as a rapper, record producer, and fashion designer. He has also won twenty-one Grammy Awards and started a family with another popular public figure, Kim Kardashian.

On the night we hosted West, he was supposed to hit the stage at 10:30 p.m., but we couldn't get him to go on until midnight. The fans were justifiably complaining. When he finally came out, wearing a white suit, all was forgiven and he received thunderous applause. The excitement of the crowd pumped him up and his show was magnificent.

Eric Danton, who reviewed the show for the *Hartford Courant*, noted West addressed some heavy issues: "He rapped on 'We Don't Care' about struggling with poverty and its accompanying statistics on drugs, incarceration and mortality rates." Danton added that West also rapped about the pain of missing relatives who have died or gone to prison. West played his hit at that time, "Slow Jamz." The crowd went wild when the pianist introduced it with the song's main hook.

That keyboard player backing West that night was John Legend, little known at that time but destined to go on to become a big star too. He and West were long-time friends. The people who saw that show had a memorable night in an intimate setting.

We lucked out twice with another rapper when we snagged Snoop Dogg in 2012 and 2014. Both shows sold out easily. He wanted to play a smaller venue and we were chosen. This is a guy who has sold more than thirty-five million albums worldwide since releasing his first album, *Doggystyle*, in 1993. His hits include "Gin & Juice," "Snoop's Upside Ya Head," and "What's My Name?"

During one of his shows he was holding what looked like a huge joint. It turned out to be a prop but it was funny to watch. After he performed, he did photo ops with the audience and signed autographs. As he was leaving that first time, he said, "I want to play here again!" Naturally I replied, "Come on back!"

Things didn't go nearly as smoothly with ODB (Ol' Dirty Bastard, whose real name was Russell Tyrone Jones). He was the lead singer/rapper for Wu-Tang Clan.

There was a memorable night in September 2003 when we had booked ODB as a solo act. We were packed. We waited and waited, but no ODB. At about 10 p.m. we got a call from ODB's manager: ODB was stuck in New York City and he couldn't make it. The manager said ODB's parole officer was sitting in the singer's driveway and had told him if he left the state he would be arrested.

Meanwhile, the crowd was getting louder and louder as fans waited for ODB to appear. I decided to take the wireless microphone, which is hooked up to our main speaker and bring it upstairs to my office. I wanted to be away from the crowd in case they went berserk. I was sitting in my office when I made an announcement: "Ladies and gentlemen, I have some good news and some bad news to report. First, the bad news: ODB will not be performing tonight due to circumstances beyond our control." I heard the people downstairs moaning and swearing; I was worried there might be a riot. So I quickly delivered the second part of my message: "The good news is that we now have an open bar for everybody!" The cheers were louder than the moans.

We kept the bar open for about a half-hour and most of the crowd seemed somewhat happy. We gave approximately a dozen refunds to people who complained about ODB's no-show. We also handed out free tickets to another hip-hop performance that was coming up a couple of weeks later by Gang Starr along with Dilated Peoples. Almost everybody left happy on the night of ODB's aborted gig. That was a scary experience but we managed to get through it.

ODB did make it to Toad's in March 2004 but the turnout wasn't good (maybe people remembered what had happened at the first show and figured he wouldn't show up). Unfortunately, his performance wasn't that good either. Quoting Kenneth Partridge of the *Hartford Courant*: "He was singing wildly out of key . . . rambling with a trademark incoherence."

The crowd was happier and much larger when we brought in the reunited Wu-Tang Clan in February 2006 during its first US tour in nearly a decade. The line-up included Method Man but not ODB—he had died of a drug overdose in November 2004. "Meth" told the audience, "We are not going to mourn Ol' Dirty Bastard's death. We are going to celebrate his life." And so the group performed ODB's hits "Shimmy Shimmy Ya" and "Brooklyn Zoo." *Rolling Stone* had a reviewer, Dan Leroy, on hand for that show; he said Method Man "ignited fans with his easy charisma."

On another night when we had Wu-Tang Clan it was the last week in December (2011) and we knew a blizzard was headed our way. Again we had a sell-out crowd and I was worried about people making it home safely, including our staff and the artists. We got Wu-Tang Clan to start the show early and finish around midnight instead of the usual 1 a.m. But during the show, the storm hit hard. We had about a foot of snow already on the ground and more falling when the show ended and people began to leave. I was praying nobody would get into a motor vehicle accident on the way home. Meanwhile, the band quickly departed and got on one of the entourage's several buses. But one of the later buses couldn't make it out of New Haven and had to double back for an overnight stay at a hotel. Our general manager Ed Dingus and I had to stay later than everybody else to close up. Fortunately he had a Jeep and I had an all-wheel SUV. That night was a reminder of what a first-class staff we have assembled.

Method Man wasn't as charismatic the night he was supposed to perform with Redman and Ghostface Killah. I had taken the day and night off, leaving Ed Dingus to work the event. He was dealing with a sell-out crowd and, as the night got later and later, anger mounted because Method Man and Redman had not shown up. All we had was Ghostface. Finally, as midnight approached we learned that Method and Redman were in New York and, it being a time before GPS, their driver was lost. They said they would be at Toad's in about an hour. Ed told them they would have to reschedule the show because it was a Sunday and state law required us to close at 1 a.m. Ed and I were exchanging a lot of phone calls with each other. We decided to offer Ghostface some extra money to go on alone. He agreed and did an excellent ninety-minute show. He saved us! He was our hero.

As we booked these newer acts, we were learning we needed to take extra precautions for hip-hop shows. Sometimes the crowd got too rowdy and fights would break out. During one such show somebody flung a chair or table and cut another guy's head, arm, and hand, sending him to the hospital. After that we started taking out all the furniture before we opened our doors for a hip-hop performance. We also removed all glassware and bottles, anything that could be wielded in a brawl. (We now do that for all of our shows.) As another precaution during hip-hop nights, we installed a "panic mode" feature on our console. If some knucklehead acted up, the panic button would light up the whole dance floor and all the exits.

One night around 2003 we booked a local hip-hop group whose members were having a feud with somebody. During the show, a guy in the audience jumped on stage wielding a knife that he had managed to sneak in because he came through the side door with the band and hadn't been frisked. "Choppa Jim," a member of the band, pulled out a .22 and shot the person who had the knife, hitting him in the arm. One of our guys got hit too, the bullet going through his thigh but fortunately missing his arteries. He crawled upstairs to my office and told me, "I got shot!"

"Are you sure?" I asked.

"Yeah, I'm sure!" he said. We got him to the hospital where he was, thankfully, treated and released that night.

The show had ended as soon as the gunfire erupted. Everybody in the crowd ran out of there as fast as they could move. There were no arrests because nobody wanted to talk. That was the last time we did a local hip-hop show. I said, "Never again."

We still booked national hip-hop acts, though, even though they sometimes could be big trouble. When Lil Herb (who became G Herbo) did a show in August 2015, he got mad at us after we ejected somebody in his posse because that guy got into a fight. Our head of security said the guy was violent, so we didn't let him back in. When word of this reached Lil Herb, he finished his show but then took off his neck chain and jumped on one of our security people. Then the rest of his posse, about fifteen of them, attacked our security guys. We fought back while the cops outside called for back-up. They got there too late to help us. Most of my guys sustained some injuries, mainly cuts and bruises. The posse took off when they heard the sirens. Lil Herb was not invited back to Toad's.

On another night, DMX, who had scored many years earlier with his debut album *It's Dark and Hell Is Hot*, was keeping our crowd waiting. At about 10:30 p.m. we got a call from his manager.

"DMX is bleeding from his ears! he said. "He can't make it."

I asked him where they were.

"At an urgent care center somewhere in Connecticut," he explained.

DMX never showed up; that was another night when I had to offer an open bar for everybody. It was a total fiasco. Sometimes DMX would show up and do a good show; you just never knew. We were upset to hear of his heart attack and death in April 2021.

Not all hip-hop bookings ended badly. We have had many successful nights with our audience leaving happy after seeing a great show. In June 2009 we had the Canadian rapper Drake, who has sold more than one hundred million records. We did his show in conjunction with DJ Buck, the program director for the radio station WZMX ("HOT" 93.7), broadcasting out of the Hartford area.

Buck told Randall Beach in a November 2020 interview, "When we brought Drake into Toad's, he had maybe one record out that we were playing. We had no idea what was going to happen with him. But with just that one song on the radio, he was able to sell out Toad's. The line of fans outside stretched down the street and all the way to the corner. Every kid there that night knew every word to every song! That's when I knew he was going to be a superstar."

Buck has been working with us for about fifteen years, bringing in reggae acts as well as hip-hop artists. While acknowledging, "Every bar has little scuffles," he can't recall any serious problems with the crowds.

Buck has been a real asset to Toad's because he brings us into the current music scene. In addition to Drake, he and his radio station promoted our shows for performers such as Post Malone, Kendrick Lamar, and Cardi B, who was named one of the most influential female rappers of all time by *Forbes* magazine. We quickly sold all our tickets for that night.

Sometimes an artist will try to mellow out his crowd if something is brewing, but that doesn't always work. In April 2008 the rapper KRS-One, which stands for Knowledge Reigning Supreme Over Nearly Everyone, was at Toad's as part of a tour to support his "Stop the Violence" movement. But a fan who was upset about being escorted off the stage by our security guys threw a beer bottle that hit KRS-One in the face and hand.

"Let it go," he told the crowd. "When negativity comes your way, let it go. Let this be an example of how we stop the violence." While KRS-One was able to keep his fans calm, during the last fifteen minutes of his performance his right hand started to swell, and we had to call an ambulance. He was treated at Yale New Haven Hospital for a fractured right hand.

The rapper Wiz Khalifa is another example of a performer with a good heart. In 2019, after he had made it big, he was doing a tour of large theaters but remembered his positive experiences with us a decade earlier. And so, with an open night on his tour, he called us about coming back. It was a win-win. That show sold out almost immediately. We appreciated his loyalty to Toad's.

Black Eyed Peas also came back to us in February 2001 after a successful show three years earlier. We had a lot of Yalies in the crowd that night as the group, led by Stacy "Fergie" Ferguson, performed their hits from their first two albums, *Behind the Front* and *Bridging the Gap*.

When Lucinda Williams performed for us on October 6, 2003, she was unlucky to be appearing on the same night the Boston Red Sox were playing the Oakland Athletics in the deciding game of the American League Division Series. New Haven is between New York and Boston, so it has plenty of passionate Yankee and Red Sox fans. On that day I fielded many calls from people asking if we were going to have the game on TV.

Williams knew nothing about any of this. She's a Louisiana native admired for her blend of country, folk, and rock styles. By then she had already garnered three

Grammy Awards. Her show was sold out, but still we had those Red Sox fans who wanted to keep track of what was happening with their ball club.

The *Yale Daily News* had a reviewer there who described Williams's sexy appearance in "tight blue jeans, black tank top, leather jacket, and shaggy blond hair." The reviewer said Williams was downright erotic as she sang her hit "Passionate Kisses." Williams was grooving on the intimacy of our club..

"I so much prefer these kind of shows," she told the crowd. That was before the baseball game heated up.

Williams was near the end of her show, belting out Howlin' Wolf's "Come to Me Baby," when a group of Red Sox fans at the bar screamed for joy as their team defeated the Athletics, 4 to 3. Williams, angry and bewildered, gave the screamers her middle finger and stomped off the stage.

Not wanting her to leave angry, I ran out to her tour bus and tried to explain what had happened. I gave her a brief history of "the curse of the Bambino" (Babe Ruth) that Red Sox fans had been enduring ever since 1918 as they awaited a World Series championship (at that point still one year away). I also gave her a Toad's leather jacket. She seemed to have calmed down and I got off the bus before saying anything that might set her off. A few minutes later I bumped into one of the guys in her band, who told me he had been watching the ball game with great interest while playing on stage! He thanked me for having the game on.

In 2008 we had a memorable night with the British-born rapper Slick Rick. He lived up to his name; he was wearing a lot of gold chains and diamond and gold rings. After his show he asked six of our security guys to walk him downstairs to "the Green Room," our nickname for the dressing room. He then asked the six to stand guard outside the door. When he was ready to leave, he asked them to escort him out to his bus. As our security guys were standing at attention, Slick Rick walked slowly in front of them like a general inspecting his troops. He then reached into his pocket, pulled out a wad of bills, and gave each of them a $100 bill! They couldn't believe it.

But after Slick Rick climbed onto his bus and started putting all of his jewelry away, he realized he had lost one of his diamond rings. We searched our entire building but couldn't find it. The next day, while one of our guys was sweeping up, he found the ring. We sent it to Slick Rick, with a note telling him who had found it. Our guy figured that since Slick Rick had given six of our security people $100 each, he was going to get a nice bonus for recovering that expensive ring. About a week later he got an envelope from Slick Rick and opened it with great excitement. What did he get? A thank you note and an autographed photograph of Slick Rick! Our guy shook his head and went back to pushing his broom.

Another character was the rapper Action Bronson. He was also a chef and had written a book entitled *Fuck, That's Delicious*. Befitting a man who liked to sample food, he decided during the middle of his show to walk off stage, go out the door, and walk over to the adjacent Yorkside Pizza. All the while he was doing this, he continued rapping on a wireless mic. He got his slice, went back on stage, and continued his performance. There must have been about a hundred people who went outside with him and followed him to Yorkside. Even though Yorkside, which specializes in Greek pizza, isn't as well known as Sally's or Pepe's, he was probably thinking, *Fuck, That's Delicious!*

We were also proud to bring in the rapper Nas, originally Nasir bin Olu Dara Jones. *Billboard* put him on its list of "10 Best Rappers of All Time." When he was at Toad's in 2008 he was riding high on his latest single, "Hero," which had followed a string of earlier hits, including "Made You Look" and "Shoot 'Em Up." His occasionally violent lyrics had drawn the ire of Bill O'Reilly of Fox News and the two of them got into a well-publicized debate a few months before his show with us.

We have done multiple bookings with Atmosphere, and we almost always sell out those shows. Our office manager Holli Martin is good friends with the members of the band and so they have a special relationship with us. The *Yale Daily News* had a reviewer at one of Atmosphere's shows, in September 2017, who wrote their lead singer Slug "was in fine form, giving fans unfamiliar but still excellent renditions of his most-loved songs, including 'God Loves Ugly' and a new favorite, 'Sunshine.'"

In August 2013 we brought in the Australian rapper and former model Iggy Azalea. Her popular song and video "Pussy" had helped to launch her musical career. It was a beautiful performance. Nobody knew she was going to get so big so fast.

Chris Webby, a local rapper out of Norwalk, Connecticut, began an annual tradition with us in 2010: his Black Friday show on the day after Thanksgiving. This became a popular fixture, especially after his first studio album, *Chemically Imbalanced*, was released in 2014. Webby's shows attract sell-out audiences, people who'd rather go to a rap show than scramble for Black Friday bargains at the mall.

In the summer of 2016 we had an almost disastrous night with the hip-hop artist Tory Lanez. The show was sold out and everything was going great until Tory jumped into the crowd and began to body surf. The crowd lifted him up and he grabbed onto a gas pipe, swinging on it. Everybody was having a fine old time. We didn't realize until the next day that several seals had been broken on the pipe. We finally became aware of the leak when our lighting chief smelled the gas. We had to call the gas company and evacuate the building for an hour.

We were in a hurry to fix the gas leak because we were getting ready to host George Clinton and his band Parliament-Funkadelic. He first came to Toad's in the mid-nineties and has returned many times. Clinton sometimes performs for four hours. P-Funk shows are wild scenes; members of the band dress up in unique costumes. One of my favorites was the diaper man, who really did parade around the stage in diapers. When the band began to play "We Got the Funk," everybody in the club would stomp their feet and chant that phrase. But in order to keep Clinton and his large entourage happy, I learned I absolutely had to pay his tour manager the total amount we owed, in large bills at least six hours before show time.

Another old favorite of ours was Johnny Winter, the albino blues singer who played a scorching guitar. For decades he did shows at Toad's every January. Winter, a native of Texas who later moved to Connecticut's Fairfield County, helped revive Muddy Waters's career. Winter produced three albums for Waters, and each one of them won a Grammy Award. We also had Winter's brother Edgar Winter at Toad's as a solo act and in a show with Johnny. We dearly miss Johnny—he died in 2014 at age seventy.

Winter played at Woodstock in 1969; he is one of many Woodstock veterans we have hosted. Some of the others include Richie Havens, Arlo Guthrie, Joan Baez, Santana, Bob Weir, Jefferson Starship (not the Airplane but close enough), Joe Cocker, David Crosby, Stephen Stills, Alvin Lee of Ten Years After, Paul Butterfield, and John Sebastian.

We also have great affection for Patti Smith, the punk rock laureate who has been with us many times and is a sweetheart. Our crowd has always loved the ferocity of her shows, especially when she sings her hit "Because the Night," which she co-wrote in 1978 with Bruce Springsteen. In 2010 she published a best-selling memoir, *Just Kids*, about her experiences in New York City in the seventies with the photographer Robert Mapplethorpe.

She waited a long time to get inducted into the Rock & Roll Hall of Fame and finally her day came on March 12, 2007. A month or two later she came to Toad's for "An Evening with Patti Smith." She was going to do two sets, with a short break in between. Then an idea came to me; I asked her tour manager if anyone had put together a champagne toast to celebrate her remarkable achievement. He said he didn't think anybody had done so. I thought it would be important for Toad's to commemorate this and the manager enthusiastically agreed.

And so between her sets we called Patti and her band down to "the Green Room" and everyone sat down at the table. I had procured the Dom Perignon and eight champagne glasses. I popped the cork, poured the champagne, then held up my glass and announced, "Patti Smith, Rock & Roll Hall of Fame. No one was ever more worthy." The room was silent for a couple of seconds as everyone tapped their glasses together. But then Patti popped her head up and said, "Even Elvis!" We all cracked up and hugged each other. This was a special Toad's Place moment.

We don't have such sweet feelings about Lauryn Hill, who was with us in December 2010. She had been with the Fugees until the band broke up in 1997. Her show with us sold out quickly, and she was fine during the sound check. Then she went back to her hotel. We knew sometimes she could be late to a show, and this turned out to be one of those times. When it got to be past show time, we were trying to calm people down. Finally Hill showed up at 11:50 p.m. We had been getting more and more nervous because state law mandated we stop selling alcohol and close at 1 a.m.

Her performance was superb, but she didn't have enough time to finish what she wanted to do. At 1 a.m. she got the signal by the police through the sound engineer that she had to stop, immediately. She asked if she could do one more song, but she was told no; this was a hard curfew. She was not happy, nor was the crowd.

And another thing: The rule was she had to be called Ms. Hill by everybody. If any member of our staff called her Lauryn or anything besides Ms. Hill, heads would roll. We complied with her edict.

On a happier note: We have had a couple of great shows in 2011 and 2013 by Alkaline Trio, a punk rock band out of Chicago. They're one of my personal favorites; great musicians with superb attitudes. When Matt Skiba starts singing, backed by bassist Dan Andriao and drummer Derek Grant, the crowd starts moving.

Beres Hammond is my favorite of all the reggae performers we have hosted. (No, we were never able to get Bob Marley.) Hammond's message is always positive and he has to be labeled the king of dance hall reggae. He's been visiting our stage for twenty years.

One of our perennial crowd-pleasers is Marion Meadows, the jazz tenor saxophone player, who has put on a show just before Christmas for more than two decades. I always look forward to that night and so do plenty of other people.

For two decades we have also had "Funksgiving" shows the night before Thanksgiving by Deep Banana Blackout. Many of those in the band hail from Connecticut. Their soul and R&B covers, mixed with original material and backed by a full horn section, never fail to get us ready to celebrate Thanksgiving.

We've hosted the gothic metal band Type O Negative a half a dozen times. The mood of the night is always positive; I wish all our shows could be like that. The ironic thing is that their lyrics focus on death and depression, so they got saddled with the nickname "the drab four." But they were great guys and I made it a point to chat with everybody in the band, especially their lead singer Peter Steele.

Often their shows sold out but one night we were maybe half full. I was okay with that but at the end of the night Steele knocked on my door. He shook my hand and apologized for the small turnout. Never had a performer done that. I told him it was not a problem, that sometimes it happens and it had no bearing on the band or our relationship. I hope he left feeling better. Soon afterward I heard he had been diagnosed with a serious heart condition. He died in 2010; he was just 48. When I heard the news, I had to sit down and catch my breath. I will never forget his apology and that deep, penetrating look in his eyes.

There are some bands I like to think we helped nudge toward the top. Hatebreed, out of Bridgeport, Connecticut, is one of them. They're a hard-core metal band, with lead singer Jamey Jasta, a close friend of mine. He always puts on his best performance when he's on our stage. We honored his twenty years of Toad's shows by commissioning an artist's painting of the band. We're proud we assisted them in making it onto the national scene.

Another member of the Toad's family of bands is New Found Glory, pop rockers out of Florida. They've got a satiric bent. In 2017, their ninth studio album, *Makes Me Sick* (Hopeless Records) had the single "Happy Being Miserable." They also recorded "Better Off Dead" and "Party On Apocalypse." I thought of their body of work often during 2020, as they expressed how we were all feeling. Their shows are energetic, fun, and pumped up; their fans come back year after year.

Let's talk about the fastest sell-outs. The alternative rock band O.A.R. (Of A Revolution) sold out in nineteen minutes. Sarah Borelli, the singer-songwriter-actress-author, had her show sell out in fourteen minutes, although it was a seated show, so just five hundred tickets were put on sale. The all-time champion is Ella Mai, the British singer-songwriter-rapper with the song "Boo'd Up." Those tickets were all gone in four minutes. Attention should also be paid to Dirty Heads, those reggae rockers from California—they sold out nine shows in a row.

But for sheer screaming hysteria reminiscent of the height of Beatlemania, Hanson takes the prize. This pop band out of Tulsa, Oklahoma, with brothers Isaac, Taylor, and Zac, drew a large and excited crowd of teen girls and young women for a show in October 2011. The night before the performance the fans set up tents on the sidewalk in order to get spots close to the stage. They had to hunker down amid rain that poured throughout the night.

The *Quinnipiac Chronicle*, the student newspaper of Quinnipiac University, sent its reporter Shannon Corcoran to cover the event. She wrote, "Every time a Hanson brother looked into the crowd, fans erupted in screams." Corcoran described it as an hour-and-forty-five-minute dance party in "a club full of screaming girls, many in their twenties." The songs included the band's megahits "MMMBop," "Penny and Me," and "Give a Little."

Those fans knew every word of every song; you could see them mouthing the lyrics. I felt like I was watching a clip of the Beatles on *The Ed Sullivan Show*.

At the end of the night, when it was time for us to escort the brothers out of there, we had to ask police to block the street so no cars could follow the tour bus. The vehicle needed to get a head start to make it onto the highway. I asked one of the New Haven police lieutenants, who was working extra duty with some other officers, if he could help us. He said he could get it done but first he had a request: Could we arrange a photo op of a couple of his nieces and nephews with the band? The brothers agreed and the photo was quickly taken. Then we got them through their fans outside, onto their bus, and on their way.

And then there was . . . "the Nuge," Ted Nugent. He had performed for us twice without incident before his ill-fated appearance in August 2013. This was one month after a jury found George Zimmerman, a white neighborhood watch captain, not guilty of murder in the shooting death of black, seventeen-year-old Trayvon Martin in Florida. The case had resulted in protests across the country. Nugent, always eager to express his views, had publicly called Martin "a dope-smoking, racist gangsta wannabe" and "a thug" who "got justice."

We paid no attention to his political views when we booked him. For us it was just another rock show, not a political statement by Toad's. But plenty of people in New Haven, which has a sizable black community, were angry when they learned he was coming to Toad's as part of what he called his Black Power tour. They called on us to cancel it. The problem was, we had already put up a huge deposit—$25,000—for Nugent's performance. The show had sold out, so if it went forward we would make about $30,000 rather than losing $25,000. We weren't in a position where we could walk away from that kind of money.

On the night of the show, there were about fifty anti-Nugent demonstrators marching outside Toad's and they got into shouting matches with the Nugent fans who were coming in. The cops did a good job keeping them separated, and there were just a few shoving incidents. Of course reporters were on the scene too. I told a *New Haven Register* reporter that Nugent's views "have nothing to do with his show here, nor does it have anything to do with Toad's Place. This is just a music show. His political views are his."

When Nugent got on stage, he asked the crowd, "Do you feel the fucking love tonight?" He added, "It's going to be all right, everything's going to be all right." After he played a couple of songs, he said the protesters should just "eat shit and die." Before he launched into "Free for All," he asked, "Is it still legal to love freedom in Connecticut? Who the fuck is gonna stop me?"

That was the last show by "the Nuge" at Toad's. He will not be invited back.

CHAPTER 8

The Local Bands

LONG BEFORE WE IMAGINED WE COULD EVER BRING SUPERSTAR ACTS LIKE BOB DYLAN and the Rolling Stones to Toad's, local bands were our lifeblood, helping us pay the bills and keeping us in business. Even after we began booking nationally known bands, we continued to offer our stage to local musicians, often as opening acts. We learned our audiences didn't demand acts who were on the cover of *Rolling Stone* to spend an evening with us; they were happy to enjoy the homegrown talent we shared with them.

Peter Menta formed the Ten Years Late Jug Band in 1975 (our first year), but he also booked bands for us from 1975 until 1978.

"We were the house opening act for Toad's," Menta said. "We got in from the ground up. We opened for the heavyweights of that time: Willie Dixon, Aztec Two-Step, NRBQ, and George Thorogood. In the early days, the local bands were important to the survival of Toad's Place," he recalled. "Local bands had draw."

The members of some of the first bands to perform at Toad's laugh as they recall the conditions back in 1975. "We played on a stage that, to my memory, was plywood up on some cinderblocks, or some such primitive thing," remembers Christine Ohlman, called "the Beehive Queen" because of her amazing tower of platinum blond hair. She was a founder of the Scratch Band, described by Dave Marsh in *Rolling Stone* as playing "contemporary rock R&B."

Rob Jockel, co-founder and singer of Eight to the Bar, recalls the night Big Mike told the band, after they played their four forty-five-minute sets, that Toad's was "closing for a couple of weeks to do some renovations."

"We're expanding into the back warehouse space," he said. The bands had been using that area as a dressing room.

"When the doors closed and the patrons left," Jockel adds, "we were all given hammers and large tools of destruction and told we could help tear down the walls and get them started on the new room. I have no clue why we were game, but we did chip in. There was plaster, wood bits, and dust all over the place. We stayed a few hours, drank beer, and left around 3 a.m."

Budd Tunick, the drummer for the Simms Brothers Band, which blended rock, jazz, and R&B, says he and his bandmates were also recruited to be part of the wrecking crew. "I remember getting off the stage and Mike gave us all sledgehammers and axes to knock down the wall. He told us, 'Look, you guys made me a lot of money; you made it possible for me to expand.' It made us feel that we were an important part of the plan. It was obvious Mike was really building something."

Bandmember Frank Simms, who with his brother George would later sing backup for David Bowie on his *Let's Dance* album and go on Bowie's Serious Moonlight tour, looks back on the early days of Toad's as "a wonderful part of my life."

Simms recalls how everybody at Toad's made the band feel appreciated. "Mike took us to Mory's for meals and to Sally's. We were paid well and got bonuses. Other clubs didn't do that. In other places there were rats, water on the floor. But Toad's had this attitude: Make the band feel good, make them happy. They've got to be in a good mood when they go on stage. A performer has to feel supported and taken care of. They treated us like royalty. There were no dickheads there."

Tunick, who went on to become a management and production consultant in the music industry, remembers Mike asking, "What should I do? What do you guys want?" Tunick and the others in the Simms Brothers Band told him, "Give us a good stage, good lights, and a good sound system." Tunick notes that many bands didn't get that. But when such professional touches were provided at Toad's, the musicians remembered and wanted to come back.

"Mike had his security crew so well-trained," Tunick adds. "He gave them all a manual. They had to read it and adhere to those rules. If something happened on the dance floor, like a fight, those guys were like flies swarming quickly over to it. I never saw anything get out of hand."

Simms, who still uses his vocal talent for commercials and *Saturday Night Live*, credits Toad's management for the club's success. "They care, they're into it. They

Clockwise from top left: Albert Collins, Jack Barakat of All Time Low and Peter Wasilewski of Less than Jake, B-52's, "Weird Al" Yankovic, Blind Melon, Alannah Myles, Peter Steele of Type O Negative and a fan, Mark Tremonti of Tremonti, George Thorogood, The Cramps, and Howie Mandel.

understand. They don't say, 'We can't afford it.' Brian has always had the same work ethic as Mike."

Tunick and Frank and George Simms had formed their band (joined by vocalist David Spinner and guitarist Mikey Leonard) in 1974 in their hometown of Stamford, Connecticut. For them it was a kick, only a few years later, to be drawing large crowds at Toad's, people who would actually listen and watch the band rather than just talk or try to pick up somebody.

"In that era," said Tunick, "those people came to see you. There would be several hundred people crowding up to the stage, watching everything we did. That was exciting! That's my best memory of Toad's: all those people who appreciated what we were doing."

"At other clubs we'd play some of our original songs and people would just sit there," Tunick adds. "Then we'd play a cover tune and they'd all jump up to dance. It was different at Toad's. They appreciated everything we did." (Tunick notes the Simms Brothers Band was booked as the headliner, not an opening act; he estimates they played at Toad's about a hundred times.)

Toad's gave another wonderful gift to Tunick: "One day at the club, Mike said, 'I want to introduce you to a friend of mine. This is Karen.' We ended up getting married," said Tunick. "Mike was the best man at our wedding."

After Toad's started attracting national acts, including visiting band members who dropped in following their concerts at the New Haven Coliseum, the local musicians sometimes got a chance to meet them.

"One night Roger Taylor and Brian May from Queen came down to our dressing room after their sold-out Coliseum show," remembers Tunick. "Mike said, 'Hey Queen, smile for the birdie' while snapping a photo."

Tunick left the Simms Brothers in 1980; two years later he began working at Toad's, helping with the bookings. During his two years in that position he specialized in booking opening acts to give them the exposure they wouldn't get anywhere else. He recalls Mike sometimes needing to be brought up to speed on a band that was about to hit it big.

"One day he asked me, 'What about this band Squish?' I said, 'Mike, that's Squeeze!' We quickly booked Squeeze, who put on a great show for us."

Phil Cutler, who owned Cutler's Records around the corner from Toad's and worked on our security crew on Fridays and Saturdays from about 1978 to '83, says that apart from the Rolling Stones and Billy Joel shows, his favorite nights were when the Simms Brothers Band or Beaver Brown played their weekend gigs.

"The local bands kept the place rolling," Cutler recalls. "Toad's was jammed, and it was just good, clean fun. And the Simms Brothers were great guys. They were easy-going and friendly. I loved their music. I was so excited when their *Back to School* album came in to my store."

Eight to the Bar, which was one of our long-running local bands out of North-ford, Connecticut, drew good crowds through the years because of their upbeat mix of American roots music, swing, boogie-woogie, and Motown, with four-part vocal arrangements. They formed in 1975, the same year Toad's got started.

Cynthia Lyon put the band together, calling on her sisters Barbara and Todd Lyon, along with Jockel, Polly Messer, John "Bubbs" Brown, John Baker, Tommy McNa-mara, and Matt Simpson. Later Collin Tilton would come on board, playing tenor and alto saxophone and flute. He played the flute solo on Van Morrison's hit "Moondance."

Cynthia Lyon believes Eight to the Bar first played at Toad's in 1975. "We were really green; we were just babies! But when we were in the dressing room before the show, one of the people in our band came in and said, 'There's a line around the block—and it's for us!' I was really scared. But it was the thrill of a lifetime."

In later years, as Toad's reputation grew and the big acts appeared, Lyon felt a new sense of "the thrill" when Eight to the Bar performed on that stage. "When you play at Toad's you feel like you've hit the big time. It has that aura. I've seen Bonnie Raitt and the Neville Brothers play there. To be on that same stage as them!"

Lyon treasures the nights at Toad's when her band opened for three prominent acts: Manhattan Transfer, blues icon John Lee Hooker (he tried to pick up one of Lyon's sisters), and George Thorogood. "George made a bet that he could play fifty shows in fifty nights," remembers Lyon, "and boy, did he put on an incredible show! He was on fire."

Eight to the Bar recorded their first album, *The Joint Is Jumpin'*, at Toad's in 1981. They have stayed together, with some changes in their line-up, since 1975. Lyon esti-mates they have played at Toad's nearly fifty times. Periodically they do a reunion show, always at Toad's. She especially remembers the thirty-fifth reunion in 2010 with Washboard Slim and the Blue Lights and the Helium Brothers.

The Helium Brothers also got started in 1975, as friends at Yale University, doing shows on campus. As their eclectic blend of bluegrass, country swing, rock, and California acoustic grew popular, they landed gigs at Toad's.

"We practically christened Toad's Place," says Andy "A.J." Gundell, who cofounded the Helium Brothers and was lead guitarist. The other original members were bassist Kim Oler, banjo player Oscar Hills, drummer Paul Fargeorge, and fiddler Michael Platt.

Gundell recalls he also played a few solo acoustic shows at Toad's. "The first time I did a show there, I forgot to get paid! I went back the next day and saw Mike at the bar. I said, 'Mike, I forgot to get my money,' and he said, 'Yeah, I know.' He reached into his pocket, pulled out two twenty-dollar bills and said, 'Don't make a habit of it.' That was classic Mike."

"It was an incredible time," Gundell says of the 1970s. "There was so much opportunity for local musicians, such a great vibe. Everybody was partying, people were drinking. It was the baby boomers hitting the drinking age (then eighteen). There were bars on every corner, they were jammed and they had music. We'd play for three to four hundred people on Sunday nights at the Arcadia Ballroom (a short-lived Toad's competitor about a mile away), then play for another three to four hundred on Mondays at Toad's. We had a Monday night residency there. WPLR played a jingle we came up with: 'Head on down the road to a Monday night at Toad's!'"

Gundell, who has persevered in the business as a full-time musician-songwriter, says the Helium Brothers played at Toad's seventy-five to a hundred times. Sometimes they were the headliners and other times they were the opening act. He recalls they were the openers for Dan Hicks and the Hot Licks.

"We never disbanded; we took long hiatuses," Gundell adds. He shares Lyon's fond memories of that thirty-fifth reunion show. "Whenever we reunited, we did it at Toad's."

Praising "the professionalism of the room," Gundell says, "I credit both Mike and Brian. They were a great team. Brian was Mike's man on the ground. They worked together well to bring in quality acts and treat them nice. They assembled a good staff too, a great cast of support."

Christine Ohlman, who remains a featured vocalist for the Saturday Night Live Band, which has also included former Scratch Band guitarist G.E. Smith, recalls, "There was always a heightened sense of excitement when you played at Toad's. Everybody knew it was the best place to play. And Toad's had this active roster of national acts coming through, which was very attractive. A great place to see a show and hang out."

Ohlman's favorite shows she's seen at Toad's include Stevie Ray Vaughan, who she remembers as having "maybe fifty people in the house." She also loved Mink DeVille and Lucinda Williams with Los Lobos. But the other thing Ohlman loved about playing at Toad's?

"Sally's pizza being brought in for you as a special perk," she said. "This was the mark that you had really made it at Toad's. The first time that pizza came in through the door, we were all so thrilled!"

In addition to Ohlman, the original members of the Scratch Band were drummer Vic Steffens, bassist Paul Ossola, vocalist and harmonica player Robert Orsi, guitarists Doug Schlink and Bill Durso, and keyboard player Ray Zeiner. Mickey Curry later replaced Steffens.

Ohlman notes Toad's eventually began having many dance party nights with a DJ playing recorded music rather than booking live bands seven nights a week. She acknowledges those dance nights draw a younger crowd, and plenty of them.

Ohlman is absolutely right about that; we've made more money on dance parties than the live shows. People will always love to dance and drink. If we didn't have those dance parties we'd be out of business.

Ohlman pulled together a special night at Toad's in April 2005 in honor of Thomas "Doc" Cavalier, who had died on New Year's Day of that year. Doc had encouraged and promoted many rising musical artists through the years at his Trod Nossel Studios in Wallingford, Connecticut. He and Mike were fishing buddies. Of course I immediately agreed to have Toad's host that tribute show when Christine asked me.

The line-up was amazing. The performers included the reunited Scratch Band and another of our early local acts, the reunited B. Willie Smith Band, Phoebe Snow, Marshall Crenshaw, and James Velvet, a beloved local musician who died in 2015.

The B. Willie Smith Band, who did a blistering version of Roy Head's "Treat Her Right" during the tribute show, was on our stage many times through the early years. They came out of North Haven High School, class of 1973. That band played rock, swing, and especially the blues. Their line-up included lead singer and guitarist Bruce Smith, guitarist Steve Baldino, drummer and vocalist Jerry Connolly, Mike Cavadini on keyboards and saxophone, Bob Elliott on bass, and Bill Hollomon on saxophone and trumpet.

Early Toad's regulars also remember Jake and the Family Jewels, led by Allan "Jake" Jabobs. He had been in a New York City folk duo, Bunky (Andrea "Bunky" Skinner) and Jake. In 1970 he put together the Family Jewels, which included Jerry Burnham, Michael Epstein, and Dan Mansolino. They could be counted on for doo-wop, folk rock, and Motown tunes. On many a night at Toad's they were the opening act for NRBQ, our veritable house band that always played to sell-out crowds.

We also booked Jasper Wrath many times. They were progressive rockers out of New Haven and they scored a regional hit with "You." They were founded by drummer Jeff Cannata, joined by keyboardist Michael Soldan, guitarist Robert Giannotti, and bassist Phil Stone. Later, James Christian became a member. After Jasper Wrath broke up in 1976, Christian, Stone, and Jeff Batter formed the band Eyes.

Peter Menta, who had formed the Ten Years Late Jug Band with his friend Howard H. Horn, recalls that after the two of them started Washboard Slim and the Blue Lights in 1986, they continued to play at Toad's as the opening act. Those they opened for included Taj Mahal, Jonathan Edwards, and Richie Havens.

"Jonathan Edwards was huge at Toad's," Menta says, remembering the large, enthusiastic audiences. "A tremendous performer."

"It was great to play at Toad's because you could see the headliners and sometimes hang out with them," Menta recalls. "I got harmonica lessons from some of the famous Chicago blues players: Carey Bell, who was with Willie Dixon, and Jerry Portnoy, who was in Muddy Waters's band."

In his role as entertainment director for Toad's, Menta had to see to many details, including making sure the musicians were provided with what had been specified in their contracts.

"I didn't read it carefully enough one night when Muddy Waters came in," Menta remembers. "He always required a bottle of Piper Heidsiek champagne or he wouldn't perform. I got him a bottle of New York State champagne instead, and when he saw that, he sent one of his bandmates back to their hotel to pick up an emergency stash bottle of Piper Heidsiek. Then Muddy sat me down in his dressing room and told me, 'Now you'll see why Piper is the right champagne.' I got to drink 'the right stuff' with Muddy Waters! He was gracious; he didn't hold it against me that I'd bought the wrong kind."

The members of those long ago local bands who got their shot at Toad's never forget it. Gregory Sherrod, who was with the band the Clarke Bros., had dreamed about being on stage at Toad's. Finally, on a momentous day in 1991, Mike offered Sherrod and his band the opening slot for Tower of Power. "It was one of the greatest nights of my life," Sherrod says. He and other bands he had formed returned to Toad's as openers, the last time in 2014, again with Tower of Power.

"After the show Brian made a personal effort to hunt me down and give me love," Sherrod recalls. "Mike also became a personal friend. Toad's Place treated me like family and treated locals like every other act. Brian and Mike personally pulled for me, lost money on me. Although it's a gruff business, they showed an awkward kid a lot of love and that a musical life was possible for me. I owe them a whole lot."

Guy Tino, the guitarist, vocalist, and percussionist for a local band the Providers (1994–2002), was awestruck when his band landed the opening gig for Roomful of Blues in 1998. "To actually stand on that stage for the first time was amazing." The Providers were invited back as opening acts six more times after that.

"Like a lot of local bands, we never did quite get that springboard to the next pinnacle," Tino says. "But those nights at Toad's were special, and no one can take that accomplishment away from us."

Another local musician, known as Opus, (actually Christian Francis Lawrence) first appeared on our stage in the early 1990s with the metal-rap-funk band Gargantua

Soul. Their lead singer Kris Keyes entertained the crowd with theatrical flourishes, such as painting his body and rising out of a coffin.

After Gargantua Soul imploded, Opus began organizing an annual Opus's Blizzard Birthday Bash held in January. He assembles a variety of bands (these have included the hardcore punk band Murphy's Law and the tech metal band Candiria, both out of New York) to perform. Opus's shows always draw five hundred to six hundred people.

"It's an honor and a blessing to play Toad's," Opus says. "It's still one of the premier spots. The sound, the room, the wood, the other artists who've played there! And the people, the crew. You feel at home and comfortable on that stage. I've played there so much that I feel like a part of my energy lives in those walls of Toad's."

CHAPTER 9

The Celebrities

THROUGH THE YEARS TOAD'S PLACE HAS ATTRACTED A WIDE VARIETY OF FAMOUS folks who weren't musicians but wanted to make the scene or knew somebody who was there to perform. We've also had a few big names who dabbled in music and could handle a guitar well enough to be part of a band.

All of this made for some interesting happenings. It also kept us, especially our security crew, on high alert for potential trouble. This included whenever President George W. Bush's daughter came to visit. We were definitely on high alert—we didn't want her to be hit on while she was in our club!

When "W" was elected president in 2000, one of his twin daughters, Barbara, was in her first year at her papa's alma mater, Yale. She arrived on campus that fall, accompanied by a vigilant squad of Secret Service agents. In those days Barbara would come into Toad's regularly. Our security people would tell me, "Barbara's here again," and I'd have one of our guys keep an eye on her at all times to make sure nothing happened. Of course plainclothes Secret Service agents were there too, trying to blend in with the crowd. One time she brought her twin sister Jenna in with her, so we had double the number of Secret Service agents. It was the weekend of the Yale-Harvard football game, so the place was jammed.

On another evening, this time in October 2000, Barbara came in to see a show by the rap group Jurassic 5. The legal drinking age in Connecticut had been raised from eighteen to twenty-one in 1985, so we had erected a fence going right down the middle of the dance floor. The side closest to the front door was for patrons of all ages, the other side was for those twenty-one or older. Barbara was only eighteen at the time, but like many college students she had obtained a fake ID.

Clockwise from top left: REO Speedwagon, Samantha Fish (photo by John Lane), John McEnroe, Keanu Reeves and Bret Domrose of Dogstar, Seal, Linda Blair, Eddie Murphy, Joe Lieberman, and Mick Fleetwood.

We had a former cop named Bill Coale checking IDs at the entrance to the alcohol side. When Barbara showed him the ID, he knew from seeing many other bogus IDs that it was phony, so he confiscated it. At that time he didn't know he was dealing with the daughter of the president of the United States.

"She was polite, but she definitely argued with me to get it back," Coale told the New York *Daily News.* "I told her, 'Look, if you want the ID back, go see the uniformed cop at the door.' But she didn't want to do that because it is a crime."

The fake ID identified her as Barbara Pierce, 22, of Baltimore. Pierce was the maiden name of Barbara Bush's grandmother, former First Lady Barbara Bush.

Coale, who held onto that bogus ID and even framed it for display in his home, got a little too talkative with reporters about the incident. He was basking in his fifteen minutes of fame. The Secret Service guys with Barbara didn't say anything as the ID was being confiscated, but a *Yale Daily News* reporter had been right behind her at the door, and naturally he wrote about what had happened. Then the *New Haven Register, Hartford Courant,* and other news outlets got wind of it. I told Coale to stop giving interviews, but he kept it up. This was probably the most attention he had ever gotten in his life.

We were trying to somehow keep a lid on the story, but then I got word through my Yale contact that the White House was upset and wanted the account squelched. I decided to put out a news release saying we were investigating the incident and that we had no confirmation as to who owned the phony ID. This seemed to cool things down for a while—until the following June, when *Newsweek* and the New York *Daily News* wrote stories about Barbara's and Jenna's brushes with the law. Jenna had been cited for underage drinking in Texas, where she was attending college. The stories included accounts of Barbara coming to Toad's and trying to get in with that fake ID.

The Bushes weren't the only famous Yalies we encountered. There were two others, both already famous actresses, who came through our doors while they were on campus: Claire Danes and Sara Gilbert. Danes was at Yale from 1998 to 2000, pursuing a degree in psychology. She dropped out after two years to focus on her acting career. She had already won a Golden Globe award for her role in the TV series *My So-Called Life* in 1994. During that same year she had a role in her first film, *Little*

Women. Later she would win many awards for her starring role in the Showtime drama series *Homeland*.

Gilbert was also well-known when she arrived at Yale in the fall of 1993. Starting at age thirteen she had played Darlene, a daughter in the hit TV show *Roseanne*. At Yale she majored in art, juggling her *Roseanne* work with her studies. But she did find time to make it to Toad's.

Bill and Hillary Clinton had graduated from Yale Law School in 1973, two years before Toad's existed. But they did enjoy some meals together at Hungry Charlie's, the restaurant in our space before Toad's was born. Hillary clearly became aware of us. During her speech for Yale Class Day in May 2018, two years after she lost the presidential election to Donald Trump, she remarked, "Those first months after that 2016 election were not easy. We all had our own methods of coping. I went for long walks in the woods. I had my fair share of Chardonnay, you had penny drinks at Woad's." This got a big cheer from the crowd, as it was a reference to Yalies' nickname for Wednesday night at Toad's, when we had dance parties for Yale students only and for the first fifteen minutes offered one drink for a penny, just to prime the pump and get the night rolling.

Two big-name athletes caused a buzz when they came through our door: Derek Jeter of the New York Yankees and tennis star John McEnroe.

Jeter, while in his prime as the Yanks' acclaimed shortstop, showed up at Toad's in late October 2002 because he was dating actress Jordana Brewster, who was studying English at Yale. She had won notice for her roles in the soap operas *All My Children* and *As the World Turns* in the mid-1990s. Then she really hit it big in 2001 with the movie *The Fast and the Furious*.

In his write-up about Jeter and Brewster being at Toad's, Randall Beach reported in the *New Haven Register* that Brewster, the granddaughter of former Yale President Kingman Brewster Jr., was twenty-two; Jeter was twenty-eight. They had been together for several months.

Beach reported the glam couple was at Toad's for one of those Woad's Yale dance parties. Yalie Steven Gilbert told Beach, "Brewster was trying to get him to dance, without a lot of luck. He was recognized by basically every sports fan in the club, so it wasn't any secret he was there."

I was quoted in Beach's story saying, "Yeah, they were here. They just stopped in late. No big deal."

But Beach noted, "It was a very big deal to the people who were in the club."

It's true—people were loving it. And so was our staff; for every drink Jeter ordered, he dropped a $20 tip to the bartender. I guess he could afford it.

Several New Haven cops got wind of what was happening and came in to get Jeter's autograph. In return they gave the happy couple a full-fledged vehicular escort out of New Haven.

John McEnroe often played in the Volvo and Pilot Pen Tennis Tournaments in New Haven. When he was done playing at the stadium across from Yale Bowl, he liked to come downtown to Toad's to hang out with the musicians, drink, and check out the ladies in the house.

McEnroe was a fan of the Black Crowes, and they had a show with us during one of those tennis tournaments. I had gotten to know McEnroe, so I brought him down to the dressing room to talk with the band members. They all seemed to enjoy it. (As noted earlier, the Black Crowes' lead singer Chris Robinson married Kate Hudson, the daughter of Goldie Hawn, and Hudson was at Toad's with the Crowes.)

McEnroe did not have such a sweet time with NRBQ. Since he knew how to play a guitar, on several occasions he had jammed with whatever band was at Toad's when he stopped in. He also had a show here with his own band, The Package, which did so-so business. However, during one of the many nights NRBQ was with us, McEnroe wanted to jam with them. I told him I would ask. When the tour manager asked keyboardist Terry Adams if "Johnny Mac" could jam with them on a couple of songs, Terry said, "No. He wouldn't want me jumping on the tennis court with him, and I would not want him jumping on our stage."

I broke this news to McEnroe as diplomatically as I could, but he was not at all happy to be rebuffed. He gave me that look. When he's pissed, his glare will slice right through you. And as anyone who has watched him on the tennis court knows, he can throw a fit when things don't go his way. I tried to hose him down by showing him around the club. When we got to our Rock Shop where NRBQ was selling its merchandise, I introduced McEnroe to the tour manager, who tossed a complimentary

NRBQ T-shirt to him. McEnroe looked at it and tossed it right back into the manager's face. I quickly moved McEnroe to another part of the building.

The rejection was probably not a good move by Terry Adams. McEnroe was one of the top-ranked tennis players in the world, worth millions. It always pays to be friendly. This is one thing Jimmy Koplik has taught me: "It's always better to use honey, not vinegar." McEnroe seemed to rebound, as he was enjoying the company of a woman at his booth.

Toad's was graced by the presence of another star who was studying at Yale: Jodie Foster. She began at Yale in the fall of 1980 and earned a degree in literature. She was already known for her movie roles, including her appearance in *Taxi Driver* with Robert DeNiro.

Unfortunately for her, a troubled young man named John Hinckley Jr. had seen that film many times and had become obsessed with the plot and with Foster. In the movie, the protagonist Travis Bickle, played by DeNiro, schemes to assassinate a presidential candidate. This apparently gave Hinckley an idea.

He moved to New Haven for a few days and began to stalk Foster. He had developed an infatuation with her and was searching for a way to meet her. He left love poems and notes under her dormitory door and called her a few times, but she didn't reciprocate. Frustrated by his inability to develop a relationship with Foster and wanting to impress her, he went down to Washington, D.C., where on March 30, 1981, he attempted to assassinate President Ronald Reagan. He wounded Reagan as well as a Secret Service agent and police officer. Reagan's assistant James Brady was also shot and permanently disabled. Hinckley was immediately arrested but later was found not guilty by reason of insanity.

Whenever Foster came into Toad's, she would just sit quietly at the bar. I never saw anybody bugging her. Yale students were cool about it; they knew how to behave around her.

We also had several visits from another famous actress, although she didn't attend Yale: Linda Blair. She came in a few times with one of the members of a band called Fast Fingers, from the Westport, Connecticut, area. Another time she was accompanied by Michael Bolton's former wife, Maureen McGuire.

During one visit we did some photo ops with Blair. I gave her a tour of our club, free drinks, and a Toad's Place jacket. Somehow she left her ID at the club. She called the next day. I spoke to her for a few minutes and looked around the club for her ID, but I came up with nothing. Somebody probably had found a nice souvenir on the floor. Linda was always very nice, even though she was in the scariest movie I have ever seen in my life: *The Exorcist*.

Another big name who arrived at our doors not old enough to drink legally was Diana Taurasi, a star player for the national champion UConn women's basketball team. Diana came to Toad's with some friends one night during the fall of 2001 to see a show by Toots and the Maytals; she was just nineteen.

I gave her a Toad's leather jacket and we did a photo op. Then she told me she wanted to hang out with her friends (who were twenty-one or older and legally allowed to drink) on the side of the room where legal drinking was permitted.

"Well, okay, but no drinking," I told her. "You're on the honor system." I didn't want to give her something and have headlines scream, "Toad's owner buys Diana Taurasi a drink!" No way.

You never know who might walk into our club on any given night. One night in May 1981, when I wasn't there, I got a call from one of my guys telling me, "Robin Williams is here."

"Take care of him," I said. "Buy him a drink."

The acclaimed actor-comedian was just hanging out, playing pinball. Later we learned he was visiting friends in the New Haven area for a few days. He came in to see a show by Robert Hunter, the Grateful Dead's guitarist, singer, and lyricist, who was doing a solo gig. Nobody bothered Williams, but of course it helped that he wasn't that well known then, unless you were a fan of *Mork & Mindy*.

Through the years we have occasionally booked comedians. When Sam Kinison did a stand-up show for us in 1992, Rodney Dangerfield also showed up to take in the performance! It was a sell-out crowd and Kinison was electrifying. The crowd was focused on every word that came out of his mouth. We escorted Dangerfield to a private seating area we had prepared for him. He was very polite. When he was introduced to the crowd he stood up and waved to everybody. They showed him a lot of respect.

In 1993 Eddie Murphy proved to a lot of people, including many of us at Toad's, that he is a talented musician as well as a superb actor and comedian. He was on tour that summer with a ten-member band, Psychedelic Soul, headed by Larry Graham, formerly of Sly and the Family Stone. Those guys played excellent rock, R&B, soul, and reggae. Murphy, who that year had released an all-music album, including the charted single "Party All the Time," played guitar and piano during the tour. He was serious about this; he wasn't there to tell jokes.

Murphy's older brother Charlie also was there that night, just to watch from our sky box. I did a double take when I saw him because they looked so much alike.

The band lit the dressing room with candles, and several of the band members carried them as they headed upstairs for the show. When they walked through the basement, each of them had a hand on the next person's shoulder, like a train.

Although Murphy didn't tell any jokes on stage, he did tell me one while we were briefly together in the Green Room. I was so nervous, though, that I can't remember the joke!

After the show I told Murphy and his band that I had heard Dylan, the Stones, U2, and Billy Joel at my club and none of them were any better than Psychedelic Soul. Murphy, realizing I was sincere and not goofing on him, started to clap and the rest of the band joined in.

The actor Harry Dean Stanton was another guy who doubled as a musician. Known for his work in *Cool Hand Luke*, *Alien*, *Repo Man*, *The Godfather Part II*, and *Twin Peaks*, he also toured as a guitarist with The Call, a Californian band led by Michael Been. The band had scored in 1983 with the song "The Walls Came Down," and Stanton toured with them in 1985. I was glad we had Stanton, but it appeared most of the crowd was there to hear the band.

Another big-name actor, Will Smith (*Men in Black*, *I Am Legend*, *The Fresh Prince of Bel-Air*), who had begun his career as a hip-hop entertainer, occasionally toured with a DJ named Jeff Townes in the duo DJ Jazzy Jeff and the Fresh Prince. We had only about four hundred people in the audience the night they came to Toad's, but those two put on a nice show.

Actor John Cusack was with us the night of the show by Seal, the British singer-songwriter ("Crazy," "Kiss From a Rose"). Cusack was dating one of the back-up vocalists. He came in unannounced, but I happened to be at the door and recognized him. I brought him up to the sky box and took care of him as best I could.

We've also had two actors from the hit HBO series *The Sopranos*: Michael Imperioli and Dominic Chianese. Imperioli, who is a guitarist and singer, had a band with him. He was pretty good, although he didn't draw a huge crowd. I gave him a tour of the club and told him about the bands we've hosted. He was fascinated. It was very cool conversing with a *Sopranos'* actor. We had only about a hundred people that night, but it was great having him.

Chianese did a solo acoustic guitar show, mostly of Italian songs. The crowd was older than our usual and the show ended by about 10:15 p.m. Afterward he did photo ops and signed his autograph for his fans. It was a delightful night. We made sure he got some pizza from Sally's. I had a nice talk with him too. Both of those guys were pleasant and personable.

Elijah Wood, who played Frodo Baggins in the *Lord of the Rings* trilogy, came to Toad's in the summer of 2008 because he was hanging out with the gypsy rock band Gogol Bordello. That band, led by Eugene Hutz, put on a tremendous show with great stage production and choreography.

Some of the loudest screaming I have ever heard at Toad's occurred on a night in August 1995 when movie star heartthrob Keanu Reeves came in with his band Dogstar. They didn't have a recording contract, but who cared? The ladies quickly snatched up every available ticket.

The *Hartford Courant's* Roger Catlin wrote a funny advance story about the show. He quoted our Katherine Blossom, who booked the band, noting the endless calls we had received from eager fans: "It's ridiculous. And it's nearly all women." Some of the females in the crowd had come from as far away as Texas.

Abiding by the contract, we had to keep Reeves's participation low-key. The ads for the show listed every member of the band, with Reeves simply getting equal billing. Who were they trying to fool?

At that time Reeves was thirty and coming off the mega-success of films such as *Bill & Ted's Excellent Adventure* and *Speed*. He was pulling in about $7 million for every movie he made, but he wanted to put together a band and go on a six-date tour of Japan, followed by a twenty-five-date tour of America.

The *Courant* dispatched correspondent Sabrina Lee to cover the Toad's show: "When Reeves walked on stage with his bass guitar strapped on, he didn't even acknowledge the pushy, territorial and idolizing throng that incessantly screamed, 'Keanu, we love you' at ear-piercing levels."

"The stubble-faced Reeves staked out one end of the stage," Lee added, "and didn't budge from the spot through the forty-minute set of typical unimpressive mainstream bar-rock. Dee Dee Ramone he's not."

I'd have to say 99 percent of the tickets we sold for that show were bought by women. For most of the show, Reeves kept his eyes lowered. But every once in a while, he'd lift his head to look at the crowd and the women would scream their heads off. It was literally painful. I'm used to loud volumes in this business, but I had to keep my fingers in my ears because I didn't want to live with chronic ear-ringing for the rest of my life. As had happened during the screaming reception for the pop band Hanson, I realized how Ed Sullivan must have felt when the Beatles hit his stage.

"Heat exhaustion overcame five people, who had to be pulled out of the sassy swarm by on-stage security," reported Lee. "After the show ended, at about midnight, groupies galore milled about in front of the band's tour bus and at each of the club's exit doors in order to get one last chance to salivate and swoon over Reeves."

Over the years we have had many events for Connecticut politicians and sometimes for national figures. New Jersey Senator Bill Bradley was at Toad's in February 2000 for a campaign event when he was running for the Democratic presidential nomination. There were about six hundred Yalies swarming the place in great excitement. He failed to get that nomination, which instead went to Al Gore.

When Joe Lieberman became a US senator representing Connecticut in 1989, we had a party for him. (We were excited for him when he went on to run for vice president in 2000, but it was not to be; that was the year George W. Bush narrowly defeated Gore). The popular oldies band the Drifters ("This Magic Moment," "Under the Boardwalk," "Up on the Roof") sang at one of the events for Lieberman. Chris Dodd also came in when he was Connecticut's US senator, and our US Representative Rosa DeLauro, known for her flamboyant outfits and ever-changing hair colors, has been here often.

When Sally's Apizza celebrated its fiftieth anniversary in 1988, the event was held at Toad's because of our long-time close relationship with the Consiglio family, owners of Sally's. Lowell Weicker Jr., who would become our governor in 1991, was on hand for that party. We have also had Connecticut governors Jodi Rell, Dannel Malloy, and Ned Lamont here.

In March 1982 Stephen Stills did a fundraiser at Toad's for US Representative Toby Moffett, who was running what would turn out to be an unsuccessful race for a US Senate seat (Weicker won that contest). Earlier that day Moffett had an appearance at Southern Connecticut State University with Carly Simon. The famous singer said very little, to the disappointment of the students; she said she was there to "learn about the issues." You wouldn't believe it if you've ever seen Simon in concert, but she has long suffered from stage fright. This might explain why she didn't make it to Toad's that night. It would have been a magic moment to have her singing on stage with Stills.

Stills returned in 1990 to do another benefit concert for Moffett when he was running for a congressional seat. (He lost that race too.) As Beach reported for the *New Haven Register,* the sell-out solo show lasted only fifty minutes. But Stills treated the crowd to a wide range of songs, including "For What It's Worth," the Allman Brothers' "Midnight Rider," "Southern Cross," "Find the Cost of Freedom," "Love the One You're With," and "Teach Your Children."

In May 1991 Stills came back yet again, this time with Simon's former husband James Taylor. Moffett must have spent a lot of money on his losing congressional campaign because Stills and Taylor were donating the proceeds of that sold-out show to help defray the costs. Stills's setlist included "Change Partners," "Southern Cross" once again, and, as an encore, "Woodstock." Taylor's setlist included "Sweet Baby James," "Carolina on My Mind," "Something in the Way She Moves," and "You've Got a Friend." Taylor and Stills joined to sing "Bluebird."

In April 2018 we brought in a local hero who had become a national star: Nick Fradiani. After he spent about five years in a band called Beach Avenue, in 2015 he became an entrant on the popular TV talent show *American Idol*. In May 2015 he won the competition with the song "Beautiful Life."

In a 2020 interview from his home in Branford, Connecticut, with Randall Beach, Fradiani said, "I'd always wanted to play at Toad's, but it wasn't until *American Idol* that I finally got to play there."

He recalled seeing a show at Toad's by the band Lit when he was thirteen. "That was my first experience of seeing people partying at a rock club. I thought, *This looks like fun!* It gave me a little push for wanting to play live music in a band."

On the day he was to perform at Toad's (joined by his dad Nick Fradiani III on acoustic guitar), he made sure he got there early. "I wanted to take it all in and get set up," he said. "It's such a famous place. I love music history and I knew all about the history of Toad's. There's something special about standing there and thinking, *Wow! I'm on the same stage the Rolling Stones were on, and Drake and Kanye West.*"

"That was one of the most fun shows I've ever done," Fradiani continued. "It was a fun crowd, a party crowd. This was a full-blown rock show. I had a seven- or eight-piece band. It was quite an experience. I'm looking forward to playing there again one day," he added. "It's a cool spot. I hope it keeps on forever. After COVID, maybe there will be a rebirth of people wanting to see live shows."

A final note about famous names at Toad's: One day in 2002 we got a phone call from a representative of the popular TV game show *Jeopardy!* The guy said they wanted to use a question that involved Toad's Place. I said, "Sure, go right ahead." The man said the show would air the following week, but I never gave it much thought. Then, one night host Alex Trebek asked the contestants, "Toad's Place in New Haven, Connecticut, is the place where they launched their Steel Wheels Tour." Of course they were supposed to respond: "Who are the Rolling Stones?" A contestant got it immediately.

We were closed the night the question aired, but I was at the club and the phone started ringing off the hook. It seemed like everybody in the world was calling to tell us we had been on *Jeopardy!* I kept saying, "Thanks. Thanks for letting me know. I know! I know!" I hadn't realized how many people loved that show and its host. All of us at Toad's were so sorry in November 2020 when Trebek lost his courageous battle with pancreatic cancer .

But I was very moved we had made it on *Jeopardy!* We had become a part of history.

CHAPTER 10

The Bouncers: Tank and Whiskey

OVER THE PAST FOUR DECADES AT TOAD'S WE'VE HAD DOZENS OF SECURITY PEOPLE who kept our crowds under control. But two of them, one nicknamed Tank and the other Whiskey, became folk heroes for their sheer size, strength, and service. They could also be characters out of a pulp fiction novel.

Anthony "Tank" Dunbar has been with us for more than forty years. Bill "Whiskey" Walkauskas worked our doors and floors from the mid-1970s to the mid-1980s. They've seen it all, from sloppy drunks to knife-and-gun-wielding yahoos, plus some of the world's biggest entertainers.

Tank met Big Mike Spoerndle during a shoot-out, although fortunately it wasn't at Toad's. Tank sat down with Randall Beach at the Three Brothers Diner, a couple of miles away from Toad's in September 2020 to describe that incident and other highlights of his time with us. Befitting his occupation, Tank is a big, big man, standing six feet, four inches tall and weighing in at 310 pounds.

"I was at this mobster place on (New Haven's) Dixwell Avenue, an after-hours social club," recalled Tank. "Mike was there gambling and drinking and hanging out. He was gonna roll the dice. Suddenly the shooting started. Mike and I knew nothing about it, but we were in the middle of it and had to get out. I said, 'Yo man, this way.' I got him out of there. A couple of people got hit; somebody got killed. That part we didn't see. Mike said he wasn't going back there. He just said, 'No more.'"

"The next time I saw him, he said, 'Hey, I've got a place downtown. You want to work there? You won't have to be dodging bullets.' I'd heard about Toad's and I'd worked security before, so I went down to see Brian and he said, 'Can you start tonight?' Forty years later I'm still there!"

"Angela Bofill was playing that first night," Tank remembers. "I made friends with her and her manager." That's one of the features of the job that has kept Tank at Toad's for four decades. "I've always liked music and there were acts I liked that came in: Sam and Dave ("Hold On, I'm Comin'") and Wilson Pickett ("Mustang Sally"), I hung out with 'em," he said. "Wilson Pickett, he was out of the church like I was. Sam and Dave were from the Miami area and I'm from Tampa."

Tank also recalled the night soul and jazz poet Gil Scott-Heron ("The Revolution Will Not Be Televised") came to Toad's. "This was at the end of the Black Panthers' time in New Haven. Mike was worried about revolution-type stuff happening, but Scott-Heron was the perfect person for that time. He brought everybody together, singing the songs."

In 1973, a few years before he came to Toad's, Tank had a shot at playing defensive tackle for the Philadelphia Eagles. He was with them for pre-season and practice games, but he suffered a pinched nerve in an auto accident, and that put an end to his football career.

Football's loss was our gain. As Tank told the *Yale Daily News*'s Peter Schmeisser in the early 1980s, both he and Whiskey have seen themselves as "dance floor psychologists" who can almost always talk people out of fighting.

"I'm not here to beat people up," Tank told Schmeisser. "I'm just your father away from home." Besides, Tank's size and presence are usually intimidating enough to deem physical restraint unnecessary.

Phil Cutler said of Tank and Whiskey, "Those guys were so big! I mean big! You'd have to be a fool to do something stupid. But they were great guys. Everybody had everybody's back."

Tank told Beach that Toad's benefitted by being so close to Yale. "People knew Toad's wasn't one of those wild places. It wasn't a dive. You couldn't come in intoxicated. If you defy the rules of the club, you gotta leave. If you grab a waitress or a bartender, you've gotta go. It's a team effort."

"You have to be on the spot," said Tank. "You've gotta know how to get out of that situation while it's cookin'. You just keep zigging; let them zag. Eventually they'll run out, they're gonna get dizzy."

Clockwise from top left: Anthony "Tank" Dunbar, Joe Satriani, Veruca Salt, The Neville Brothers, Jeezy (photo by Buddy Mention), Bad English, Buckwheat Zydeco, and Bill "Whiskey" Walkauskas.

But even the biggest, savviest guys are going to get hurt sometimes. The most serious injury Tank sustained came the night he broke up a wild fight between two large groups.

"It was a girlfriend-boyfriend sort of deal. The old boyfriend came in and was bickering with the new boyfriend and the girl. The new boyfriend had buddies there and so the old boyfriend got jumped by those guys. I went to stop them. This kid [the old boyfriend] had something sharp in his hand, not a knife but something real sharp. It was like friendly fire, and I got injured. But then I chased him down outside and brought him back. Thank God I'm tall or he would've got me in the groin. He got me in the upper thigh. I had to go to the hospital to get stitched up. The guy who stabbed me got arrested. A lot of these guys end up in jail because they want to be the judge and the jury."

There were times Tank was called upon to disarm a patron.

"One night a guy had a gun. It was closing time. I asked him, 'Why did you bring a gun into a club? You gotta go.' I grabbed him in a hold and took him outside. The cops were there and they took care of it."

Tank thought he had another violent situation on his hands one night in the late seventies when punk bands had become the rage and their fans showed their enthusiasm by slam dancing. Tank said the first time the Ramones came in, "the punks were all slamming, knocking each other down. I'd never seen that; it was like a zoo or a riot. I started throwing them out. I got about fifteen punks outside. Then they told me, 'You know, we're not fighting, we're dancing!' I said, 'Knocking people down is dancing?' So they gave me a demonstration on the sidewalk: Bam! Bam! They said, 'That's a mosh pit.' That was a day in school for me."

Tank continued, "But we told them, 'You can't do that here.' It's dangerous. People get hit in the head. It's like a bowling ball, knocking people down. One guy got injured pretty bad. We don't want to get sued; our insurance doesn't cover that."

Tank developed a philosophy about handling each night's situation, whether he's dealing with Billy Joel, the Rolling Stones, or a local band.

"You always have to keep it in the back of your mind that you'll be dealing with this person for a couple of hours. Let it be," he says. "You want to do the best you can to make it as smooth as possible. It's a short time in your life; why mess it up?"

"Some of the performers are really into the fans," says Tank. "Some are not. Some want to get in and get out. The encore is over and they want their driver ready. They're gone. George Thorogood is going to get in the car and leave. But a guy like Kris Kristofferson, he's going to sign autographs until the line is done."

Tank was sixty-eight when Beach interviewed him. He said he planned to come back to Toad's after the pandemic was brought under control, but he added, "Brian's not expecting me to do the stuff I did thirty-five to forty years ago. Being there keeps me in a different state of mind. It gives me a different viewpoint on life, seeing the way things are done after eight at night. Everything is different. It's a totally different world."

Tank compares Toad's to the Apollo Theater in Harlem. "There aren't many places where you can say, 'We did this. We had this.' I saw worldwide things. I'm a very lucky man."

And we've been lucky to have him. I've seen Tank wade in all by himself when there were six guys engaged in a big brawl in the middle of the dance floor. He quieted the ruckus down with no problem. Many times he would take two guys at the same time under his arms and drag them out of the crowd and out the door. Even today people brag about being thrown out by Tank. He's also great at escorting bands in and out of the club. Sometimes the band members ask for him by name. He will also bring people to their VIP areas. He moves through the crowd like a lawnmower. People part like the Red Sea when they see Tank coming.

Like Tank, our man Whiskey was a football player. He played on his high school team at South Hills Catholic in Pittsburgh, Pennsylvania, and received an athletic scholarship from Yale in the days when Ivy League colleges still made such offers. But he played only for Yale's freshman team, as a defensive lineman, and didn't make it to the varsity level. He said, "I wasn't a good fit for Yale," so he dropped out.

During an October 2020 interview with Beach at the Twin Pines Diner in East Haven, Whiskey told the story of how he got his nickname.

"My high school football coach couldn't pronounce my name (Walkauskas). But 'Whiskey' he could pronounce. That stuck with me for thirty years. It was fun, but I was never a big drinker. I must've had thirteen thousand club sodas with lime at Toad's."

After Whiskey dropped out of Yale, where he had studied philosophy and psychology (good training for his later work at Toad's), he got a job as a parking lot attendant at Yale New Haven Hospital. "I read books, listened to music on the radio, and waved to people. I liked it."

But a couple of years later, during the first or second year of Toad's existence, he got the job working security for us. And why not? He's six feet, four inches tall and at that time weighed 250 pounds.

"Working at Toad's was like working at the parking lot," he said. "I waved to people, I listened to music. Mostly I was at the front door, checking IDs." He became an expert at spotting the fake ones.

In that *Yale Daily News*'s story about our two famed bouncers, Whiskey was quoted as saying, "Tank and I work what you might call a zone defense. I take care of things coming in off the street and Tank patrols the inside. We are not here as oppressors. That's why Toad's hires big foremen. When Tank and I surround you, there is no need for any violence. I think I punched one guy this year, just one, and he had his teeth sunk in my arm."

In that Yale story, Whiskey described his job as "10 percent authority and 90 percent psychology."

During the diner interview in 2020, Whiskey said, "We were like the local cops. When a situation got out of hand, we dealt with it. We didn't over-deal with it. We didn't hurt anybody. We made it a safe place."

Whiskey noted the large number of college students he dealt with. "Toad's was a place where people came to learn how to date—with a little alcohol." It was great for his social life too. "I'd had twelve years of Catholic school. Suddenly I had a great way to meet a couple thousand women!"

In addition to dealing with people coming in the front door, Whiskey monitored the crowd during the shows from his vantage point in the sky box. "It was elevated, so I could watch over people. Tank was the physical contact. If something happened, he could dominate any situation."

"I was at Toad's for about 1,300 shows over ten years," Whiskey said. "I think the best music was the local bands: the Simms Brothers, Beaver Brown. I did see Dylan, but I got there late. I missed the Stones, I don't even know why. They weren't on the top of my list."

Asked why he left Toad's, Whiskey said, "It was just time. After 1,300 shows, it was time for something else. It wasn't going to be my whole life. I loved the music, it was a great job to have, but I was not doing much good for the world. It didn't give meaning to my life."

He found that meaning by working as a teacher's aide for Area Cooperative Educational Services, an agency serving the New Haven region. "Hey man, it gave me a reason to live! At ACES I got my missing piece. You make a contribution, that's the piece that was missing. Working with those kids, it kept me alive. That's why I was there for thirty-five years."

After he left Toad's, Whiskey became a Quaker. "It became a big part of my life. We built a meeting house in New Haven. We started a day care in the basement, the Friends Center for Children, where I volunteered."

But he said working at Toad's was "a great preparation for my real life's work at ACES. If I was in the classroom and a kid went off, I could deal with it, not hurt them. I could control the situation."

Whiskey, who is now retired from ACES, said, as does Tank, that he feels lucky to have had the chance to work at Toad's Place. "It was a good period of my life. I'm grateful for it."

CHAPTER 11

The Crowds

WHEN HUNDREDS OF LIKE-MINDED PEOPLE GATHER IN A NIGHTCLUB LIKE TOAD'S, fueled by fun music and ample quantities of alcohol, you can bet romances will sprout up and sometimes lifelong relationships will form. There are plenty of people who can boast, "I met my (future) husband at Toad's Place," or "I met my (future) wife at Toad's!"

In 2020 Randall Beach encouraged the readers of his *New Haven Register* column to tell him about their formative experiences at Toad's. It's clear from the response that the action wasn't happening only on the stage.

"I met my one and only at Toad's. He spilled his beer on me and he's been paying for it ever since," said Kathleen "Katie" Regan. "Toad's has a very special place in our hearts."

After Beach read this email message from Regan, he called her and got the full story.

"I was eighteen," she said. "Mike was twenty. He was working at Mory's (the venerable Yale-connected restaurant next door to Toad's) as a busboy. The date was August 22, 1981."

Her name then was Kathleen O'Neill. She went to Toad's that night with her sister and another friend. "I had just graduated from high school," she said. "My dad was very sick, and we needed to get out of the house for a night."

She thinks the name of the band playing that night was Fast Fingers, but what she remembers for sure is her fateful encounter with young Mike Regan.

"I'd seen him at other bars," she noted, and she liked what she saw. "I think he was dancing while drinking a beer; he's a crazy dancer! As he was moving past me, he bumped into me and spilled his beer on me and jostled my beer too. He apologized and said, 'Oh, let me buy you another beer.'"

"At first I was pissed," she recalled. "But then I saw it was him! And I thought, *Ah–ha! This is not so bad after all!*"

After he brought her that replacement beer, they began to talk and then to dance. It can be said they "danced the night away" because they stayed there until closing time. At that point she realized her sister had left, so her new love interest gallantly offered to drive her home.

Regan then met up with his buddies, who were preparing to go to Martha's Vineyard the next day. When he told one of them, "Wow, I met this girl," the friend must have seen the love light in his eyes because he said, "I think you're going to marry that girl!"

The young couple returned to Toad's many nights after that to dance, laugh, talk, and drink beer. She remembers seeing fun shows by NRBQ.

They got married in 1984. Earlier that year she had discovered she was pregnant with twins. As she was readjusting her thinking about what this news meant to her future, her friend Judy told her what she had read in a bathroom stall at Toad's: "Life is what happens while you're making plans for life."

Fast forward twenty-five years to November 28, 2009 and the couple's twenty-fifth wedding anniversary. "My sister told me James Taylor was stopping by Toad's that night," Regan said. "She knows I'm a big James Taylor fan. Mike claimed he didn't really want to go, but I said, 'We should do this.' When we got there, my sister said, 'Oh, we have to go to a special room upstairs. That's where James Taylor is going to be.'"

When they got up to Lilly's Pad, the private party room on the second floor, about seventy-five of their friends and all of their family shouted, "Surprise!" She forgot about James Taylor right away.

"It was very heartwarming, one of the biggest surprises of my life," Regan said. "Our kids had set it up. They had a play list all prepared."

Those are her two very special nights: the time she met her future husband and the surprise party for their twenty-fifth wedding anniversary. And both of them happened at Toad's Place. "Every year at Christmas," Regan said, "I have a little toad I put on our Christmas tree to remind me."

Clockwise from top left: Counting Crows, Manchester Orchestra (photo by Benji Wagner), Robin Zander of Cheap Trick, Cyndi Lauper, Drake, and Count Basie.

John Minardi also emailed Beach to recount how he met his future spouse at Toad's. This happened on December 17, 1983, a Saturday night.

Minardi said he and his buddy Pete hadn't intended to go to Toad's that night. Their destination was another New Haven club, the Keg House, which offered twenty-five-cent beer pitchers on Saturdays. These two young dudes didn't have much money, but they had "a pocket full of quarters."

"We were in shock to find the place boarded up and closed!" Minardi said. "I said to Pete, 'Now where do we go?' We were dressed in flannel shirts with torn jeans and work boots, just for drinking that night and nothing else. He said, 'Let's just see what's going on at Toad's.'

"We got to Toad's and there was a Saturday night dance party. We were reluctant to go in. We were rock 'n' roll fans and did not like that type of music and we were certainly not dressed for a dance party. Pete said, 'Look, there's no cover, so let's go in for one beer, scope the place out, and leave if it's that bad.'

"We go in and immediately realize we are out of our element. But at that point I just wanted to sit down and have a cold beer. We sit at one of the tables along the side wall and I'm just nursing that beer and enjoying every sip. Pete is looking around, and he said these two girls at a table across from us keep staring at us. I looked down at my work boots and thought, *No way, this is not our crowd.* But Pete insisted on a second beer and also insisted we talk to these girls. I looked up and he was right, they seemed to be eyeing us or just glancing over every once in a while."

"We ordered a second beer and walked over to their table. We said hi and asked if they'd mind if we sat down. Surprisingly, considering how we were dressed, they said, 'Sure!' Pete started talking with Phyliss, so I started talking to Dawn. She told me she had just turned twenty on the Monday before. She had a great smile—still does!"

"We were talking and laughing when finally the dance party DJ played a Romantics tune. I thought, *Thank God, some rock 'n' roll!* It was 'What I Like About You.' This was great timing! So I asked her if she wanted to dance and she said yes! I did whisper in her ear, and all of those corny things in the lyrics while we were dancing. It was fun."

"I got her phone number that night after a couple more beers. Pete and I didn't want to overstay our welcome. But I called her the next day, and we've been together ever since that night thirty-seven years ago. We got married in May of '86. Toad's will always have a special place in our hearts and memories."

Carolyn Martino also met her future husband, Anthony, at Toad's, in an interesting twist of fate. "My boyfriend at the time was front and center for a show by John Valby, 'the prince of porn,' and I was to meet up with him there. Well, I was with a small group of friends when we showed up and went in. One of their boyfriends met them there. In that group of friends was my future husband. I never made it much past the front door that night. We all hung out and talked for a few hours. Never did see my boyfriend that night. We left with them, and the rest is history, twenty-three years of marriage and three children later!"

Robert Rigutto recalled going to Toad's for a Friday night dance party in 1987 with a group of his friends. "We were hanging out on the dance floor when my buddies recognized two women they had picked up one night while riding their motorcycles. We all went over and I asked one of them, Lorraine, for a dance, and she accepted. We danced all night. All I remember is having a good night and my buddies saying I needed to call her the next day, which I did. We've been married almost thirty years now."

Rigutto said he was looking forward to getting back to Toad's after it reopens: "I'd love to come, if possible, on or close to our anniversary. That would be fun."

Many of the memories people have of their nights at Toad's are about the music, not romantic connections. You could have a wonderful, special experience, even if you didn't meet your future wife or husband. You might even get a big surprise.

Kurt Evans spent many nights at Toad's during the 1980s and 1990s. "I was a regular there. Every night was an event, just to be there. On a particular Wednesday night in the mid-nineties, a group of my friends and I headed over there on a whim. It was a typically high energy night, the drinks flowed." (They had paid no attention to the signs outside announcing the performer who was scheduled to be there that night.)

"Then, to our surprise and subsequent immense enjoyment, Tom Jones appeared on stage! What a show he put on, just immeasurably memorable! The crowd was so into it, and he was absolutely phenomenal. The intimate atmosphere, his sonorous voice, it all combined to make magic. It was my favorite concert experience ever. Thank you, Toad's!"

Tom Christensen spent many nights at Toad's from 1975 to the mid-1980s. Although he saw some major acts there, including Billy Joel, he said, "The one show that really stands out in my memory is the one put on by Charles Brown." (His hits included "Driftin' Away" and "Merry Christmas Baby.")

"He was one of the greatest blues piano players ever," Christensen noted. "He had a very distinctive style that was popular from the late forties to the late fifties. I had been a big fan of the blues since my junior year in high school, and when I heard that Charles Brown was coming to Toad's, I convinced my buddies to come and see a legend."

"I insisted we get there early to get the best seats possible," Christensen continued. "Toad's had rows of chairs set up. Our group of four grabbed some drinks and staked out some front row seats. Two or four rounds later the lights went down and out comes 'Mr. Smooth' himself, Charles Brown! The only problem was that besides our group, there were only about six more people in the seats and maybe a dozen people at the bar. I was heartbroken for Charles. Here was an American original, a legend of the blues genre, and only twenty or so people showed up. But he played like he was performing before a sell-out audience at Carnegie Hall. He totally blew our minds with his playing and stage persona. It was one of the greatest concerts I've ever experienced."

"After the show, the security guys at Toad's allowed me and my buddies to go backstage and get his autograph," remembers Christensen. "I'm not an autograph guy, but I really wanted to meet and thank Charles for his performance. Charles came out and signed the cassette of his that I'd brought with me and then he proceeded to talk with us for about twenty minutes! He was so incredibly gracious and generous with his time."

"When I attempted to apologize for the small turn-out, he cut me off and said it didn't matter how many people were there. He wanted to make sure those that were in attendance were entertained. What a class act!"

Brown wasn't the only act that Christensen caught at Toad's. "Seeing Billy Joel at the height of his popularity in a tiny venue like Toad's was certainly exciting, as was seeing Jack Bruce and Ginger Baker close-up (and hoping Clapton would show up!). Muddy Waters was incredible. Tower of Power always put on a great show and Buddy

Guy was just a singular experience. However, that Charles Brown show still, to this day, sends chills down my spine when I think of it."

Lisa Braman was a big fan of *The Partridge Family* show from the seventies, whose cast included David Cassidy, who of course went on to become a popular singer. The Partridge Family also had a hit single, "I Think I Love You." Another actor on that show was Danny Bonaduce, who played the wise guy, middle son. In 1991, when Braman heard that Cassidy was going to perform at Toad's, she made sure she got there, even though she had never been to the club before. She convinced her friend Melissa to go with her.

"What we didn't realize until we arrived," she remembers, "was that the opening act was Danny Bonaduce, performing a stand-up comedy act. That was an added surprise and bonus for us! It was so exciting to see him take the stage. So many memories of watching him on *The Partridge Family* came to mind and here he was in person before us. We watched and listened to Danny, with his same childish grin, entertain the crowd with stories of his life and some of the wild infamous stories of recent years. He spoke with gratitude that David had given him this opportunity to tour and get out his message that he was becoming sober and straightening out his life."

"I noticed when he left the stage that he made his way back toward the bar. Melissa and I decided we would follow him and see if we could persuade him to join us for a drink. We walked right up to him and stood next to him at the bar. He was immediately friendly and initiated a conversation. We asked him if he wanted to join us for a shot of tequila. He said, 'Sure!' I said, 'I thought you don't drink anymore.' He replied, 'Ah, that's just shtick for the act.' So we ordered up the shots, toasted, laughed, and drank up. He was very charming and fun to talk with."

"About fifteen years later, my brother, who had become a senior writer and creative producer in California, told me he was writing a reality-type show with Bonaduce. He offered to take my old Partridge Family album back to California with him so he could ask Danny to sign it for me. A week later I got a call from my brother's cellphone. Much to my surprise, I was met with a very different voice: 'Lisa, this is Danny Bonaduce. I am sitting here with your brother, and he's telling me that you and I shared a drink at Toad's Place.' I was blown away. I reminded him about the tequila toast. While he couldn't remember all the details, he said, 'That's certainly what I would do.' He added, 'I have your album here, and I'm going to sign it for you.' He said he enjoyed hearing about that night at Toad's and he appreciated that it was such a fond memory for me."

"My brother mailed the album cover back to me. I have it framed and hanging in my home for all to see. Danny Bonaduce signed it 'To Lisa—I think I love you, or at least I tried to. Toad's Place '91.'"

CHAPTER 12

"Big Mike"

THE TOAD'S PLACE STORY IS ESSENTIALLY ABOUT THE RELATIONSHIP AND PARTNERSHIP between Mike Spoerndle and me. For my first ten years or so (1976 to 1985), I was the club's manager. Then Mike offered to make me his legal partner. But by ten years after that, in the mid-nineties, Mike had become so unstable from his drug abuse that I made the painful but necessary decision to negotiate a deal severing his ties with Toad's.

At the beginning, when Mike invited me to work at the club, he was my mentor, my role model. He was almost like my big brother. We became close friends. Beyond that, I respected him for what he had accomplished as a young man still in his twenties.

Although I got to know Mike well and even shared a house with him that we bought together a year or two after I started at Toad's, he was private about personal things, despite his affable veneer. He never told me about his traumatic childhood and teenage years living with his abusive father.

Randall Beach's interviews with Mike's first wife Joan Mary Spoerndle and his younger brother Pat unearthed revelations that could explain why Mike was insecure, couldn't handle the fame and stress of Toad's, and became addicted to alcohol and other substances.

During their extended conversation with Beach at her condo in Milford, Connecticut, Joan smiled as she recalled the first time she saw her future husband—he was standing in the kitchen of her parents' Milford home, preparing dinner for her family.

"This guy filled the room," she recalled. "I said, 'Hello. Who are you?' He just gave me that big smile, with a twinkle in his eyes. Then my mom came in and said, 'Mike's cooking dinner for us!'"

To Toads
One more notch in your
on my belt! Another
show! Keep er
Rock! I
Love

JOAN JETT

Clockwise from top left: Mike "Big Mike" Spoerndle (illustration by Marc Potocsky - MJP Studios), Hootie & the Blowfish, Busta Rhymes (photo by Eileen Finegan), John Paul Jones, Crash Test Dummies, signed photo from Joan Jett, and Edgar Winter.

The year was 1970. Mike had moved from his small hometown in Ohio to Connecticut, initially living in the hotel Joan's parents owned in the suburban shoreline community of Milford. He was there to study at the Culinary Institute of America, which in those days was in New Haven. On that day when Joan met Mike, he was trying out a new meal, an informal part of his course work.

"He was always saying, 'Let me try this gravy, let me try this,'" Joan said. "He could make a meal out of a baked potato. He had such a gift. If he'd kept up with his cooking career, he would've put Emeril Lagasse to shame. Cooking was his passion. He wanted to be a French chef."

Indeed, Toad's Place began as a French restaurant. But the business just limped along; parking was a problem for customers and New Haven hadn't yet become acclaimed for high-end dining spots. However, Mike soon realized he had a better idea about how to make Toad's a successful enterprise. He didn't know much about the music scene, but as Joan said, "He was adept at everything." Everybody who knew him said he was smart, a quick study.

Above all, Mike Spoerndle had charisma. "When he gave you that smile," Joan said, "you knew everything would be okay. He could get people to do things. He was a leader. And he cared about people."

Mike and Joan married in 1973, two years before Toad's opened. Their wedding song was the Carpenters' "We've Only Just Begun."

In 1974 Joan became pregnant with their son Matt. In 1975, having graduated from culinary school, Mike launched Toad's Place with his Ohio friends Chuck Metzger and Mike Korpas. Because of his large build, unlike Korpas, Mike Spoerndle became known as Big Mike, a nickname that also fit his personality.

Over the following years he transformed his club into a national sensation, luring superstar acts such as the Rolling Stones to his small venue. But during those three decades Mike also divorced Joan; married Andrea DeNicola; divorced her; married Abigail Jacobson; became addicted to alcohol, cocaine, and heroin; and lost ownership of Toad's. In May 2011 he was found dead at his home in East Haven, his drug use given as the underlying cause of his death. He was only fifty-nine.

More than one person has said Mike was "the heart and soul of Toad's Place." But anyone who knew Mike and talks about his life inevitably uses two words: "sad" and "tragic."

"What he accomplished in his life and what he built was unbelievable," said his kid brother Pat Spoerndle. "But he couldn't get it right. He couldn't stay sober. And it ultimately cost him his life."

Speaking from his home in Ohio, Pat described their upbringing, the "rough times" that might explain why Mike was unable to deal with his meteoric ascent and why he fell so fast.

"I was Mike's little brother," Pat said. "There were four of us. The oldest was Steve, the responsible big brother who took care of everybody. The next oldest was Susan, then Mike, born in 1953, and then me, in 1956."

Their parents were Harry, an insurance salesman, and Margaret, a homemaker. The family lived in the small town of Fairview Park, a suburb of Cleveland. "It was a great community," Pat said.

But behind the closed doors of the Spoerndle house, the kids were raised in what Pat said was "an unhealthy environment."

"We had a father who was verbally and physically abusive," Pat said. "He hit my mom and he hit us. Mike probably got more of it because he was more willing to stand up for himself."

"I spent a lot of years trying to figure out what my father's problem was," Pat added. "He wasn't a big drinker. I think he was a very insecure human being. Anything that challenged him he reacted to. Mike was likely to say, 'To hell with you!' and leave for a few hours to let things calm down."

Mike exhibited this angry defiance with authority figures at high school too, Pat recalled. "He was on the football team for a little while because he was big and strong. But one day the coach said, 'Spoerndle, get your fat ass moving!' Mike told the coach, 'Let your little skinny guys play!' And he just quit the team. He wasn't going to be put down. That wasn't his nature."

Pat described his mother as "awesome" in the face of the ongoing abuse at the hands of her husband. But she finally decided she had had enough and divorced him when Mike was fourteen or fifteen. She gave the marriage a second chance, marrying

Harry again, but then divorced him once more when Mike was nineteen or twenty, Pat said. "She regretted re-marrying him."

Mike found a refuge from the chaos and violence of home; he got a job at a nearby Greek diner when he was only about fourteen. "He was washing dishes and bussing tables all through high school," Pat said.

Looking back on the abuse the kids endured from their father, Pat said, "It certainly shaped all of us. The belittling I experienced as a kid shaped me decisively. I was always trying to prove that I was okay, counter to what my father told me. A lot of my drive was to prove he was wrong. I think we were all in that same kind of a bind."

As for the effects of the abuse on Mike? "It was probably the most significant thing that happened in his life. Maybe it got him started with alcohol and drugs as a way to feel better. I don't know the answer to that," said Pat. "But I think Mike had a lot of insecurities as a result of that stuff."

"He also had one of the biggest hearts I've ever seen," he added. "Sadly, that was interrupted by drugs and alcohol."

As soon as Mike graduated from high school, he was off to Connecticut and culinary school with his friend Metzger. Joan said that while Mike was at that school, he continued to live at the hotel her parents owned by the beach in Milford. After he finished with his culinary training, Mike worked at a restaurant in Fairfield, Connecticut. But he wanted his own place, so he, Metzger, and Korpas signed a property lease at the then-vacant Hungry Charlie's in New Haven.

Joan remembers the day Mike announced their new restaurant was to be called Toad's Place, a reference to Ohio people nicknaming couch potatoes "toads." "I said, 'A French restaurant named Toad's Place?' He said people would remember that name."

After Toad's became a hot spot for music, Mike got another idea. "He came home one night and said, 'I'm changing my name to Mr. Toad.' I said, 'I'm not going to be Mrs. Toad.' I think he really would have changed his name to that if I'd agreed. He was so proud of that business."

When Matt was born, Joan recalled, "Mike did come to see the baby at the hospital, for a few minutes. When he got the keys to Toad's, he was there close to twenty-four hours a day. Even when he came home, he was always on the phone with somebody about Toad's."

Joan didn't care for the nightclub scene and was at Toad's only a couple of times. "It's a hard business to have a marriage in," she said.

In 1977 they separated. In 1978 they got divorced. Joan got full custody of Matt.

Pat Healy, who lays claim to being the first bartender at Toad's and remained at the club for decades as one of Mike's best friends, said that for a period after the separation Mike lived in an upstairs room at Toad's. Healy recalled people joking that Mike was "living on top of Toad's."

Within a year of starting Toad's, Mike, Metzger, and Korpas were arguing so much about how to run the business that Mike told them, "Buy me out or I'll buy you guys out. This isn't going to work anymore with the three of us." Metzger and Korpas, who weren't as dedicated to the business and had never envisioned remaining there for very long anyway, agreed to the split.

"It's either in your blood or not, the nightclub business," Healy said. "To stay in that business, it becomes your life. You might say, 'I could be home now.' But you miss the thrill, the action."

Healy recalled the club being a tougher place in those earlier days, sometimes attracting biker gangs. "One night a couple of knuckleheads were coming after a guy's girl. Mike got into it with one of them. He got the big guy down and the other guy was going after Mike. I jumped over the bar to help, and a guy stuck a gun in my stomach. Mike grabbed the gun and it went off into the ceiling. Mike snapped the guy's arm. He broke it. The guys ran off and Mike just said, 'All right, get back behind the bar. We've gotta make some money.'"

Our bouncer Bill "Whiskey" Walkauskas described Mike as being "super impulsive."

"He always had that sense of pushing boundaries," said Whiskey. "He tended to stir up energetic situations. I figured out that my job was to go around with Mike and make sure he didn't hurt anybody, because he'd get physically upset. If it got physical, I got in between Mike and the other guy right away, because Mike was real important to the place."

"Mike always did everything to the max," said John Dubuque, who booked bands independently of us from an office at Toad's. "He took everything beyond his capacity and everybody else's. If you were going sixty to seventy miles per hour, he'd go 110.

One day he took me out in his Porsche and he was going so fast he snapped my head to the back of the seat. I was scared shitless."

Manuel Rodriguez, a promotion manager for Warner Electra Atlantic Records who helped get bands to Toad's, had a similar experience with Mike.

"He had a big gold wing motorcycle," remembers Rodriguez. "He said, 'Let's go for a ride.' I'm in my suit and he just takes off. We're riding around New Haven, without helmets of course. I might have been screaming. I told him, 'Come on, Mike! Come on!' He just wanted to scare me."

Mike soon got tired of "living on top of Toad's." He used the money he'd made at the club to buy, with me, a nice house in the shoreline town of Branford, alongside the exclusive Pine Orchard Yacht and Country Club. Kirk Baird, who handled the banking for Toad's from 1977 to 1984 at what was then First Bank in New Haven, remembered when Mike moved into that house.

"It was fifty yards from the fourth fairway on the golf course," he said. "The house was a big, rambling thing. Mike knew I was a member of the Pine Orchard club and he said, 'Kirk, I want to join the club.' I said, 'Really, Mike? Are you sure?' He said, 'Absolutely!' I said, 'It's going to be like a horse auction; they're going to look at your teeth, put you through the wringer. You'll need a sport jacket and tie—do you have that?' He said, 'I sure do. I even have wing tip shoes!' He could dress up for an occasion and pull it off if he wanted to do it."

"Well, he got in," said Baird, "which was a dream for this kid from Ohio. For the owner of Toad's to get into the Pine Orchard Yacht and Country Club! It was pretty damn exclusive."

Baird recalled a Friday night when he and his wife were dining at the club. "Suddenly I hear, 'Hey Kirk!' It's Mike, with Al Anderson and another member of NRBQ. Mike was so excited to bring those two guys into that club for dinner. They weren't dressed up, even though most of the club people dressed in blue blazers, white pants, and Italian loafers. What I remember about that night was the grin on Mike's face. This was a big deal for him to have these two guys from NRBQ at his club."

Healy said Mike did occasionally use the golf course. "He was not a good golfer. He'd just go out and hack at the ball and have some fun. He had a golf cart."

By the early 1980s Mike had remarried and was spending a lot of time hanging out at the club's pool with his second wife, Andrea, and their kids, Jennie, Jacqueline, and Michael Jr. As for me, I no longer fit in at our house. Andrea didn't want me there, which I understood; she wanted it to be just her family. I sold my share of it to Mike and moved out. I was continuing to put in long hours at Toad's to keep it afloat. Mike, trying to live the suburban family life, wasn't there as much.

But he still didn't fit in with the country club set. I remember one night being in the car with him while he was riding around with his dogs, a Doberman pinscher and a German shepherd. He had a big Black Russian on a tray so he could sip from it while driving and a marijuana cigarette hanging out of his mouth. After we took one trip around the block, I made some excuse and got out of that car.

Mike loved his family and tried to spend time with them. But he simply couldn't resist the lure of hanging out with the band members and others in the music business.

"You could see him getting caught up in that lifestyle," remembers his brother Pat, "the drinking and doing drugs with people who were on their way to becoming famous musicians."

Joan, who by then was seeing very little of Mike except for when he came by for his scheduled time with Matt, said, "When you have a nightclub, the temptation is always there. You can say 'yes' or you can say 'no'—and he chose 'yes.' You never think it will get out of control. When you're twenty or thirty, you think you can handle everything."

Pat Healy thinks it was the late hours and the drinking and drug use that caused Andrea to leave Mike, taking the kids with her. "It's the business," Healy said. "You're working nights. You get that in your blood and it's not conducive to family life."

Healy added, "We were all drinking back then. Everybody was dabbling in those days." But he said that, unlike Mike, "I could just stop. I had the ability to do that."

Pat Spoerndle said, "When Mike and Andrea got divorced, I understood it. He was in and out of sobriety. She shouldn't have had to live that way."

"He still had that big house in Pine Orchard," remembers Healy. "He didn't want to live there alone. Mike didn't like to be alone; he liked having people around. So he invited me to live with him. He said, 'Come on, come on! For crying out loud!'"

Not long after Healy moved in, he grew weary of the late-night parties and the squalid conditions, including Mike's casual ways with his dogs. He didn't bother taking them out for regular walks.

"I told him, 'Mike, you bring one more thing that shits into this house and I'm out of here!' The next day I come home—and there's a cow tied to a tree! Mike said, 'Do you realize how much money we're going to save on milk?' He was standing there, laughing his ass off. He had gone down to a farm and rented the cow for a day. Mike liked doing that kind of stuff. After we had a laugh, he called the farmer and told him, 'Hey, you can come get your cow.'"

Healy lasted for about three years in that house, remaining because of his affection for Mike. "He was loving and caring," he said. "He'd give you the shirt off his back."

"But as he started to decline," said Healy, "I had to distance myself. It just wasn't good for me; that's why I moved out. I told him, 'If you're going to continue doing what you're doing, we'll have to distance our friendship. I love you dearly, Mike, but we've got to go our different ways now. I'm not running away from you, but I've got to get away from you.' Mike understood. After that, we drifted apart."

Meanwhile, back at Toad's Place, I was overseeing all the daily and nightly details, twenty-four hours a day. Mike would come in for the big shows, like Billy Joel. In 1985 or '86, I decided I was going to leave, do my own thing. That's when Mike said, "I'll make you a partner." This was an offer I couldn't refuse. I got 40 percent of the business, Mike got 60 percent.

Mike always liked to drink on the job, but it got worse and worse. He loved his Metaxa and his Black Russians. It got to the point where he'd come in and drink non-stop until he left. Mike was doing more than drinking. He was getting high on Quaaludes and cocaine, with pot too. Soon his erratic behavior began to mess up our business. After we'd had that successful first visit by Johnny Cash with two sold-out shows, he was going to come back. Our phones were ringing off the hook and we were going to sell out that show too. But Mike, with that crazy look in his eye, high as a kite, got on the phone with Cash's people. Mike said he was "playing hard ball," demanding a discount on the $20,000 guarantee we had already agreed to pay him in the contract. Cash's agent got really pissed and said Johnny would just go to a funeral that day instead. And so the show was cancelled. That was a terrible day for us. Soon after that, Mike was sleeping at his desk.

Budd Tunick of the Simms Brothers Band saw Mike's decline up close. He and Mike had become very close as each of their wives began having kids at about the same time. "We'd go up to Branford and Mike would put all the kids on the wagon of a tractor and tow them up into the woods," remembers Tunick. "He'd ask them, 'Who wants to go to the witch's house?' Then he'd make lobsters for us."

"For a while he was on top of the world, making money hand over fist with the dance party nights," Tunick said. "He was buying nice cars and doing new construction at his house."

But after the drugs took hold, Tunick started to receive alarming phone calls from Mike. "He called and told me, 'I was out in the woods on my snowmobile, and it flipped over. I broke my back.' Another time he called and said, 'I'm out on [Interstate] 95, going to New York. How do I get there from here?' I knew things were spiraling out of control."

Even more troubling was the day Tunick was working at Toad's and Mike came into the office, sat down, and pointed a gun at him. "It was the middle of the afternoon and he was messing around," Tunick remembers. "I think he did it for fun, but the gun was probably loaded."

However, Tunick said, "There was so much that was good about Mike. I'd rather remember that." Tunick and others who knew Mike cited his many donations and fundraisers for local charities. The events he organized helped the Connecticut Fund for the Environment, the Juvenile Diabetes Foundation, Connecticut Hospice, the Boy Scouts, and the New Haven Project for Battered Women.

"When Mike was sober," his brother Pat said, "that's when you saw his big heart."

But Pat added, "Mike was two different people—the addict Mike and the sober Mike, who was incredibly good."

Eventually Mike admitted he had a serious problem and started going to Alcoholics Anonymous meetings. WPLR DJ Mike Lapitino said Mike encouraged others to go to meetings with him, often driving them there. "He introduced me to AA, and for that I'll always be grateful."

Lapitino, like many others, still dearly misses Mike after all these years. "It was a whole lot of fun getting to be friends with Mike Spoerndle. What a character! He was New Haven's P.T. Barnum."

Lapitino said while he himself was able to stay sober, Mike "started to venture out again. It's a disease, it really is. It was uncomfortable being around him, and we became estranged. It broke my heart. You didn't want to hang out with him because you didn't know what was going to happen. It was scary. He was a big dude."

Jimmy Koplik recalled what happened on the night in the mid-nineties when Smashing Pumpkins was doing a show at the Hartford Civic Center. "I was backstage with Mike; he said bugs were crawling out of his ear. I had to throw him out. I couldn't work with him anymore."

In June 1992 the *Hartford Courant* carried the news: TOAD'S PLACE OWNER ARRESTED. Warrants issued by state drug control agents and Branford police charged Mike with sixteen counts of obtaining controlled drugs by fraud and deceit and fifteen counts of illegal possession of controlled substances. The drugs included Valium, Vicodin, and Percocet.

Another arrest hit the papers after Mike went into a supermarket while he was high on cocaine or heroin.

"We all thought he was sober," Pat Spoerndle said. "But his demons kept taking over again. We heard he'd gone into a supermarket, picked up a watermelon, sat down on the floor, pulled a knife out of his pocket, and started carving up the watermelon."

When the heroin took over, that was Mike's downfall. He was bad news for all of us at Toad's. I tried talking to him, but he wouldn't listen. I said, "Mike, you can't be getting arrested over and over again. We'll lose our liquor license."

We were at a meeting with our accountant, Henry Barron, and Mike had these scabs on his arms and hands. He said, "I've got bugs on my arms." We had to get him out of there.

Barron remembered, "Mike was having hallucinations. He carried a shoebox around with him. He said, 'There are bugs crawling around in here.' I looked but there was nothing inside."

Hugh Keefe, the attorney who represented Mike during his divorce settlements, recalled Mike calling him after a relapse. "He told me that little green men, space creatures, had surrounded his house, and he didn't know what to do. I tried to talk him down. It was the cops that had surrounded his house. Eventually they apprehended him."

We were trying to keep Mike out of Toad's because he was coming in and taking money from the cash register and our office to support his drug habit. Our general manager, Ed Dingus, recalled one incident.

"I was upstairs in the office, trying to keep the proceeds locked away. Mike was pounding on the door. I knew he'd raided the office a few times, taking money out of the drawers. On that day when I was there, he got in again. I was trying to make sure he didn't get any of the money. I had a couple thousand dollars lying around, and I needed to deposit it. I distracted Mike by showing him a newspaper story on Toad's franchising efforts. That's how I got rid of him."

Finally in 1998, Mike and I negotiated a deal with our attorneys in which I bought him out of the business. I took control of the company. It pained me, but I had to ban him from the club after that. One day when he showed up, I had to confront him.

"Stay out of here," I told him. "That's it. I've told the doorman not to let you in."

He looked at me and said, "Phelps, I made you, and I can break you."

It was really bad. I was so stressed that I was grinding my teeth in my sleep. I was trying to keep Toad's going during all this turmoil. I didn't want to close the place.

Pat Spoerndle said losing Toad's was devastating for Mike. "He anguished over that for the rest of his life."

Mike kept trying to get straight. During an AA meeting he met Abigail Jacobson, an attractive and avid horse rider. They fell in love and soon afterward they got married. But in December 2002 she died at their home. According to Branford town records, the cause of death was acute cocaine toxicity.

Pat Spoerndle said that in 2004 or 2005 he and his eldest brother Steve traveled from Ohio to Connecticut "to try to guide Mike to get help. He was so paranoid, he was out of his mind. Physically and mentally he was a wreck. We were there probably for four days. It seemed to help a little bit, to get him back on track."

But Mike's former acquaintances who ran into him over his final years saw he was in deep trouble. "He wasn't Big Mike anymore," said Tunick. "He was so gaunt. His pants were bundled up around his waist."

Hugh Keefe said, "The last time I saw Mike, he was in a line going into the New Haven courthouse. He was using a cane. And he was skinny. But as always, he was friendly."

Tank Dunbar remembered Mike at that time "talking about starting a new Toad's Place. I said, 'Mike, there's not gonna be another Toad's Place. Try to right your wrongs, not re-tracing your steps.' But he said, 'I'm gonna do it. You'll be surprised.'"

On May 6, 2011, Mike, then fifty-nine, was found dead at his home. The East Haven town records list the cause of death as poly-substance abuse and kidney failure.

One of the obituaries quoted what Mike had told the *Yale Herald* in 2000: "I made a lot of bad decisions, made a lot of bad choices, and I ended up in a place where nothing short of an act of God could get me out."

Pat Spoerndle said of his brother, "He is the poster child of addiction. Mike experienced all of the negative consequences you can have from addiction: loss of family, loss of your business, loss of your life."

Pat said it was especially agonizing for Mike to lose his children. "When he got off the rails, it cost him his kids and his relationship with Andrea. That's a lot of pain, a lot of a sense of failure. Mike loved his kids. For them not to be part of his life was very difficult."

Pat was heartened by the testimonials given at Mike's funeral. "A lot of people from AA were there who credited Mike for saving their lives. People told me about the role Mike had played in their recovery. Sometimes he paid for their treatment. That's what I want to remember about Mike: who he was when his head was on straight, not the tragic story that he became."

Healy said Mike told him that he had reconnected with his father, at least enough to have a civil phone conversation, shortly before his dad died. "He had some kind of closure. His parents were very proud of him."

"He loved helping people and he loved his children," Healy said. "But he just couldn't get that monkey off his back."

CHAPTER 13

The WPLR Connection

FOUR YEARS BEFORE BIG MIKE AND HIS ORIGINAL PARTNERS CHUCK METZGER AND Mike Korpas opened Toad's Place, a new FM radio station dedicated to playing rock 'n' roll, WPLR, "99 Rock," began broadcasting from the second floor of a small building on Chapel Street in New Haven.

Dick Kalt, who was the station's first sales and promotion director, recalled in 2020 how Bob Herpe and a group of attorneys had bought WNHC, which had a basic Top-40 format.

"On April 29, 1971," Kalt said, "Bob and I launched WPLR." The first song was "Up, Up and Away" by the 5th Dimension.

WPLR was already well-established as the premier rock station in the New Haven area in 1975 when we opened our doors to musical acts. Initially we booked blues and bluegrass bands, most of them local. But within a couple of years we were bringing in many rock 'n' rollers, both locally and nationally known.

WPLR was there to play music by those bands and promote upcoming shows at Toad's.

"Toad's was PLR's clubhouse," said Rick Allison, who was a morning DJ for the station and eventually became program director. He noted it was an easy walk from the station to our club.

"Toad's was one leg of a stool in this marvelous time," Allison noted. He said there were forces that came together in a synchronicity that "can never be repeated."

"The legs of this stool wouldn't have stood if it weren't for the baby boomers and this wonderful audience waiting to hear this great music," Allison added. "And the drinking age was eighteen."

But what happened in the Elm City didn't happen everywhere at that time.

Clockwise from top left: Queen Latifah, John Mayall, New Found Glory stage, Huey Lewis, Chris Kampmeier from WPLR, Jeff Lorber, Indigo Girls, and Jefferson Starship.

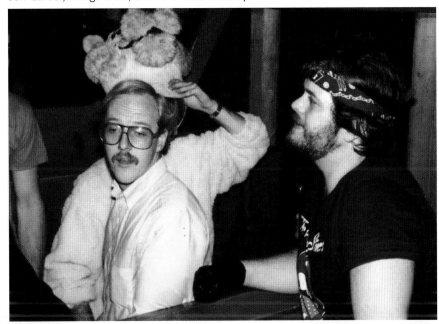

"We were fortunate in New Haven to have all the parts," Allison said. "You had a city of only about 125,000 people, but it was blessed with having this great institution called Yale and all the arts that spun off of it and an institution called Toad's Place. It was perfect." Allison added, "It was like growing up with this band called the Beatles but not knowing how great it was at the time. Everything was working in our favor."

Working in tandem with the emerging Toad's Place, Allison noted, "You had PLR, Jimmy Koplik, the *New Haven Advocate*, and local record stores like Cutler's, Rhymes, and Festoon's. It was one big organism connecting to this thing we all got to share. We experienced life-changing moments. I loved it."

As Allison said, everything came together, and we at Toad's rode that baby! The recently opened (in 1972) New Haven Coliseum was also part of the mix, with Koplik, promoting the action on WPLR, bringing in major bands to that arena like the Who and the Grateful Dead. Sometimes those performers, including Bruce Springsteen, would come over from the Coliseum and do an encore for us. (But not the Who or the Dead, unfortunately.)

Everyone in New Haven County and beyond who loved rock music was listening to WPLR. And they were reading the *New Haven Advocate*, the arts and news weekly that was distributed for free in street boxes throughout the region. WPLR and the *Advocate* became our two principal avenues of advertising. We also had people putting up posters, but that didn't carry the clout of radio and print.

In the late seventies, the *New Haven Register* also became part of the synergy. Randall Beach, who was covering suburban towns for the *Register* as a young reporter, realized there was a void in the paper's approach: Nobody was writing about the fabulous bands who were coming to New Haven to perform at the Coliseum, Toad's, and other local clubs. Beach convinced his editors to let him review those shows and interview many of the performers. When Beach left the *Register* for a hiatus in 1984, another young reporter, Thom Duffy, became the main rock music writer for the *Register* and its sister paper, the *Journal-Courier*. All of those stories propelled more people to the shows.

Our relationship with WPLR was solid. We bought weekly ads at the station and they co-sponsored many of our shows. Our relationship got tighter in 1980 when Billy Joel did his two shows at Toad's, which Koplik made happen. WPLR broadcast the announcement about Joel's shows and where and how to get tickets. The station announced many other Toad's shows too.

Koplik and WPLR DJ Mike Lapitino did weekly on-air shows together to promote upcoming concerts, and naturally Toad's was frequently mentioned. Often the band members who were playing in the area would come into the WPLR studio to do interviews with Lapitino or another DJ, Eddie Wazoo. Kalt remembers spending an entire afternoon at the station with Frank Zappa when he was performing at the Coliseum. Kalt also hosted Billy Joel at WPLR, circa 1972. "He looked like a thirteen-year-old," Kalt said. "*Piano Man* had just come out."

The WPLR guys hung out with us and we talked about what was up on the music scene. We were all one big family. Kalt remembers spending lots of time with Big Mike at the station, discussing the up-and-coming bands. "I looked at Toad's as a great promotion opportunity for the station; Mike looked at the station as his audio extension. It was the perfect combination at the right time."

Phil Cutler said, "Nobody had it better than me. Between my store and walking over to Toad's, I had the best of both worlds. And I could walk over to PLR and hang out there! Between Cutler's, Toad's, and PLR, it was like the hot triangle. I couldn't get enough of it."

Those WPLR guys were characters. One of the favorites for listeners was Stoneman, whose real name was Joe Demaio. He always signed off at midnight with John Prine's "Illegal Smile" and Led Zeppelin's "Stairway to Heaven."

John Griffin, who used "the Wigmaster" as his radio name, was a program director and DJ at WPLR for many years, and he loved coming to Toad's. "It's truly where the legends came to play," he said. "Rickie Lee Jones, Living Colour, Johnny Cash! Seeing King Crimson in a small hall like that, my God!"

In the late seventies we started doing live radio broadcasts from Toad's that were broadcast on WPLR. Kalt said it was an innovative concept that proved "we didn't want to be your mother's radio station. We were part of the pulse of New Haven."

Kevin Garrity, who was one of our sound men from 1975 to '85, was instrumental in pulling together those live broadcasts. He said there were about forty of them, starting on January 17, 1979, with George Thorogood. "George was having so much fun that he did a dance contest."

"Those shows were fantastic," Garrity said. "But I never got to see the bands. I was upstairs, doing the mixing, so we could get it out on the air."

Garrity said one of the last broadcasts was a show by Marshall Crenshaw on June 27, 1982.

Gordon Weingarth, WPLR's program director from 1977 to '81, said the live broadcast with Ian Hunter was almost a disaster. "We had all the wires put in from the mixing board to the station. But then a technician from the phone company was doing a check and he pulled out the wires. He said, 'What's this?' We had no idea he had done that. When we did a test just before the live broadcast, the people at the station said, 'We're not getting anything.' Our DJ, Bob Nary, checked everything and got it fixed. Still, we had to announce, 'We'll have the entire broadcast, but not until about 11 tonight.' The show started at 8:30. It wasn't carried live."

Peter Menta, who was our club's entertainment director from around 1975 to 1978, said one of those live broadcasts stands out for him. "When the rockabilly craze hit, Robert Gordon had the song 'Red Hot,' with the lyrics 'My gal is red hot, your gal ain't doodley squat!' It was all over PLR. Link Wray was one of the guitarists that night."

Lapitino said he can remember live broadcasts by the Gregg Allman Band, the Black Crowes, John Hiatt, and Living Colour. "I'd go on stage and warm up the crowd. When I told them, 'This is a live broadcast, try not to swear,' they would yell, 'Fuck you!' But the shows were exciting and people were excited, because it was a happening."

Allison, Weingarth, and the others who were at WPLR speak fondly of the days when they could play whatever songs they wanted. This was before corporate ownership came in and mandated tight play lists. "We got to break a lot of acts," Weingarth said. "We helped break the Steve Miller Band and Springsteen, outside New Jersey. We became known in the music business."

Manuel Rodriguez, who after his record company days became WPLR's station manager and then its vice president and general manager, said, "We created magic. Every day somebody would come in with an idea. And we'd do it!"

That kind of free-form radio ended long ago at WPLR. Its current owner is Connoisseur Media, who acquired the station in 2013. The Wigmaster couldn't take the corporate control and tight play lists; he left in 2020.

But an echo of that original WPLR spirit survives on Sunday nights. Allison, who now has his own weekday show on Cygnusradio.com, continues to do "The Local Bands Show," which has endured for more than three decades on WPLR. On his show Allison highlights the latest music by local bands with co-host Frank Critelli, who took that position after James Velvet died in 2015. Allison noted a key reason he enjoyed Toad's in the seventies and eighties was our promotion of local musicians. "The bands that opened for the national acts were as much a revelation as the headliners." But he recalled with a grin what happened during Meat Loaf's performance: "I got some of the big man's sweat on me. I was sitting up front."

Allison added, "Thank God Mike didn't succeed with that French restaurant!"

In recent years we've continued to work with WPLR (celebrating its fiftieth anniversary in 2021) for shows that align with their classic rock formula. I will never forget the friends I made there and the great shows we put on together.

CHAPTER 14

The Yale Connection

Yale has always been our biggest, most prominent neighbor and friend during Toad's long history. We've had a wonderful relationship with generations of Yale students for more than forty years. Close neighbors do have their arguments but through it all I believe we share a mutual affection and respect.

As Ed Dingus, our general manager told a reporter from the *Yale Daily News* in 2018, "It's kind of like two siblings fighting. We had the fight, and now we're back on speaking terms."

Toad's Place is in the middle of the sprawling and ever-expanding Yale University campus, so inevitably we have had turf disputes. It's no secret that Yale's leaders would have loved to buy our building (unfortunately, we've never had a parking lot) as the university has done with property near us.

But they couldn't do it! Sometimes David does beat Goliath, and this was one of those times.

Our confrontation arose in 1986 when the Kligerman family, who owned our building and from whom we had been leasing the property for eleven years, decided they wanted to sell it. They hired a lawyer from the prestigious New Haven law firm Wiggin and Dana. Big Mike and I figured we could get the property for a reasonable price, but unknown to us, the lawyer contacted Yale officials to see if they wanted to bid on the property.

Mike and I offered $800,000, knowing the building had been appraised at about $1 million. But then Yale offered $1.3 million. Mike and I said, "What?! That's a lot of money." However, we knew that as the lease holders we had the right of first refusal on the property (this was specified in our lease) and we had thirty days to match Yale's offer. Our challenge was that we had to come up with about $500,000. Fortunately, we had the money in the bank; we had been doing a good business with the dance parties and live music. When we pulled together the $500,000 with the bank's help, we matched Yale's $1.3 million bid. Once we matched their offer, Yale wasn't legally permitted to make a higher bid. We had won; we beat Yale!

The Yale officials were upset, to say the least. They never dreamed we could match their offer.

Our victory over Yale and our resulting purchase of the building meant we would probably not be in big financial trouble down the road. After that day, we no longer had to worry about a landlord raising our rent.

Yale students knew nothing about this. All they cared about was being able to come to Toad's in the middle of the week for the first round of penny drinks during "Woads" (Wednesday at Toad's), returning on Saturdays for another dance party and maybe even checking out a great band on another night of the week. Many Yalies strutted around campus with shirts carrying the message "All roads lead to Toad's."

We decided to come up with a special honor for any Yale student who came to every Wednesday night, all year long. He or she would be dubbed a "Woads Scholar." Maybe their parents would have been happier if they had become Rhodes Scholars, but our scholars had also worked hard for their recognition. At the end of the year we gave them a free gift, such as a commemorative Toad's souvenir.

Yale's sorority and fraternity members, especially those from the DKE fraternity, have a long tradition of coming to Toad's. The older members bring in freshmen (now called "first-years") to commemorate their being accepted into the fraternity. The new member is ordered to go up on stage with a date, kneel down, and sing, "You're just too good to be true; can't take my eyes off you." If you can't name that tune, it's Frankie Valli's "Can't Take My Eyes Off You."

We have also built strong relationships with members of Yale's athletic teams. For decades we've invited the Yale football team's offensive line to Toad's for a photo op and free Toad's T-shirts. Other teams are called in after their victories for toasts and parties.

Sometimes the Yale dance parties can get a little too crazy. On one particular night, just before 1 a.m., a Yalie was on the stage dancing like a maniac. Then out of some odd impulse, he jumped (he was a tall dude), latched onto the sprinkler pipes, and started

Clockwise from top left: Was (Not Was), UB40, A Toad's Record by Fountainhead, Donovan, Randy Newman, Tom Tom Club, sixth year celebration on the cover of *Connecticut Music Magazine*, and Peter Frampton.

TOADS RECORDS

SIDE A
7-1025A

TIME: 3:25

FOUNTAINHEAD
"DON'T BLOW ME UP"
RENEGADE RHYMES

© 1982 Ken Griffith
Recorded & Produced by
Bill Dale
Recorded at The I.B Studio
So. Glastonbury, Ct.

swinging. The pipes broke with a loud rumble and water gushed out at a high speed. I heard the blast from my auxiliary office in the basement and raced upstairs. Water was all over the dance floor, and the Yalies just kept on dancing. I guess they thought this was all part of the show. We quickly shut off the water supply, turned up all the house lights, and told everybody to leave. The Fire Department came in, but it took some time to pump out all the water.

Hey, they're college students; they love it. Emma Gardner, Class of 2006, told the *Yale Daily News* in 2014: "Toad's was drunken and crazy. It had a wild hook-up scene. I would definitely say that one of my most distinct memories of Yale is being at Toad's."

And so you can see why Yale administrators might not always like having such a wild party site in the middle of their campus. We had another legal battle with Yale that started in 2010 and lasted for about five years. The university's officials sued us for trespassing because they got angry about some of our patrons exiting our back doors while "smoking, littering and drinking" on Yale property. Eventually we agreed to seal those back doors and use them only in emergencies. The whole drawn-out process cost us a ton of money in lawyers' fees, but we reached a mutually acceptable solution and survived.

I admit there are some Yale students who don't like to party and dance and drink and listen to music. I think they are in the minority, but they're not shy about expressing their views. In 2015 a student named Alex Fisher wrote an op-ed for the *Yale Daily News* entitled CLOSE TOAD'S NOW. He referred to our club as "a citadel of vulgarity."

But some members of the Yale community, even as high up as University President Peter Salovey, really dig Toad's. It helps that Salovey is a musician, playing bass in the Professors of Bluegrass. They performed at our club four times from 1993 to 1994. Big Mike helped make it happen.

Barbara Shaw, who in the nineties was in that band with her husband Frank Shaw, sent a short essay to Randall Beach explaining how the Professors got to Toad's.

Shaw recalled that her husband sometimes played guitar with his cub scout den in the Shaws' basement. One of the cubs was the son of Kelly Brownell, a Yale psychology professor. One night, when Brownell picked up his son and noticed Frank playing guitar, he said he too was a guitar player and suggested they get together to play some bluegrass. Frank said his wife was also learning to play guitar, so she was recruited too.

Brownell invited his friend and colleague Salovey to join as well. Salovey was then also a Yale psychology professor. Another person who joined the band was Brownell's wife Mary Jo, who played autoharp and sang harmonies.

Big Mike, who knew Brownell because both of them belonged to the Pine Orchard Yacht and Country Club in Branford, dubbed the new group the Professors of Bluegrass. Mike had been named a fellow at Yale's Trumbull College, one of its residential colleges, and he wanted to put on a party for the Trumbull students. Why not do it at Toad's, with music by the Professors of Bluegrass? It all came together on February 11, 1993.

"The show happened as suggested," wrote Shaw, "despite my fear of dying on stage. The kids screamed with joy at the sight of their popular professors (Brownell and Salovey) playing bluegrass. We all felt like rock stars, with the colored lights, blasting sound system, and full wall monitors around the room. The Yale singing groups New Blue and Baker's Dozen were also part of the entertainment."

Shaw said Mike invited them back. During one of those shows, Mike asked his buddy Al Anderson of NRBQ to sit in on guitar for "Will the Circle Be Unbroken." She recalled Anderson's "dazzling guitar breaks" as she sat next to him "with wide eyes and gaping mouth."

Shaw also recalled that during a rehearsal for a Toad's gig, as she struggled to play three chords on her guitar, she laughed and said, "When I grow up, I'm going to be a great bluegrass star!" Salovey chimed in, "And when I grow up, I'm going to be president of Yale!" Everybody laughed. But guess whose dream came true?

Brownell, who left Yale to become director of the World Food Policy Center at Duke University, said of those shows, "It was nice of Mike to do that. He gave us more visibility than we deserved."

In September 2020 when Beach asked Salovey to reflect on his feelings about Toad's and what it has meant to Yale, Salovey quickly responded in an email. He first noted the Professors of Bluegrass still get together occasionally and that their current banjo player is Oscar Hills, a former member of the Helium Brothers. They were a mainstay of the Toad's local bands scene starting in the 1970s.

"When I think of Toad's," Salovey said, "I tend not to focus on Yale students [pre-COVID] heading there for Wednesday night dancing. Rather, I think of the importance of the club as a small venue for testing out material by incredible artists like Bob Dylan and the Rolling Stones. I was not at either of those events, alas, but I have caught other similarly exciting moments over the years. I have always appreciated Brian and Mike's commitment to musicians and their talent."

CHAPTER 15

Sex and Drugs and Rock and Roll

"If those walls could talk, we'd all be in big trouble!" said Emilio Castillo, the saxophonist for Tower of Power when we asked him for a testimonial about Toad's Place for this book.

But those walls aren't talking, and neither is Castillo. We didn't ask him, nor did we expect him to do that. This is not a "tell all" book, and we're not about to violate the privacy of the band members who have frolicked in our Green Room (which was our dressing room) or perhaps in our hot tub. And so, to a large extent, we're not talking either. But we are willing to pull back the curtain just a little bit and give you a peek.

Now that we've got you wondering about that hot tub, here's the story. Back around 2004 I had what I thought was the great idea of hauling that big, heavy tub downstairs and installing it in the bathroom next to the Green Room. I figured the bands would enjoy it, using the thing to relax in after their shows.

But guess what—very few people wanted to get into it. They were afraid of what might have been in it and who might have used it before them.

"That hot tub was a science project!" said Christine Ohlman, whose bands spent a lot of time in the Green Room. "I never knew anybody who got into it. We thought it was hysterical. We all said, 'I'm not getting in it—you get in first!' A hot tub in a rock 'n' roll club? Seriously?"

I can name only a few people who dared step into it. One was Billy Joel's daughter, Alexa Ray Joel, also a singer, songwriter, and pianist. She was going out with a guy in her road crew, and the two of them used the tub. As far as I know, the only band that ever used it was Gwar, the "shock rock" group that favors heavy make-up and crazy alien costumes. This was a band that sprays their audiences with fake blood, urine, and

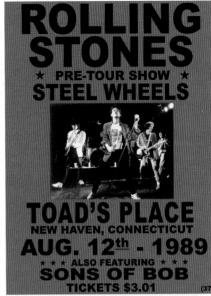

Clockwise from top left: Rick Derringer, The Smithereens, They May Be Giants, Rolling Stones poster (made as a commemoration after their surprise appearance), David Bowie, Mary Chapin Carpenter, Ace Frehley, Men at Work, Belinda Carlisle of the Go-Go's, Kooks & Spooks, and Graham Parker.

semen, so they weren't concerned about germs in a hot tub. They just climbed in and relaxed. "This is nice," they said.

But since they still had all their make-up on when they got into the tub, when they got out it looked like green pea soup.

We also allowed some of the Yale fraternity members to have hot tub parties. They would go into the tub in their bathing suits and have a wild time of heavy drinking. Then they'd get dressed and go upstairs for the dance party. (Yale's seniors also flock to Toad's every year at graduation time for Exotic Erotic night, when they all show up in their underwear.)

Eventually I decided I was all done with that hot tub. But getting it upstairs and out of the building was a nightmare. The whole main staircase had to be yanked out and then we had to take out part of our front door to squeeze the tub through.

Of course many musicians see sex as a fringe benefit of their job; they will indulge as often as they can. And there are plenty of fans hanging around who aren't musicians but have sex on their minds too. They want to get with a rock star; that's their thing. The feeling is mutual and they take advantage of each other. As Bob Seger sang in "Night Moves," "I used her, she used me, and neither one cared."

Our long-time bouncer, Tank Dunbar has seen that horny hunger many times at our front door. "The groupies are out there, and they want some extra-curricular activities," he said. "So do the guys in the bands. They'll tell me, 'See that blond over there? Give her a backstage pass and let her come downstairs.'"

Tank told a *Yale Daily News* reporter a wild story about what happened at a Saturday night show during the seventies: "There was this woman mud wrestler who got the hots for the keyboard player. She tried to climb up on stage, and when she couldn't get there, she started taking off her clothes. By the time I got to her, all of her clothes were lying at her feet. I told her, 'You can't go downstairs and see him after the show unless you put your stuff back on.'"

Sometimes the band members flaunt their groupies for the crowd. John Valby, "the prince of porn" who told X-rated jokes during his shows, liked to get women to flash their breasts or strip on stage. He could get as many as ten of them to do it. The band L.A. Guns had a ton of women following them around who would routinely disrobe and hang out in the Green Room. The band would bring a few of them onto the stage semi-naked during the middle of their shows and have them parade around.

When the Jim Rose Circus came here to unleash its crazy sideshow troupe, they had a topless woman lie on a bed of nails. The circus also featured Mr. Lifto, who had many pierced body parts, swinging an anvil around on his penis.

Some of the musicians didn't mind using their sex appeal as part of their performances. Wendy O. Williams of the Plasmatics, who was a former stripper and porn star, did a show at our Waterbury club. She wore pasties on stage, with black masking tape on her nipples and a bikini bottom. As part of her crazy act, she also cut a guitar in half with a chain saw.

When Courtney Love of the band Hole performed, she wasn't wearing any underwear. She put her foot on top of the amplifier throughout the night, much to the delight of our security guys stationed directly in front of the stage and members of the audience standing up front. She was at our club six months after the suicide of her husband, Kurt Cobain of Nirvana.

Tank notes that during his years at Toad's, he saw some interesting things. "Oh yeah, I've seen intercourse and masturbation going on. You tell them, 'Get out, this is not a hotel. Take it to a hotel room.'"

Tank remembers a New Year's Eve sex stunt that took place downstairs in our ladies' room: "I was told just before midnight, 'There's a couple having sex down in the bathroom.' It turned out this girl had come up from Georgia to visit her friends. The plan by her and her boyfriend was to ring in the new year by having sex at Toad's. I went down to the women's room and interrupted them. I had to break up the whole thing; it was getting to be a sight. The other girls were peeking through the stall at the couple and horsing around. They took all the clothing from the girl having sex and hung a piece of it on top on each stall. There were panties on one stall, a bra on the other, panty hose, and so on. The guy had a pink condom, and all the girls were laughing at that."

There were other times when "extra-curriculars" would spill out of Toad's and happen off-site. When I was sharing a house with Big Mike, he told a member of one of the local bands that he could crash with us overnight; this man didn't leave Toad's by himself. When I got home late that night, there was a partially naked woman asleep in my bed. Mike thought that was hilarious.

As for the drugs, it's no secret rock musicians love to indulge themselves with all kinds of narcotics: marijuana, cocaine, heroin, hash, meth, you name it. They claim it enhances their performances, gets them more in touch with the music—or that it's just fun, cuts the stress, and they're entitled to it. As I noted earlier, we have no problem supplying alcoholic beverages for the musicians, especially when it's in the riders of their contracts; Muddy Waters got his Piper Heidsieck champagne. But we don't get involved in supplying anybody with drugs. Wouldn't be prudent.

CHAPTER 16

The Road Ahead

When COVID-19 roared into Connecticut as part of its murderous march across America and the rest of the world in the first week of March 2020, we had a full slate of upcoming shows set to go. We were primed for another great spring season.

Our line-up included electronic DJ music by Bear Grillz and Jauz and guaranteed sell-outs for the reggae band the Movement, the rockers Angels & Airwaves, the rapper Fetty Wap, the rock band the Wonder Years, singers Jeremy Zucker and Skip Marley, the grandson of Bob Marley.

One by one, those performances were cancelled. We also had to cancel twenty-three private parties and our Wednesday and Saturday night dance parties. Suddenly nobody felt safe being in an enclosed space with lots of other people. The thrill of being packed together with hundreds of other sweaty dancing people, the essential lure of Toad's for more than four decades, was replaced by a fear of strangers and getting infected with a deadly virus.

On March 8 we were forced to shut down. The state of Connecticut mandated at least temporary closure for indoor gathering spots such as Toad's.

At that time I assumed it would be only for a few weeks. The owners of other nightclubs, bars, and restaurants were anxiously hoping for the same thing. None of us could have imagined then that this virus would kill hundreds of thousands of people across America, make millions of others sick, and keep us in lockdown into 2021. As of this writing in April 2021, it appears COVID-19 will force us to remain closed for a total of about a year and a half. We might open mid-summer but certainly hope to do so by the fall of 2021

I know the students and others have been missing us. A Yalie named Julia Hornstein reported in 2020 in a Yale publication, *The New Journal*, that "Toad's Place is shut down like a damn morgue." She said that seeing our windows blank instead of listing upcoming acts and walking through a deserted campus felt "apocalyptic."

The year 2020 was depressing for everybody and deeply troubling for business owners wondering if they could hold on. Here's what I told Randall Beach in April 2020 when he interviewed me in my empty club for his *New Haven Register* column: "This coronavirus has been a nightmare for me. It hit me in the last two and-a-half months of my busy season. As long as social distancing remains in place, we are in very, very bad shape. Think about it, if you have a small bar, what do people do? They sit next to one another and talk. If you want to meet someone, you can't do it from six feet away. If you want to dance, six feet apart is not going to work. We are a tribal people. We want to be close to each other in nightclubs, people want to go where the crowds are."

Toad's received $106,000 in the first round of the federal government's Paycheck Protection Program (forgiven loans) in the spring of 2020. This was a huge help for us. We used it for our utilities, our staff's medical insurance, upgrades such as painting, and salaries for a few months. But eventually I had to furlough forty-five of my part-time employees and ten full-timers.

I am waiting for a second shot in the arm from the Shuttered Venue Operators Grant, passed by Congress in December 2020. This will provide $15 billion for the arts. The funds from that pot of money will help with costs for utilities and maintenance, among other expenses.

Fortunately, I also have some money saved from our many good years. I think I can see the light at the end of the tunnel now. We will survive. We have a destiny in front of us!

These long months of having Toad's closed has given me time to look back on the club's history and appreciate what we have accomplished, thanks to so many loyal, dedicated, and hard-working people on our staff.

Ed Dingus, our general manager, started at Toad's in 1991 as a bar back, bringing supplies to the bartenders. In 1999, after he had become a bartender himself, he met his future wife, Michele, at Toad's during a St. Patrick's Day party. She ordered a Kahlua and club soda from him, they got to talking, and off they went! They have been together ever since.

"I've spent my entire adult life as part of Toad's Place," Dingus said. "This club has given me everything I have: my wife, my home, and the majority of my memories."

Holli Martin has been our office manager since October 1999. She's in charge of marketing, dealing with all the tour managers and many of the agents. She has complete knowledge of what it takes to make each show happen.

The invaluable workers in our office in our earlier years included the band bookers Lucy Sabini and Katherine Blossom. (Interviews with them are in chapters two and three). Jack Reich has been our booking agent for more than fifteen years and is still with us. He was also the manager for NRBQ, starting in the late seventies. In addition, agents Cara Lewis and Peter Schwartz have become like Toad's family members while bringing us some of the biggest bands in the industry.

Jimmy Day started doing our lighting in 1977 and stayed with us full time until Marty Weiand became our lighting director. Jimmy, who stands out in his long beard and turban, still does maintenance work for us whenever our plumbing, electrical system, or phones need repair.

Our accountant Henry Barron has been with us ever since we began. He saved our bacon in 1975 when Big Mike and his partners were in so much financial trouble that United Illuminating shut off the power. Henry got the lights back on by setting up a payment plan, and he's remained with us, watching the books.

Even our bartenders have stayed with us for decades. Pat Healy was our first, and he has become almost like a partner in the operation. Paul Liberti has been behind our bar for more than a quarter-century, and Kevin Meehan was our assistant manager and spent many hours as bartender. Jim Torello, now our assistant manager and permitee, has been with us for more than fifteen years.

When people talk about why Toad's has been so successful and has been able to remain in business in an ever-changing music landscape, the reason given always points to the teamwork here and how long our employees remain with us. I appreciate the kind words about me from the people Randall Beach has interviewed.

Jimmy Koplik, who is Live Nation's regional president for Connecticut and upstate New York and who I'm partnering with for some shows, was kind enough to say, "The secret of Toad's success is Brian. He runs a tight ship. He knows how to get every dollar out of the business. He's got that knack."

As to why he thinks Toad's will carry on, Koplik said, "It's the brand. Toad's as a brand is multi-generational."

Others know what it takes to keep such a brand running. "Brian is a workaholic!" says Jack Reich. "He comes in at about 5 p.m. and he's there until 3 or 4 a.m., five or six nights a week. He pays attention to every detail, including the sound, lighting and staffing. That's the reason the club has been able to survive and go through all the changes in music. It's largely because of Brian's work ethic. Many nightclubs have come and gone. Because of Brian, Toad's is still hopping."

Ed Dingus explains, "Most of us have been here for ten to twenty years. Brian is very loyal to his people. And the bands feel they're being treated as part of the family. One of our traditions is that when a band gets a sell-out crowd, we do a Dom Perignon champagne toast for them at the end of the night. You can see in the band members' reactions that this is not what they usually get. We build good relationships, so they'll want to come back."

Looking at the future of Toad's Place, Dingus said, "I'm optimistic. We've gone through each phase of new music and stayed relevant. Hopefully, after COVID is under control, there will be a resurgence of people wanting to hear live music, which they haven't been able to do for so long. And we'll keep adapting to the new kinds of music."

WPLR DJ Mike Lapitino says, "When you walk into Toad's, there's an atmosphere that you're going into a professionally run place, a class operation. The fact that Toad's has stayed open is a testament to Brian's great business mind. He's kept that place afloat, God bless him. It's been a hell of a run, better than anybody could have dreamed."

We've had our competitors. In New Haven alone there's been the Oxford Ale House, the Agora, the Grotto, Ron's Place, the Great American Music Hall, and the Arcadia Ballroom. All of them are gone.

Beach asked some people in the music business why a select few nightclubs have stayed alive while others haven't. Dave Brooks, a senior director at *Billboard* magazine, noted that the Stone Pony in Asbury Park, New Jersey (Springsteen's turf, opened in 1974) and First Avenue in Minneapolis (opened in 1970) are national success stories.

In addition, the Troubadour in West Hollywood (opened in 1957) and the Iron Horse in Northampton, Massachusetts (opened in 1979) are still humming along.

"I think the main thing that has kept them open all these years is staff or current ownership who feel a sense of guardianship and strive to protect these venues because of their cultural and historical impact on popular music," Brooks said.

Audrey Fix Schaefer, communications director for the National Independent Venue Association, listed these components needed to keep a nightclub operating through economic uncertainties: The owners must have their ears to the ground so they are hip to local tastes in music; know how to draw people in and win their trust so as to take them to the next level, introducing them to acts they don't know; have business acumen; be able to adapt to changing musical styles; have good connections with their employees; and develop audience loyalty, earned through the years and ensuring that when customers walk in they know they're going to have a good time.

In addition to naming the Troubadour and First Avenue as long-running clubs, Fix Schaefer cited the 9:30 Club in Washington, D.C. (started in 1980) and the Bitter End in New York City (started in 1961).

She also relayed this sad statistic: About three hundred clubs closed permanently during the pandemic.

Members of the music media are well aware of what Toad's has been doing for the last half a century. In 1998 *Performance* magazine named us the number-one nightclub in the country. In 2013, *Rolling Stone* ranked us fourteenth in its list of "best big rooms in America." In 2015, *USA Today* voted us the number-one small venue in the country.

"What a long, strange trip it's been"—I have to quote the Grateful Dead as I look back on these past years. I'm still coming into this now-empty, silent club on most days to do whatever office work I need to do as we all wait out COVID. I walk past the wall facing the stage and see the faces painted there: David Bowie, Billy Joel, the Rolling Stones, Bob Dylan, Kendrick Lamar, Cardi B, the Ramones, Stevie Ray Vaughan, Bon Jovi, Talking Heads, Snoop Dogg, Drake, Chick Corea, Johnny Cash, U2, Phish, and so many more. I walk downstairs, past our "Wall of Fame" on the corridor's ceiling, all those painted names: Peter Tosh, Beck, the B-52s, the Kinks, Blondie, Bruce

Springsteen, Muddy Waters, Jose Feliciano, King Crimson, Tom Waits, Frankie Valli, Santana . . . It goes on, too many to count, all of them bringing back memories of those nights.

Sometimes people ask me how much longer I plan to stay here, doing this work. I want to keep going a while longer, at least to our fiftieth anniversary. My co-workers Holli Martin, Ed Dingus, and others have devoted their lives to Toad's. I feel an obligation to them. I want to make sure they have a way to move forward with their lives. This means a lot to me. I'm a businessman, but I'm also looking at these people and what they've done for me and for this club.

I know Toad's will be back up and running. And that's that!

When the crowds return, they will notice some changes. We are re-painting the entire building. I might also put in a new dance floor and install more laser lights. We've booked comedy acts in recent years and we will continue to do that, maybe more than before. The comedians on our stage have included Matt Bellassai, Harry Anderson, Sandra Bernhard, Eric D'Alessandro, and Sam Kinison.

One thing that hasn't changed, the limitation we've always had is, no on-site parking. If you want to come to Toad's, you might have to walk a couple of blocks. This bothers the "older" crowd a bit more than the younger generations. People also need to understand why our music acts have changed. People of my generation, the rock 'n' rollers who are over sixty, often ask me, "What's with all this hip-hop stuff? Why don't you bring back those good old bands?" My answer? I'm still making money from hip-hop acts and dance parties. I've got to keep the business going. People over sixty say they want to see an early show, they want to sit down, they want parking nearby. They tell me, "I don't want to come out because it's a pain in the ass." Younger people who come for the DJ dance parties will show up as long as we play the music they like. They dance and drink and go home. That's the way it works now.

For those of a certain age who are Toad's veterans, let's remember this from Mark Twain: "Wrinkles should merely indicate where the smiles have been."

People of all generations can still have a fun time at Toad's Place, enjoying either a DJ or a newer cutting-edge band. The thing about Toad's is, you've got everybody gathered around, the sound is good, the crowd is all screaming in unison at that last note. The band members are smiling, the vibe is great. When the people leave, they're smiling. They're saying, "I had a good night. I'm not going to forget this night." To me, that's what's important.

I have always liked to think about Toad's as a place that makes people forget about all the problems in their lives for a short time, a place where people can let loose without anybody being bothered.

There's a bar I've visited in Williamsburg, Virginia, with this overhead inscription as you're walking in that reads: "Frivolity is the offspring of wisdom and good life." We offer that to our audiences in New Haven.

Toad's Place has been my passion. This is my legacy. This is my life.

Clockwise from top left:
Steve-O, Yellowman, U2,
Suzanne Vega, Rory Gallagher
(photo by Ray Cote), Winger,
John Cafferty, and Robert Cray.

List of the Bands Who Have Played at Toad's Place

Because Toad's Place is nearly fifty years old and rock 'n' roll record-keeping is far from perfect—especially true for us in the early years—this is not a complete list of every band that has appeared on the Toad's stage. Also, many of the opening acts are not included.

* member of the Rock & Roll Hall of Fame

.38 SPECIAL
10,000 MANIACS
2 CHAINZ
2 SKINNEE J'S
3 (CARL PALMER AND KEITH
   EMERSON)
30H!3
311
3RD BASS
5TH ELEMENT
808 STATE
999
A BOOGIE WIT DA HOODIE
A ROCKET TO THE MOON
A STATIC LULLABY
A TRIBE CALLED QUEST
A$APFERG
A$APROCKY
AARON CARTER
AB-SOUL

ACE FREHLEY*
ACOUSTIC JUNCTION
ACTION BRONSON
ADDISON GROOVE PROJECT
ADRENALINE MOB
ADRIAN BELEW
ADRIAN LEGG
ADVENTURES
AESOP ROCK
AFGHAN WHIGS
AFTER 7
AGAINST ME!
AGNOSTIC FRONT
AIMEE MANN & MICHAEL PENN
AL DIMEOLA
AL KOOPER
AL STEWART
ALAN HOLDSWORTH
ALANNAH MYLES
ALB. SURE!

ALBERT COLLINS
ALBERT KING*
ALEXA RAY JOEL
ALKALINE TRIO
ALL STAR WEEKEND
ALL THAT REMAINS
ALL TIME LOW
ALLGOOD
ALMOST QUEEN
ALTER BRIDGE
ALVIN LEE & TEN YEARS AFTER
AMANDA PALMER
AMERICAN AUTHORS
AMINE
AMPHIBIAN
AMY RAY
AN EMOTIONAL FISH
ANBERLIN
AND YOU WILL KNOW US BY
    THE TRAIL OF DEAD
ANDERSON .PAAK
ANDREW MCMAHON
ANDREW W.K.
ANDY FRASER
ANDY PRATT
ANGEL CITY
ANGELA BOFILL
ANGELA STREHLI & LOU ANN
    BARTON
ANNIE HASLAM
ANTHONY B

ANTHONY GREEN
ANTHRAX
ANTIBALAS AFROBEAT
    ORCHESTRA
ANTI-FLAG
ANTIGONE RISING
ANVIL
APATHY
APPETITE FOR DESTRUCTION
ARC ANGELS
ARIKA KANE
ARKANSAS TRAVELER REVUE
ARLO & ABE GUTHRIE
ARMOR FOR SLEEP
ARRESTED DEVELOPMENT
AS I LAY DYING
ASIA
ASLEEP AT THE WHEEL
ASSEMBLY OF DUST
ATMOSPHERE
ATREYU
AUGUST BURNS RED
AVERAGE WHITE BAND
AZTEC CAMERA
AZTEC TRIP
AZTEC TWO-STEP
B. WILLIE SMITH BAND
B.A.D. II
B.B. KING*
B.O.B.
BABY CHAM

BAD BRAINS
BAD ENGLISH
BAD FISH
BAD MANNERS
BADFINGER
BADLANDS
BALAAM AND THE ANGEL
BALANCE
BAND OF HORSES
BANG TANGO
BARENAKED LADIES
BAROOGA
BAS
BASEMENT
BASH & POP
BATON ROUGE
BAY CITY ROLLERS
BAYSIDE
BEANIE SIGEL
BEAT FARMERS
BEATNUTS
BEAU BOLERO
BEAUSOLEIL
BECK
BEENIEMAN
BELA FLECK & THE FLECK
    TONES
BELL BIV DEVOE
BELLY
BELOUIS SOME
BEN FOLDS
BEN JELEN

BERES HAMMOND
BETH HART BAND
BETTER THAN EZRA
BETWEEN THE BURIED AND ME
BIG AUDIO DYNAMITE
BIG D AND THE KIDS TABLE
BIG GIGANTIC
BIG HEAD TODD & THE
    MONSTERS
BIG K.R.I.T.
BIG SEAN
BIG SHOT
BIG STREET
BIG WRECK
BILL BRUFORD
BILL CHINNOCK
BILL KREUTZMANN TRIO*
BILLY BRAGG
BILLY COBHAM
BILLY IDOL
BILLY JOEL*
BILLY OCEAN
BILLY RANKIN
BIOHAZARD
BIRTHDAY MASSACRE
BLACK 47
BLACK EYED PEAS
BLACK REBEL MOTORCYCLE
    CLUB
BLACK SABBATH*
BLACK SHEEP
BLACK STAR RIDERS

BLACK UHURU
BLACKALICIOUS
BLACKFOOT
BLANC MANGE
BLASTERS
BLESS THE FALL
BLIND MELON
BLONDE REDHEAD
BLONDIE*
BLOODLINE
BLOTTO
BLUE MURDER
BLUE OCTOBER
BLUE OYSTER CULT
BLUE RODEO
BLUES BLOCKBUSTER
BLUES BUSTERS
BLUES TIME
BLUES TRAVELER
BLUESTIME WITH MAGIC DICK
BLUR
BLUSHING BRIDES
BO DIDDLEY*
BOB DYLAN*
BOB GELDOF
BOB MOULD
BOB SEGER*
BOB WEIR*
BOBBY & THE MIDNITES
BOBBY BROWN
BOBCAT GOLDTHWAIT
BODEANS

BOGMEN
BON JOVI*
BONE THUGS-N-HARMONY
BONGOS
BONHAM
BONNIE RAITT*
BOOK OF LOVE
BOOMBOX
BORGORE
BORIS GREBENSHIKOV
BORN JAMERICANS
BOUNTY KILLER
BOWLING FOR SOUP
BOW-WOW-WOW
BOY HITS CAR
BR5-49
BRASS RING
BRAZILIAN GIRLS
BREAK SCIENCE
BREAKFAST
BRETT DENNEN
BRIAN AUGER
BRITNY FOX
BROKEN SOCIAL SCENE
BROTHER ALI
BROTHER CANE
BROTHERS GRIM SIDESHOW
BRUCE COCKBURN
BRUCE DICKINSON
BRUCE HORNSBY* &
    THE RANGE
BRUCE SPRINGSTEEN*

BRUFORD LEVIN
BRYAN ADAMS
BRYNDLE
BRYSON TILLER
BUCKCHERRY
BUCKETHEAD
BUCKWHEAT ZYDECO
BUDDY GUY*
BUDDY RICH
BUFFALO TOM
BUILT TO SPILL
BUJUBANTON
BULLETBOYS
BUN B & KIRKO BANGZ
BUNJI GARLIN
BURNING SPEAR
BUSBOYS
BUST A RHYMES
BUSTER POINDEXTER
BUTTHOLE SURFERS
BUZZCOCKS
C.S. ANGELS
CAKE
CAKED UP
CAMPER VAN BEETHOVEN
CAM'RON
CANDIRIA
CANDLEBOX
CANDY DULFER
CANDYLAND
CANNIBAL CORPSE
CAPITAL CITIES

CAPLETON
CAPTAIN BEEFHEART
CARCASS
CARDI B
CARL PALMER BAND
CARL PERKINS*
CARL WILSON
CARLA BLEY
CARLENE CARTER
CARNIVORE
CAROLYN MAS
CARTER THE UNSTOPPPABLE
    SEX MACHINE
CASH CASH
CATCH 22
CATHERINE WHEEL
CHARLATANS UK
CHARLES BROWN
CHARLIE HUNTER
CHARLIE SEXTON
CHEAP TRICK*
CHERRY POPPIN DADDIES
CHERUB
CHERYL "PEPSI" RILEY
CHEYENNE KIMBALL
CHICK COREA
CHIEF KEEF
CHILDREN OF BODOM
CHIMAIRA
CHON
CHRIS DE BURGH
CHRIS DUARTE GROUP

CHRIS HILLMAN
CHRIS WEBBY
CHRIS WHITLEY
CHRISTIAN DEATH
CHRISTINA PERRI
CHRISTINE OHLMAN
CHUCK MANGIONE
CIRCA SURVIVE
CIRCUS OF POWER
CITIZEN
CITIZEN COPE
CITIZEN KING
CITY AND COLOUR
CKY
CLARENCE "GATEMOUTH"
    BROWN
CLARENCE CLEMONS
CLEAN BANDIT
CLIPSE
CLUTCH
COAL CHAMBER
COLD WAR KIDS
COLLECTIVE SOUL
COLLIE BUDDZ
COMBICHRIST
COMMANDER CODY
COMMON
CONCRETE BLONDE
CONOR OBERST & THE MYSTIC
    VALLEY BAND
CONSPIRATOR
COREY SMITH

CORROSION OF CONFORMITY
COSMIC DUST BUNNIES
COUNT BASIE
COUNTING CROWS
COWBOY JUNKIES
COWBOY MOUTH
CRACKER
CRADLE OF FILTH
CRANBERRIES
CRASH TEST DUMMIES
CRISS
CROSSFADE
CROWDED HOUSE
CRY OF LOVE
CRYSTAL SHIP
CULTURE
CUPCAKKE
CURREN$Y
CUTE IS WHAT WE AIM FOR
CYNDI LAUPER
D GENERATION
D-12
DADA
DAG
DAMIAN MARLEY
DAN BAIRD
DAN HICKS
DAN REED NETWORK
DANCE HALL CRASHERS
DANGER DANGER
DANIEL JOHNSTON
DANIEL LANOIS

DANNY BROWN
DAR WILLIAMS
DARIK AND THE FUNBAGS
DARK LOTUS
DARK STAR ORCHESTRA
DARK TRANQUILITY
DAS EFX
DAS RACIST
DASHBOARD CONFESSIONAL
DAVE DAVIES
DAVE EAST
DAVE EDMUNDS
DAVE GRISMAN QUARTET
DAVE MASON*
DAVE MATTHEWS BAND
DAVE VALENTIN
DAVE WAKELING
DAVID BENOIT
DAVID BOWIE*
DAVID BROMBERG
DAVID BYRNE
DAVID CASSIDY
DAVID COOK
DAVID CROSBY*
DAVID DREW
DAVID GARZA
DAVID GRISMAN QUARTET
DAVID JOHANSEN
DAVID LINDLEY
DAVID TORN QUARTET
DAVID WILCOX
DAVID WOLF AND EYES

DB'S
DEAD BY WEDNESDAY
DEAD MILKMEN
DEADEYE DICK
DEADPHISH ORCHESTRA
DEAN WEEN GROUP
DEEE-LITE
DEEP BANANA BLACKOUT
DEEP BLUE SOMETHING
DEER TICK
DEL FUEGOS
DEL LORDS
DEL THE FUNKY HOMOSAPIEN
DELA SOUL
DELAMITRI
DELBERT MCCLINTON
DENNIS BROWN
DENZEL CURRY
DEREK TRUCKS BAND
DESCENDENTS
DESIIGNER
DEV
DEVILDRIVER
DEXTADAPS
DIAMOND RIO
DICK DALE
DICK DALE TRIBE
DICKEY BETTS
DIG
DIGABLE PLANETS
DILATED PEOPLES
DILLINGER ESCAPE PLAN

DIMMU BORGIR
DINOSAUR JR.
DIO
DION*
DIPSET
DIRTY DOZEN BRASS BAND
DIRTY HEADS
DIRTY LOOKS
DISCO BISCUITS
DIVINYLS
DIXIE DREGS & STEVE MORSE
    BAND
DIZZY GILLESPIE
DJ BL3ND
DJ JAZZY JEFF & THE FRESH
    PRINCE
DJ LOGIC AND PROJECT LOGIC
DJ SPOOKY
DMX
DOCTOR & THE MEDICS
DOGSTAR WITH KEANU REEVES
DOKKEN
DONNA THE BUFFALO
DONNIE IRIS
DONOVAN*
DOPAPOD
DOPE
DOUG AND THE SLUGS
DOWN
DR. DOG
DR. JOHN*
DRAGONFORCE

DRAKE
DRAKE BELL
DRAMARAMA
DREAD ZEPPELIN
DRIVE-BY TRUCKERS
DRIVIN''N' CRYIN'
DROPKICK MURPHYS
DUKE JUPITER
DWIGHT TWILLEY
EAGLES OF DEATH METAL
EARL KLUGH
EARL SCRUGGS
EARL SWEATSHIRT
EARTH CRISIS
EARTHGANG
ECHO & THE BUNNYMEN
ECHOBRAIN
EDDIE MONEY
EDDIE MURPHY
EDGAR WINTER
EDIE BRICKELL & THE NEW
    BOHEMIANS
EDWIN MCCAIN TRIO
EEK-A-MOUSE
EELS
EHANK III
EIGHT TO THE BAR
ELECTRAFIXION
ELECTRON
ELEPHANT MAN
ELLA MAI
ELLEN SHIPLEY

EMANCIPATOR
EMF
EMMURE
ENGLISHTOWN PROJECT
ENUFF Z'NUFF
ENVO
ENVY OF THE COAST
ERIC BURDON*
ERIC GALES BAND
ERIC HAMILTON BAND
ERIC MARIENTHAL BAND
ESCAPE THE FATE
EUROGLIDERS
EVAN & JARON
EVELYN CHAMPAGNE KING
EVERCLEAR
EVERLAST
EVERY TIME I DIE
EVERYONE ORCHESTRA
EXODUS
EXPLOSIONS IN THE SKY
EXPOSE
EXTREME
EYES
EZO
FABOLOUS
FABULOUS RHINESTONES
FABULOUS THUNDERBIRDS
FAINT
FAITH NO MORE
FAMILY FORCE FIVE
FAMOUSDEX

FANTOMAS
FASTBALL
FATES WARNING
FATHERS OF AFRIKA TOUR
FELIX CAVALIERE*
FELLY
FIEND FEST
FIERY FURNACES
FIGHT
FIGURE
FINCH
FINGER PRINTZ
FIONA
FIREHOSE
FIREHOUSE
FISH
FISHBONE
FIVE BLIND BOYS OF ALABAMA
FLATBUSH ZOMBIES
FLESHTONES
FLO & EDDIE
FLOBOTS
FLOCK OF SEAGULLS
FLOGGING MOLLY
FLOTSAM & JETSAM
FOGHAT
FOREIGNER
FOREVER THE SICKEST KIDS
FOUNTAINHEAD
FOUNTAINS OF WAYNE
FOUR NON BLONDES
FOUR YEAR STRONG

FRANK BLACK
FRANKIE COSMOS
FRANKIE VALLI & THE FOUR
　　SEASONS
FREDDIE MCGREGOR
FREDDY JONES BAND
FREEDY JOHNSTON
FRENCH MONTANA
FRENTE!
FROG WINGS
FROM AUTUMN TO ASHES
FROM FIRST TO LAST
FROM GOOD HOMES
FUDGE TUNNEL
FUEL
FURTHER SEEMS FOREVER
FUTURE
G. LOVE & SPECIAL SAUCE
G. LOVE IN THE KING'S COURT
GAELIC STORM
GALACTIC
GANG OF FOUR
GANG STARR
GARGANTUA SOUL
GARLAND JEFFREYS
GARY MYRICK
GARY U.S. BONDS
"GATEMOUTH" BROWN
GEEZER
GENE LOVES JEZEBEL
GENTLE GIANT
GEOFF TATE

GEORGE CLINTON & PARLIA-
　　MENT FUNKADELIC*
GEORGE HOWARD
GEORGE THOROGOOD & THE
　　DESTROYERS
GEORGIA SATELLITES
GET THE LED OUT
GETTER & AFK
GETUP KIDS
GHOSTEMANE
GHOSTFACE KILLAH
GIL SCOTT-HERON
GILBY CLARKE
GIN BLOSSOMS
GIPSY KINGS
GIRL TALK
GLADIATORS
GO AHEAD
GO WEST
GOD LIVES UNDERWATER
GOD STREET WINE
GODFATHERS
GODSMACK
GOGOL BORDELLO
GOLDFINGER
GOOD CHARLOTTE
GOOD RATS
GORKY PARK
GOV'T MULE
GRACE POTTER & THE
　　NOCTURNALS
GRAFFITI

GRAHAM PARKER
GRAMATIK
GRAND ALLIANCE
GRANDMASTER FLASH*
GRANT LEE BUFFALO
GRATEFUL DEAD*
GRAVEL PIT
GRAVITY KILLS
GREAT BIG SEA
GREAT WHITE
GREEN APPLE QUICKSTEP
GREENSKY BLUEGRASS
GREG KIHN BAND
GREGG ALLMAN*
GREGORY ISAACS
GREYBOY ALL-STARS
GROUNDATION
GUIDED BY VOICES
GURU
GUSTER
GWAR
GYPTIAN
GZA
HALIFAX
HAMMER OF THE GODS
HANDSOME BOY MODELING
   SCHOOL
HANOI ROCKS
HANSON
HARRY ANDERSON
HARRY DEAN STANTON
HATEBREED

HAWKWIND
HAWTHORNE HEIGHTS
HELEN SCHNEIDER
HELIUM BROTHERS
HELLOGOODBYE
HELMET
HENRY LEE SUMMER
HENRY ROLLINS
HERBIE HANCOCK
HEY MONDAY
HIGH KINGS
HIGH ON FIRE
HIIO
HINDER
HIT THE LIGHTS
HOBO JOHNSON
HOLE
HOLLYWOOD UNDEAD
HONOR SOCIETY
HOODIE ALLEN
HOODOO GURUS
HOOKAH BROWN
HOOTIE & THE BLOWFISH
HORATIO SANZ & THE KINGS
   OF IMPROV
HORRORPOPS
HORSE THE BAND
HOST AGE CALM
HOT ROD CIRCUIT
HOT TUNA
HOTHOUSE FLOWERS
HOUND MOUTH

HOUSE OF LORDS
HOUSE OF LOVE
HOUSE OF PAIN
HOWIE DAY
HUEY LEWIS AND THE NEWS
HUGH MASEKELA
HUMAN RADIO
HUNTER HAYES
HURRICANE
HUSKER DU
I AM THE AVALANCHE
I MOTHER EARTH
IAN HUNTER
IAN MATTHEWS
IAN MOORE
ICE CUBE*
ICEHOUSE
ICICLE WORKS
IGGY AZALEA
IGGY POP
ILL BILL
IMMORTAL TECHNIQUE
IN FLAMES
INDIGENOUS
INDIGO GIRLS
INDUSTRY
INFORMATION SOCIETY
INGRID MICHAELSON
INNER CIRCLE
INSANE CLOWN POSSE
INSIDERS
INSPIRAL CARPETS

INTERPOL
INTO IT OVER IT
INXS
IRATION
IRON BUTTERFLY
IRON CITY HOUSEROCKERS
ISRAEL VIBRATION
IVAN NEVILLE
J. GEILS BAND
J.I
J.J. CALE
JACK BRUCE & GINGER BAKER*
JACKOPIERCE
JACK'S MANNEQUIN
JACO PASTORIUS
JADAKISS
JAHMALLA
JAKE AND THE FAMILY JEWELS
JAKE MILLER
JAM STAMPEDE
JAMES COTTON BLUES BAND
JAMES MCMURTRY
JAMES TAYLOR*
JAN HAMMER
JANE JENSEN
JANE SIBERRY
JANE'S ADDICTION
JANIS IAN
JARS OF CLAY
JARULE
JASON BONHAM BAND
JASPER WRATH

JAY CRITCH
JAY ROWE
JAYHAWKS
JAZZ IS DEAD
JAZZ MANDOLIN PROJECT
JBOOG
JEAN-LUC PONTY
JEDI MIND TRICKS
JEEZY
JEFF BUCKLEY
JEFF HEALEY
JEFF LORBER
JEFFERSON AIRPLANE*
JEFFERSON STARSHIP
JEFFREY GAINES
JEFFREY OSBORNE
JELLYFISH
JEN DURKIN
JENNY & JOHNNY
JERRY HARRISON
JERRY JEFF WALKER
JESSE COLIN YOUNG
JESUS JONES
JEWEL
JID
JIDENNA
JIM CAPALDI*
JIM CARROLL AND THE RINGS
JIM ROSE CIRCUS SIDESHOW
JIMMIE DALE GILMORE
JIMMIE VAUGHAN
JIMMIE'S CHICKEN SHACK

JIMMY CLIFF*
JIMMY HERRING BAND
JOAN BAEZ*
JOAN JETT & THE BLACKHEARTS*
JOAN OSBORNE
JOANNA NEWSOM
JOE BONAMASSA
JOE BUDDEN
JOE COCKER
JOE ELY
JOE JACKSON
JOE KING CARRASCO
JOE PERRY PROJECT
JOE SATRIANI
JOE STRUMMER*
JOE WALSH*
JOE ZAWINUL
JOEY BADA$$
JOEY BELLADONNA
JOHN BROWN'S BODY
JOHN CAFFERTY & THE BEAVER
    BROWN BAND
JOHN ENTWISTLE
JOHN HALL
JOHN HARTFORD
JOHN HIATT
JOHN KADLECIK BAND
JOHN KAY & STEPPENWOLF
JOHN LEE HOOKER*
JOHN LYDON*
JOHN MAYALL'S
    BLUESBREAKERS

JOHN MCENROE
JOHN MCLAUGHLIN TRIO
JOHN PAUL JONES*
JOHN PRINE
JOHN PRING
JOHN SCOFIELD BAND
JOHN SEBASTIAN*
JOHN VALBY
JOHN WAITE
JOHN WESLEY HARDING
JOHNNY BRAVO
JOHNNY CASH*
JOHNNY CLEGG
JOHNNY CLYDE COPELAND
JOHNNY OTIS
JOHNNY VAN ZANT BAND
JOHNNY WINTER
JOHN CENA
JON BUTCHER
JON SPENCER BLUES
    EXPLOSION
JONATHAN EDWARDS
JONATHAN RICHMAN
JONATHON COULTON
JORMA KAUKONEN BAND
JOSE FELICIANO
JOSEY WALES
JOSH KELLY
JOSHUA KADISON
JOSHUA RADIN
JOSHUA REDMAN
JUDY MOWATT

JUDYBATS
JUELZ SANTANA
JUICY J
JULIAN LENNON
JULIAN MARLEY
JULIANA HATFIELD
JULUKA
JUNIOR WELLS
JUNKYARD
JURASSIC 5
KANSAS
KANYE WEST
KAP SLAP
KARL DENSON'S TINY UNIVERSE
KARYN WHITE
KATE VOEGELE
KATELL KEINEG
KATRINA AND THE WAVES
KEITH EMERSON & CARL
    PALMER
KEITH SWEAT
KELLER WILLIAMS
KENDRICK LAMAR
KENNY G
KENNY RANKIN
KENNY WAYNE SHEPHERD
KENTUCKY HEADHUNTERS
KEVIN MARTIN & THE HIWATTS
KICKING DAISIES
KID INK
KILL THE NOISE
KILLSWITCH ENGAGE

KIM CARNES
KIM WATERS
KING CRIMSON
KING DIAMOND
KING OF THE HILL
KING SUNNY ADE AND THE
    AFRICAN BEAT
KING SWAMP
KINGS
KINGS OF LEON
KINGS OF THE SUN
KINGS X
KITTIE
K'NAAN
KNOCKS
KOKO TAYLOR
KOKOMO
KONSHENS
KOOL KEITH
KORN
KOTTONMOUTH KINGS
KREATOR
KREWELLA
KRIS KRISTOFFERSON
KROKUS
KRS-ONE
KT TUNSTALL
KUNG FU
KY-MAN! MARLEY
KYUSS LIVES!
L.A. GUNS
LADY SAW

LADYSMITH BLACK MAMBAZO
LAIDBACK LUKE
LAMB OF GOD
LARRY CARLTON
LAURA NYRO*
LAURYN HILL
LE TIGRE
LEE "SCRATCH" PERRY
LEE RITENOUR
LEFTOVER SALMON
LENE LOVICH
LENNY KRAVITZ
LEO KOTTKE & MIKE GORDON
LEO SMITH
LEON REDBONE
LEON RUSSELL
LES CLAYPOOL
LES TETES BRULEES
LESLIE WEST
LESS THAN JAKE
LET'S ACTIVE
LETTERS TO CLEO
LETTUCE
LEVEL 42
LIFE OF AGONY
LIFEHOUSE
LIL BABY
LIL BIBBY
LIL DICKY
LIL DURK
LIL HERB
LIL KIM

LIL TJAY
LIL UZI VERT
LIL YACHTY
LINDA PERRY
LINDSEY STIRLING
LINK WRAY
LISA LISA & CULT JAM
LISA LOEB
LIT
LITTLE AMERICA
LITTLE FEAT
LITTLE RICHARD*
LITTLE RIVER BAND
LITTLE STEVEN
LIVE
LIVING COLOUR
LLOYD BANKS
LMFAO
LOCK UP
LONDON QUIREBOYS
LONE JUSTICE
LONG BEACH SHORTBUS
LONNIE MACK
LORD HURON
LORDS OF THE NEW CHURCH
LOS CAMPESINOS!
LOS LOBOS
LOTUS
LOUDON WAINWRIGHT III
LOUDPVCK
LOVE AND ROCKETS
LOVE SPIT LOVE

LOVE/HATE
LOVERBOY
LUCERO
LUCIANO
LUCINDA WILLIAMS
LUPE FIASCO
LURA
LUSCIOUS JACKSON
LUSH
LUTHER "GUITAR JR." JOHNSON
LUTHER ALLISON
LYLE MAYS
LYNCH MOB
M. WARD
M.O.D.
MAC MILLER
MACEO PARKER
MACHINE GUN KELLY
MACHINE HEAD
MACHINES OF LOVING GRACE
MACKLEMORE & RYAN LEWIS
MACYGRAY
MAD BALL
MAHAVISHNU
MAHLATHINI & THE MAHO-
    TELLA QUEENS
MANCHESTER ORCHESTRA
MANHATTAN TRANSFER
MANU DIBANGO
MARC COHN
MARIA MULDAUR
MARIANAS TRENCH

MARIANNE FAITHFUL
MARILLION
MARILYN MANSON
MARIO
MARION MEADOWS
MARK ISHAM
MARK WILSON
MARKY RAMONE
MARSHALL CRENSHAW
MARSHALL TUCKER BAND
MARTHA AND THE MUFFINS
MARTI JONES & DON DIXON
MARTIN SEXTON
MARY CHAPIN CARPENTER
MARY WILSON*
MASON RUFFNER
MASTADON
MASTERS OF REALITY
MAT KEARNEY
MATERIAL ISSUE
MATES OF STATE
MATISYAHU
MATT COSTA
MATT NATHANSON
MATT AND KIM
MATTHEW SWEET
MAX CREEK
MAXI PRIEST
MAYDAY PARADE
MAYNARD FERGUSON
MCAULEY SCHENKER GROUP
MEADE BROTHERS

MEAT BEAT MANIFESTO
MEAT LOAF
MEDESKI, MARTIN & WOOD
MEGADETH
MELI'SA MORGAN
MELISSA ETHERIDGE
MELISSA FERRICK
MELVIN SEALS AND JGB
MEN AT WORK
MEN WITHOUT HATS
MERCYFUL FATE
MERKULES
MERL SAUNDERS & THE RAIN-
    FOREST BAND
ME'SHELL N'DEGEOCELLO
METAL ALLEGIANCE
METHOD MAN
METRO STATION
MICHAEL BOLTON
MICHAEL FRANTI &
    SPEARHEAD
MICHAEL GLABICKI
MICHAEL IAN BLACK
MICHAEL PENN
MICHAEL STANLEY BAND
MICHELLE SHOCKED
MICK FLEETWOOD*
MICK JONES*
MICKEY HART*
MIDGE URE
MIDNITE
MIGHTY PURPLE

MIKATA
MIKE DOUGHTY'S BAND
MIKE GORDON
MIKE PETERS
MIKE POSNER
MIKE STUD
MIMOSA
MIND FUNK
MINDLESS SELF INDULGENCE
MINISTRY
MINK DEVILLE
MINUS THE BEAR
MIRACLE LEGION
MISFITS
MISSION OF BURMA
MISSION UK + BALAAM
MITCH RYDER
MIXMASTER MIKE
MOBBDEEP
MOBY
MODERN ENGLISH
MOE.
MOJO NIXON
MOLLY HATCHET
MONEYBAGG YO
MORBID ANGEL
MORGAN HERITAGE
MORPHINE
MOS DEF
MOSE ALLISON
MOTION CITY SOUNDTRACK
MOTORHEAD

MOUNTAIN
MOXYFURVOUS
MR. BIG
MR. BUNGLE
MR. CROWE'S GARDEN
MR. VEGA$
MUDDY WATERS*
MUDVAYNE
MURMURS
MURPHY'S LAW
MUSHROOMHEAD
MUSIQ SOULCHILD
MUTEMATH
MY CHEMICAL ROMANCE
MY LIFE WITH THE THRILL
    KILL KUL T
NADASURF
NAHKO & MEDICINE FOR THE
    PEOPLE
NAJEE
NANTUCKET
NAPALM DEATH
NAPI BROWNE
NAS
NASHVILLE PUSSY
NAUGHTY BY NATURE
NEUROSIS
NEVER SHOUT NEVER
NEW DEAL
NEW FOUND GLORY
NEW KIDS ON THE BLOCK
NEW POTATO CABOOSE

NICK FRADIANI
NICK LOWE
NICK SILVER
NICOLETTE LARSON
NIGHT RANGER
NIGHTHAWKS
NILS LOFGREN
NIT GRIT & TWO FRESH
NONA HENDRIX
NORMA JEAN
NORTH MISSISSIPPI ALL-STARS
NOT WEEN
NRBQ
NUCLEAR ASSAULT
NUNO
NUSHOOZ
O.A.R.
OCEAN BLUE
OCTOBER PROJECT
OF MONTREAL
OINGO BOINGO
OKGO
OKKERVIL RIVER
OLD 97'S
OLD SCHOOL REUNION
OLIVER TREE
OMAR & THE HOWLERS
OMD
ONCUE
ONYX
ORION THE HUNTER
ORLEANS

OTEP
OTIS DAY & THE KNIGHTS
OTTMAR LIEBERT & LUNA
    NEGRA
OUR LADY PEACE
OUTLAWS
OVERKILL
OZOMATLI
P.LL.
PABLO CRUISE
PABLO MOSES
PACKAGE
PACO DE LUCIA
PALE DIVINE
PANCHO SANCHEZ
PANDORAS
PANTERA
PAPA ROACH
PAPADOSIO
PAPOOSE
PARAMORE
PARTICLE
PARTYNEXTDOOR
PAT BENATAR
PAT MCGEE BAND
PAT METHENY
PATO BANTON
PATRICK MORAZ AND BILL
    BRUFORD
PATTI SMITH*
PAUL BUTTERFIELD*
PAUL CARRACK AND NICK LOWE

PAUL RODGERS

PAUL STANLEY*

PAUL YOUNG

PAULA COLE

PAW

PENNYWISE

PEPPER

PERIPHERY

PERPETUAL GROOVE

PETE FRANCIS

PETER FRAMPTON

PETER MURPHY

PETER TOSH AND JIMMY CLIFF

PETER WOLF

PHANTOM PLANET

PHIL ALVIN

PHISH

PHOEBE SNOW

PHYLLIS HYMAN

PHYSICAL GRAFFITI

PIEBALD

PIECES OF A DREAM

PIGEONS PLAYING PING PONG

PINBACK

PINEGROVE

PINK TALKING FISH

PIXIES

PLAIN WHITE T'S

PLASMA TICS

PNBROCK

POCO

POE

POI DOG PONDERING

POISON THE WELL

POLYPHIA

POP SMOKE

POPACHUBBY

PORK TORNADO

PORNO FOR PYROS

POSIES

POST MALONE

POSTMODERN JUKEBOX

POUSETTE-DART BAND

PRESIDENTS OF THE USA

PRETTY & TWISTED

PRETTY POISON

PRIMAL SCREAM

PRINCE PAUL

PROCOL HARUM

PROFESSIONALS

PROFESSORS OF BLUEGRASS

PROJECT TWO

PROJECT/OBJECT

PRO-PAIN

PSYCHEDELIC FURS

PUBLIC ENEMY*

PUDDLES PITY PARTY

PURSUIT OF HAPPINESS

PUSH PLAY

PUSHA T

QUEEN LATIFAH

QUEENNAIJA

QUIET RIOT

R.E.M.*

RA
RACHAEL SWEET
RADIOHEAD*
RAEKWON
RAGING SLAB
RAHZEL
RAILROAD EARTH
RAINDOGS
RAINER MARIA
RAKIM
RAMONES*
RANDY HANSEN
RANDY NEWMAN*
RANK AND FILE
RANKIN ROGER
RAQ
RARARIOT
RASPUTINA
RATT
RAVE-UPS
RAY DAVIES
REBELUTION
RED HOT CHILI PEPPERS*
RED ROCKERS
REEL BIG FISH
RE-FLEX
REGINA SPEKTOR
REID GENAUER
RELIENTK
RENAISSANCE
REO SPEEDWAGON
REVEILLE

RHETT MILLER & THE
    BELIEVERS
RIC OCASEK*
RICHARD THOMPSON
RICHIE KOTZEN
RICHIE SPICE
RICK DERRINGER
RICK JAMES
RICK SPRINGFIELD
RICKIE LEE JONES
RIDERS ON THE STORM
RIFFRAFF
RIGGS
RIVAL SCHOOLS
RJD2
RO JAMES
ROB WASSERMAN & JOHN WES-
    LEY HARDING
ROB ZOMBIE
ROBBEN FORD
ROBBY KRIEGER*
ROBERT CRAY BAND
ROBERT ELLIS ORALL
ROBERT FRIPP AND THE
    LEAGUE OF GENTLEMEN
ROBERT GORDON
ROBERT HUNTER*
ROBERT RANDOLPH & THE
    FAMILY BAND
ROBIN LANE
ROBIN TROWER
ROBYN HITCHCOCK

ROCK & HIDE
ROCKATS
ROCKY BURNETTE
ROGER MCGUINN
ROHN LAWRENCE
ROLLINS BAND
ROMEO VOID
RON WOOD
RONNIE EARL
RONNIE LAWS
RONNIE SPECTOR*
ROOMFUL OF BLUES
ROONEY
ROOTS
RORY GALLAGHER
ROY AYERS
ROY BUCHANAN
ROYCE DA 5'9"
RUFIO
RUFUS WAINWRIGHT
RUN-DMC*
RUPEE
RUSTED ROOT
RXBANDITS
RYAN CABRERA
RYAN DOWNE
RYAN MONTBLEAU BAND
RYO KAWASAKI
SAGE FRANCIS
SAM KINISON
SAM & DAVE*
SAMANTHA FISH

SAMMY ADAMS
SANCHEZ
SANCTUARY
SANDRA BERNHARD
SANTANA*
SARA BAREILLES
SARA HICKMAN
SARAYA
SAVOY BROWN
SAVUKA
SAVES THE DAY
SAY ANYTHING
SCARY KIDS SCARING KIDS
SCATTERBRAIN
SCHOOL OF FISH
SCHOOLBOYQ
SCREAMIN' CHEETAH
    WHEELIES
SCREAMING BLUE MESSIAHS
SEAL
SEAN PAUL
SEBADOH
SEBASTIAN BACH
SECOND CITY COMEDY
SECONDHAND SERENADE
SECRET AFFAIR
SENSES FAIL
SEPULTURA
SET YOUR GOALS
SEVEN MARY THREE
SEVENDUST
SHABBA RANKS

SHABOO ALL STARS
SHADOWS FALL
SHAGGY
SHAI
SHAKEDOWN
SHANNON CURFMAN
SHAWN COLVIN
SHEILA E.
SHELTER
SHERYL CROW
SHINEDOWN
SHIRLEY ALSTON*
SHOTGUN MESSIAH
SHPONGLE
SHWAYZE
SHYGLIZZY
SICK OF IT ALL
SILENCERS
SILVERSTEIN
SIMMS BROTHERS BAND
SIMON TOWNSHEND
SIMPLY RED
SINEAD O'CONNOR
SIR DOUGLAS QUINTET
SISTER HAZEL
SISTER MACHINE GUN
SISTERS OF MERCY
SIX FEET UNDER
SIZZLA
SKATALITES
SLAUGHTER
SLAUGHTERHOUSE

SLAYER
SLEEZE BEEZ
SLICK RICK
SLIGHTLY STOOPID
SLIVERSTEIN
SLOW BURN
SLY FOX
SNARKY PUPPY
SNOOP DOGG
SOCIAL DISTORTION
SOJA
SOMETHING CORPORATE
SOMO
SON SEALS BLUES BAND
SON VOLT
SONIC YOUTH
SONNY OKOSUN
SONS OF ANGELS
SONS OF BOB
SOPHIE B. HAWKINS
SOUL ASYLUM
SOUL BRAINS
SOULFLY
SOULIVE
SOUND TRIBE SECTOR 9
SOUP DRAGONS
SOUTHERN CULTURE ON THE
    SKIDS
SOUTHERN PACIFIC
SOUTHSIDE JOHNNY & THE
    ASBURY JUKES
SPARTA

SPEARHEAD
SPECIAL BEAT
SPIRITUALIZED
SPITALFIELD
SPONGE
SPOON
SPORTS SECTION
SPRING HEELED JACK USA
SPYRO-GYRA
SPYS
SQUEEZE
ST. LUCIA
STABBING WESTWARD
STANLEY CLARKE
STANLEY JORDAN
START MAKING SENSE
STATE RADIO
STATIC X
STEEL PULSE
STEELHEART
STELLA
STEPHEN KELLOGG & THE
    SIXERS
STEPHEN LYNCH
STEPHEN MARLEY
STEPHEN STILLS*
STEPS
STERLING
STEVE EARLE & THE DUKES
STEVE FORBERT
STEVE HACKETT
STEVE HOWE

STEVE MORSE BAND
STEVE STEVENS' ATOMIC
    PLAYBOYS
STEVE VAL
STEVE-O
STEVEN LYNCH
STEVIE RAY VAUGHAN*
STORY OF THE YEAR
STORYVILLE
STRANGE DESIGN
STRANGEFOLK
STRANGLERS
STRAY CATS
STRAYLIGHT RUN
STREETLIGHT MANIFESTO
STREETS
STRING CHEESE INCIDENT
STRUTTER
STUART HAMM
SUBURBS
SUGAR
SUGAR TOOTH
SUGARCUBES
SUICIDAL TENDENCIES
SUM41
SUNNY DAY REAL ESTATE
SUNRA
SUPERCAT
SUPERDRAG
SUPERSUCKERS
SUSAN TEDESCHI
SUZANNE FELLINI

SUZANNE VEGA
SWEETWATER
SWOLLEN MEMBERS
SWORN ENEMY
SYMPHONY X
SZA
T. MILLS
T.S.O.L.
TAJ MAHAL
TAKE6
TALIBKWELI
TALKING DREADS
TALKING HEADS*
TALKPECK SOUNDSYSTEM
TALL STORIES
TALLY HALL
TANITA TIKARAM
TANTO METRO & DEVONTE
TARRUS RILEY
TAYLOR DAYNE
TEA LEAF GREEN
TECHNOTRONIC
TED LEO + THE PHARMACISTS
TED NUGENT
TEENAGE FANCLUB
TEGAN AND SARA
TELEVISION
TERENCE TRENT D'ARBY
TESLA
TESTAMENT
TEXAS FLOOD
TEXTONES

THAT PETROL EMOTION
THE ALARM
THE ALL-AMERICAN REJECTS
THE ALTERNATE ROUTES
THE AQUABATS
THE ATTIC
THE AVETT BROTHERS
THE B-52's
THE BAND*
THE BAND FROM UTOPIA
THE BANGLES
THE BEARS
THE BELLTOWER
THE BLACK CROWES
THE BLACK KEYS
THE BOUNCING SOULS
THE BREEDERS
THE CALL
THE CHURCH
THE CLANCY BROTHERS
THE CLICK FIVE
THE COMMITMENTS
THE CONNELLS
THE CRAMPS
THE CRAYONS
THE CULT
THE DAMNED
THE DARKNESS
THE DEAN'S LIST
THE DECEMBERISTS
THE DESERT ROSE BAND
THE DIXIE DREGS

THE DONNAS
THE DOVES
THE DREAM
THE DREGS
THE DRESDEN DOLLS
THE DRIFTERS*
THE ENGLISH BEAT
THE EXPENDABLES
THE FALL OF TROY
THE FARM
THE FEELIES
THE FIXX
THE FLAMING LIPS
THE FOUR SEASONS*
THE FRONT BOTTOMS
THE GAME
THE GATHERING
THE GERMS
THE GO-GO'S*
THE HACKENSAW BOYS
THE HATTERS
THE HAUNTED
THE HEAD AND THE HEART
THE HOLD STEADY
THE HOOTERS
THE INTERRUPTERS
THE ITALS
THE JOY FORMIDABLE
THE KINKS*
THE KOOKS
THE LA'S
THE LONG RIDERS

THE LOX
THE MACHINE
THE MAINE
THE MARS VOLTA
THE MELVINS
THE MEMBERS
THE MEN
THE MICK TAYLOR BAND
THE MIGHTY LEMON DROPS
THE MIGHTY MIGHTY
   BOSSTONES
THE MODELS
THE MOONEY SUZUKI
THE MOTELS
THE MOTHER STATION
THE NAKED AND FAMOUS
THE NEIGHBORHOODS
THE NERDS
THE NEVILLE BROTHERS
THE NIELDS
THE NITECAPS
THE NIXONS
THE ODDS
THE ORIGINAL WAILERS
THE OUTFIELD
THE OUTLAWS
THE PHARCYDE
THE PIETASTERS
THE POGUES
THE PRETENDERS*
THE PROCLAIMERS
THE PRODIGALS

THE PRODUCERS
THE RADIATORS
THE READY SET
THE REMBRANDTS
THE REPLACEMENTS
THE REVEREND HORTON HEAT
THE REVIVALISTS
THE RIPPINGTONS
THE ROCHES
THE ROCKET SUMMER
THE ROLLING STONES*
THE ROMANTICS
THE SAINTS
THE SAMPLES
THE SAW DOCTORS
THE SCRATCH BAND
THE SELECTOR
THE SILVER BEATS
THE SLEEPING
THE SLIP
THE SMITHEREENS
THE SPILL CANVAS
THE SPIN DOCTORS
THE STARTING LINE
THE STOOGES*
THE SUBDUDES
THE SUNDAYS
THE THE
THE TOASTERS
THE TOLL
THE TONY LEVIN BAND
THE TRIBE

THE TUBES
THE UNDERWORLD
THE URGE
THE VENTURES*
THE VERVE PIPE
THE VOIDS
THE WAILERS
THE WALLFLOWERS
THE WEAKERTHANS
THE WOLFE TONES
THEORY OF A DEADMAN
THEY MIGHT BE GIANTS
THIRD EYE BLIND
THIRD WORLD
THREE DOG NIGHT
THRICE
THROWDOWN
THROWING MUSES
THURSDAY
TIL TUESDAY
TIMBUK 3
TIMEFLIES
TIN MACHINE
TIREBITER
TITUS ANDRONICUS
TOAD THE WET SPROCKET
TOADIES
TODD RUNDGREN*
TODD SNIDER
TOM BROWNE
TOM JONES
TOM TOM CLUB

TOM VERLAINE

TOM WAITS*

TOMAHAWK

TOMMY CONWELL & THE
  YOUNG RUMBLERS

TOMMY DORSEY ORCHESTRA

TOMMY STINSON

TOMMY TUTONE

TONY REBEL

TONY YAYO

TOOTS AND THE MAYTALS

TORI AMOS

TORTOISE

TORY LANEZ

TOURISTS

TOWER OF POWER

T'PAU

TRAGICALLY HIP

TRANSATLANTIC

TRAPT

TRIBAL SEEDS

TRICKY

TRINA

TRIPPIE REDD

TRIVIUM

TRIXTER

TURKUAZ

TURNOVER

TWIDDLE

TY DOLLA $IGN

TYGA

TYPE O NEGATIVE

U2*

UB40

UFO

ULTRA VOX

UMPHREY'S MCGEE

UNCLE KRACKER

UNCLE TUPELO

UNDEROATH

UNEARTH

URGE OVERKILL

US THE DUO

VANDENBERG

VANILLA FUDGE

VAST

VERTICAL HORIZON

VERUCA SALT

VICTOR WOOTEN

VIDA BLUE

VILLAGE PEOPLE

VIOLENT FEMMES

VIXEN

VNVNATION

WAKA FLOCKA FLAME

WALE

WALK OFF THE EARTH

WALL OF VOODOO

WAR

WARGASM

WARRANT

WARREN ZEVON

WARRIOR SOUL
WASHBOARD SLIM AND THE
 BLUE LIGHTS
WASP
WEBB WILDER BAND
WEEN
WEEZER
"WEIRD AL" YANKOVIC
WESTSIDE GUNN & CONWAY
WHITE ANIMALS
WHITE PANDA
WHITE TRASH
WHITE ZOMBIE
WIDESPREAD PANIC
WIDOWMAKER
WILCO
WILD FLAG
WILLIE DIXON
WILSON PICKETT
WINERY DOGS
WINGER
WIZ KHALIFA
WOLF PARADE
WOLFGANG GARTNER
WONDER STUFF
WOODENTOPS
WOODY HERMAN

WU-TANG CLAN
X
XAVIER RUDD
X-ECUTIONERS
XYZ
YEASAYER
YELAWOLF
YELLOW CARD
YELLOW JACKETS
YELLOWMAN
YFNLUCCI
YG
YNGWIE MALMSTEEN
YOGOTTI
YOLATENGO
YOUNG DOLPH
YOUNG DUBLINERS
YOUNG M.A
YOUSSOU N'DOUR
ZACHDEPUTY
ZAPPA PLAYS ZAPPA
ZED'S DEAD
ZIGGY MARLEY & THE MELODY
 MAKERS
ZILLA
ZULU SPEAR

ACKNOWLEDGMENTS

Brian Phelps

My adult life was built in several areas. One main piece was choosing Toad's Place to be my career. Even though I stayed active in the martial arts over those many decades, as well as maintaining a more subdued interest in chess and finding the time to earn a pilot's license over many years and raise a family, Toad's encompassed a large part of my time.

There were many folks along the way who were important supports to the structure that eventually developed. It was a long, long road to somewhere I could never have imagined. During that journey I was knocked down over and over again. For some unknown reason, I kept getting up. Now, at sixty-seven years old, I'm still trying to move forward. Maybe this is why all of us, as a species, are destined to keep going, no matter how hard the path.

In no particular order, I should start by mentioning the audio team of Horizon Sound, overseen by Fred Santore. Many of his inner staff eventually moved on to bigger stages, but they included Keith Dupke, Matt Diamond, Chad Emerson, Dave Barata, Bob Elliot, Jake Rosenfeld, O.T., and others. They were extremely important to what people came to Toad's for: primarily the sounds of music.

I had two key guys on the lighting crew: Marty Weiand and Jim Day. They were the second part of the technical team that gave people the experience they were looking for.

We had other people who lent a great hand in holding all the parts together over the years. Those were Katherine Blossom, whose sixteen years at the helm are beyond words, and her predecessor Lucy Sabini; Heather Orser (McDonald); Jeff Petrin; Jim Torello; Paul Liberti; Kevin Meehan; Pat Healy; Jack Reich; WZMX Program Director DJ Buck; the KC101 Saturday Dance Party team, DJ Thomas "Action" Jackson and former security guy/jazz aficionado Rohn Lawrence, as well as the dearly departed security guy and later WPLR point man Sam T., as well as our security men Anthony "Tank" Dunbar and Bill "Whiskey" Walkauskas. These people all played an important role here at Toad's and deserve to be highly commended. Of course Hollis Martin and Ed Dingus have been the anchors of my staff for the past couple of decades. They devoted a huge part of their lives to this company and this will not be forgotten.

Behind the scenes, my dear friend and advisor on countless issues, Lou Buccino, as well as former bookkeeper Barbara Galba have spent a part of their lives dealing with the happenings at Toad's. Another important advisor for me was C. Mike Cunningham, who helped direct me through the many pitfalls that befall a nightclub guy. He was also part of my martial arts experience that helped keep me sane through the years. The key professionals who guided me these many years from the very start were attorney Jim Segaloff and my accountant Henry Barron.

Randall Beach did a fabulous job putting the text together for this story. His effort and focus are to be highly commended. Very few people could have looked as deeply and transparently as he did in accurately describing what happened here inside during those forty-six years.

Jim Koplik has to be at the very top of my list. Without him as the guiding light through this crazy world of rock 'n' roll, the "legendary" part of Toad's would not have existed.

Jim has been "the godfather" of rock 'n' roll music in Connecticut almost from its beginning. This is a reality not just for myself, but for the entire state. He deserves a proclamation and a statue in his honor. There is no other person who comes close to his contributions here in the Nutmeg State. There is no one I respect more than this man.

My family whom I raised while in the middle of this crazy era of rock in Connecticut deserves an award for having to mature through the decades as I spent so many hours of my life away from them and here at Toad's. My wife, Maria, and my three children Jessica, Kaylie, and Brian Jr. all did their part without complaint. It was not an easy task for any of us as we juggled our family time with my countless hours at the club. They deserve a tremendous amount of credit for holding up their end of things.

Finally, there is that unknown guy who smashed the glass door to my karate school around the corner from Toad's. Whoever he is, without him doing that insane stunt I would not have connected with Mike Spoerndle and ended up where I did. My life would have taken another direction. Life's decisions can be so strange and you may not realize it until a long time thereafter. What you first think is a bad thing can turn out to be a good thing.

Randall Beach

There were many people who helped me tell the story of Toad's Place. At the beginning of this process, Stephen Spignesi, John White, and Jim Motavalli gave me expert advice on how to find a publisher. Once I began doing interviews, four people in particular were especially generous with their time and insights: Joan Mary Spoerndle, Pat Spoerndle, Pat Healy, and Jimmy Koplik. I also learned a lot about Toad's Place security from Anthony "Tank" Dunbar and Bill "Whiskey" Walkauskas.

Thom Duffy, my rock 'n' roll companion for many years, provided leads and a great sidebar on his many nights at Toad's. He lined me up with his colleague at *Billboard*, Dave Brooks, and with Audrey Fix Schaefer of the National Independent Venue Association, and they, too, were helpful. Rick Allison, another longtime friend of mine, let loose with a string of memorable quotes about nights at Toad's and set me up with his former colleagues at WPLR. (On August 12, 1989, Rick also gave me the best tip I ever received in my years as a reporter: "There's a real good chance that the Stones are playing at Toad's tonight!") The WPLR chapter was enhanced through information provided to me by Dick Kalt, Manuel Rodriguez, Kevin Garrity, John Griffin, and Mike Lapitino.

Some of the musicians who have been on stage at Toad's gave me fine reminiscences: Christine Ohlman, Budd Tunick, Frank Simms, Al Anderson, Nick Fradiani, Opus (Christian Francis Lawrence), Cynthia Lyon, Rob Jockel, Guy Tino and Andy "A.J." Gundell. A special thanks to Ted Canning and James Polisky, former members of the Sons of Bob, for recalling what it was like to suddenly be the opening act for the Rolling Stones. And thanks to Dean Falcone and Troy Church for helping me find those two "Sons."

The always-competent and helpful bookers of the bands, Katherine Blossom and Lucy Sabini, also helped me understand how the process worked and provided backstage stories. Peter Menta, who was the first such "booker," assisted me with tales and information on the early years at Toad's.

Others who set aside some time for me included: attorneys Hugh Keefe and James Segaloff; accountant Henry Barron; WZMX Program Director DJ Buck; Phil Cutler (whose Cutler's Records is sorely missed in New Haven); Wayne Nuhn, the former head waiter of Mory's; Kirk Baird; Charles Rosenay; Nick Pastore; Jerry Zajac; Steve

Mednick; Timothy Wood; Gregory Sherrod; Lawrence Dorfman; Kelly Brownell; Barbara Shaw; and Yale University President Peter Salovey.

Those who described for me their memorable nights as people in the crowd at Toad's included: Katie Regan, Thomas Christensen, John Minardi, Carolyn Martino, Lisa Braman, Kurt Evans, and Robert Rigutto.

These staffers at Toad's Place also provided valuable insights and assistance: Office Manager Holli Martin, General Manager Ed Dingus, Booking Agent Jack Reich, and Lighting Man Jimmy Day.

I am indebted to my collaborator on this book project, Brian Phelps, for taking me on. I learned through my interviews for this book and by spending time with Brian that he is the one who made it possible for Toad's Place to survive all these years of change and challenge. I also owe a debt to Mike Spoerndle, whose original vision got Toad's rolling.

During the nearly two years of work on this book, my wife Jennifer Kaylin has been my able assistant, advisor, consultant, line editor, and guiding light. She worked with me day by day to keep this book moving forward.

TOAD'S PLACE
300 YORK STREET · NEW HAVEN

1ST DOMESTIC DRAFT WITH ALL MEALS

= ONLY 10¢ =

SHRIMP BASKET *with french fries · beer batter fried shrimp* 2.95

CHICKEN BASKET *with french fries · honey dipped chicken* 2.75

FISH in the BASKET *with french fries · 2 large wedges of breaded white fish* 1.35

CLAM BASKET *with french fries · generous portion of clams deep fried* . 1.45

BUCKET of STEAMERS 1.65 *served with butter & lemon wedge*	**FRESH GROUND ROUND** 2.65 *onion rings or french fries*

= SIDE ORDERS =

SOUP DU JOUR   FRENCH FRIES .45   SALADS

cup .45   bowl .65   ONION RINGS .75   tossed .55 chefs 2.35

= SANDWICHES =

HAMBURGER .95   CHEDDAR DOG .95

CHEESEBURGER 1.05   CHILI DOG .95

ROQUEFORT BURGER 1.25   FISH SANDWICH .85

HOT DOG .85   ~10¢ extra for tomato & lettuce   ROAST BEEF 1.45

= DESSERTS =

Special homemade CHEESECAKE 1.25   SHERBET .65

CHOCOLATE BAVARIAN CREAM PIE .65   ICE CREAM .65

= BEVERAGES =

COFFEE .25   TEA .25   ICE TEA .35   SODAS ~ small .40 large .55

~ above orders available for carry out ~

Clockwise from top left: Marillion, Los Lobos, Michael Bolton, Mike Patton of Faith No More, Leo Kottke, Melissa Etheridge.

About the Authors

Brian Phelps was born in New Haven, Connecticut. His music background was nothing more than listening to AM radio or watching an Elvis Presley flick. He had no idea where his path in life was about to lead. Brian met Mike Spoerndle, owner of the new Toad's Place in 1975. One year later Big Mike invited Brian to start working at the club, following college. Several years later, Mike made Brian an offer to become business partners. In January 1995 Brian took control of the company and bought the rest of the business in 1998. Brian later

met with longtime associate Randall Beach and decided to write a memoir. He took "a road less traveled," but one we think you will enjoy reading about.

Randall Beach was the rock music critic for the *New Haven Register* from 1978 to 1984, covering many shows at Toad's Place. He later wrote about rock music for the *New Haven Advocate,* the *Hartford Courant,* and *Billboard* magazine. He was also a reporter and columnist for the *New Haven Register* from 1997 to 2020. In addition, he writes the "Beachcombing" column for *Connecticut* magazine. He lives in New Haven.

MARA LAVITT